Working with the]
Survivor

Working with the Human Trafficking Survivor fills a void in existing literature by providing students, faculty, and professionals in applied, helping disciplines, with a comprehensive text about human trafficking with a focus on clinical issues. This book gives an overview of the medical care, options for psychological treatment, and beyond. *Working with the Human Trafficking Survivor* is a great resource for social work, counselling, and psychology courses on human trafficking or domestic violence.

Mary C. Burke is an associate professor in the Department of Psychology and Counseling at Carlow University, where she is the program director of the doctoral program in Counseling Psychology. She has been involved in anti-human trafficking efforts since 2004 and is the founder of the Project to End Human Trafficking (www.endhumantrafficking.org).

Although there are a variety of books on human trafficking at national and international level, many fail to address victims. Burke's *Working with the Human Trafficking Survivor* provides information on "real world" treatments to better the lives of both children and adult survivors of human trafficking.

– **Kim McCabe**, *Professor and Chair, Criminology, Lynchburg College*

Working with the Human Trafficking Survivor

What Counselors, Psychologists, Social Workers and Medical Professionals Need to Know

Edited by
Mary C. Burke

Routledge
Taylor & Francis Group

NEW YORK AND LONDON

First published 2019
by Routledge
711 Third Avenue, New York, NY 10017

and by Routledge
2 Park Square, Milton Park, Abingdon, Oxon OX14 4RN

Routledge is an imprint of the Taylor & Francis Group, an informa business

© 2019 Taylor & Francis

The right of Mary C. Burke to be identified as the author of the editorial material, and of the authors for their individual chapters, has been asserted in accordance with sections 77 and 78 of the Copyright, Designs and Patents Act 1988.

Library of Congress Cataloging-in-Publication Data
Names: Burke, Mary C., editor.
Title: Working with the human trafficking survivor : what therapists, human service, and medical health care providers need to know / edited by Mary C. Burke.
Description: 1 Edition. | New York : Routledge, 2018. |
Includes bibliographical references and index. |
Identifiers: LCCN 2018024566 (print) | LCCN 2018036818 (ebook) | ISBN 9781315684468 (Master Ebook) | ISBN 9781317409243 (Web pdf) | ISBN 9781317409236 (ePub) | ISBN 9781317409229 (Mobipocket) | ISBN 9781138924284 (hardback) | ISBN 9781138924307 (pbk.) | ISBN 9781315684468 (ebk)
Subjects: LCSH: Human trafficking victims--Services for. |
Human trafficking.
Classification: LCC HQ281 (ebook) | LCC HQ281 .W67 2018 (print) | DDC 364.15/51--dc23
LC record available at https://lccn.loc.gov/2018024566

ISBN: 978-1-138-92428-4 (hbk)
ISBN: 978-1-138-92430-7 (pbk)
ISBN: 978-1-315-68446-8 (ebk)

Typeset in Bembo
by Taylor & Francis Books

Contents

vi   *Contents*

Illustrations

Figures

Tables

1 Human Trafficking in the 21st Century

An Overview for Healthcare Providers

Mary C. Burke

"Human trafficking" or "trafficking in persons" and "modern slavery" are terms often used interchangeably to refer to a variety of crimes associated with the economic exploitation of people. Human trafficking, regardless of its form, violates a number of basic human rights, as outlined in the United Nations Declaration of Human Rights (1948). While there are many articles contained within the Declaration that pertain to trafficking, the following are most relevant:

Article I

> All human beings are born free and equal in dignity and rights. They are endowed with reason and conscience and should act towards one another in a spirit of brotherhood.

Article 3

> Everyone has the right to life, liberty and security of person.

Article 4

> No one shall be held in slavery or servitude; slavery and the slave trade shall be prohibited in all their forms.

Human trafficking occurs worldwide, and despite popular depictions in the media that primarily involve young girls, children and adults from all cultural backgrounds are trafficked. Common among trafficking survivors is their economic vulnerability, which can be caused by any number of variables (e.g., political instability, social class structure, insufficient family or other network of support). In addition to individuals being trafficked by those known to them, such as family or friends, trafficking has been associated with transnational organized crime groups, small, more loosely organized criminal networks and local gangs, violations of labor and immigration laws, and government corruption (Richard, 1999; US Government Accountability Office, 2006; Väyrynen, 2003). At the international level, the United Nations Convention against Transnational

Organized Crime, which was adopted by UN General Assembly resolution 55/25, is the primary legal instrument used to combat transnational organized crime.[1] The Convention is supplemented by three Protocols, each of which focuses on specific types of organized crime and are: the Protocol to Prevent, Suppress and Punish Trafficking in Persons, Especially Women and Children; the Protocol against the Smuggling of Migrants by Land, Sea and Air; and the Protocol against the Illicit Manufacturing of and Trafficking in Firearms, their Parts and Components and Ammunition. Article 3 of the Protocol to Prevent, Suppress and Punish Trafficking in Persons, Especially Women and Children defines human trafficking as follows.

> Trafficking in persons shall mean the recruitment, transportation, transfer, harboring or receipt of persons, by means of the threat or force or other forms of coercion, of abduction, of fraud, of deception, of the abuse of power, or of a position of vulnerability or of the giving or receiving of payments or benefits to achieve the consent of a person having control over another person, for the purpose of exploitation. Exploitation shall include, at a minimum, the exploitation of the prostitution of others or other forms of sexual exploitation, forced labor or services, slavery or practices similar to slavery, servitude or the removal of organs.
>
> (United Nations, 2000)

For the purpose of this text the definition above will be used.

The definition comprises three essential parts: recruitment, movement, and exploitation, all of which point to critical aspects of the trafficking process. It is important to note that it is not necessary for "movement" to include crossing from one country into another; an individual can be trafficked within the borders of her or his own country or town and can even be trafficked from the home in which she or he lives. As an example of an in-country situation, it is not uncommon for a girl or woman to be trafficked from the rural areas of Costa Rica to the coastal regions where the commercial sex industry is thriving. Another example of in-country trafficking that happens often in the United States, is for children to be sold by adults who are strangers, acquaintances or even caregivers for money in exchange for sex to a third party. Also critical to understanding human trafficking is understanding what is meant by **coercion**. The term "coercion" in this context specifically refers to: (a) threats of harm to or physical restraint against any person; (b) any scheme intended to cause a person to believe that failure to perform an act will result in harm or physical restraint against any person; or (c) the abuse or threatened abuse of the legal process. However, it is essential to take other factors into consideration with regard to coercion, in particular when working with victims of sex trafficking and prostitution, such as whether the individual had any legitimate alternatives to support her basic needs (Hernandez, 2001) when approached by the pimp (trafficker). If not, then the thinking is that desperation to perform responsibilities such as support a child, and feed and keep one's self safe, can be a form of coercion.

Technically, people are trafficked into a slavery-like situation; however, that distinction is not often made in reference to these terms, meaning that the terms human trafficking and slavery are sometimes used interchangeably. This leads to an incomplete and therefore inaccurate representation of human trafficking. Coercive and sometimes forcible exploitation of one human over another has occurred in a variety of forms throughout history. The primary characteristics of this phenomenon have remained the same over time and include one person exercising fear and sometimes violence-based control over another for economic gain. What is typically different in the twenty-first century is that it is far less expensive to purchase or otherwise secure a person today than previously. For example, costs as low as US$10 have been reported in places like South East Asia, with the average cost for a person being US$90 (Free the Slaves, n.d.). A second difference is that the relationship between the trafficker and the victim is shorter in duration. This is primarily a consequence of the large number of individuals vulnerable to trafficking (i.e., available to be exploited) and the care and healthcare costs associated with a lifelong or longer-term relationship (i.e., it's easy and less costly to find a healthy replacement). A trafficker would rather purchase another person for US$90 than invest hundreds or thousands of dollars into maintaining the health and profitability of a victim.

Forms of Human Trafficking

Categorization of trafficking by the nature of the work performed is a common although misleading practice. Categories of labor and sex trafficking are most often used; however, concerns have been raised that this separation may serve to make invisible the sexual exploitation that occurs for most women in this situation, even if they are involved in what might be described as a labor-trafficking situation. In other words, a woman may be trafficked primarily for domestic servitude; however, it is likely that she will be forced to engage in sex acts as well—this speaks to the unique vulnerabilities of women and girls. It is impossible to note all of the various types of labor performed by victims, both in sex and labor trafficking; however, typically tasks that are reimbursed at the lower end of the wage continuum are those in which trafficking survivors can be found.

The Trafficked Person

The popular stereotype of victims of human trafficking is innocent young girls who are lured or kidnapped from their home countries and forced into the commercial sex industry (Bruckert and Parent, 2002). While this is not necessarily an erroneous depiction, girls are by no means the only victims of trafficking. Women, men, and children of all ages can be trafficked for sex and labor. Those at risk of trafficking most often come from vulnerable populations including undocumented migrants, runaways, LGBT and other at-risk youth, females, members of other oppressed or marginalized groups, and the poor. Traffickers target individuals in these populations because they have few resources, and limited social support and work options. This makes them easier to recruit through deception or force and they tend to be easier to control.

At-risk youth and runaways are targeted by traffickers and by pimps for labor exploitation, begging, and very often for commercial sex (Estes and Weiner, 2002; Finkelhor and Ormrod, 2004). Pimps and sex traffickers manipulate child and adolescent victims and are known to make use of a combination of violence and affection in an effort to cultivate loyalty in the victim. The phrases "Romeo trafficker" or "Romeo pimp" are used to refer to human traffickers who rely heavily on psychological manipulation to control victims. These traffickers recruit victims by cultivating romantic feelings in the victim and making promises of security. Once these feelings are in place, the trafficker typically uses a combination of strategies to maintain control of the victim. Such psychological manipulation often includes controlling all decision making (e.g. insisting that the victim ask permission to use the bathroom or to eat) to take away the victim's sense of agency in her environment. Other methods are more overtly violent and often include rape, physical violence, and forced drug use leading to addiction, threats to family, and more. Such strategies can result in **Stockholm syndrome**, a psychological phenomenon wherein hostages experience and express empathy and positive feelings for their captors. This is more likely to develop with children and adolescents than with adults, although it is a possibility with the latter as well. This psychological manipulation reduces the victim's likelihood of acting out against the trafficker.

A combination of factors make undocumented immigrants extremely vulnerable to being trafficked (Human Rights Watch, 2012). Some of these factors include lack of legal status and related protections, poverty, few employment options, immigration-related debt, limited language skills, and social isolation. It is not uncommon for undocumented immigrants to be trafficked by those from a similar ethnic or national background, which may play into the victims trust in a way that makes her or him more easily deceived.

Regions impacted by political instability and war create an environment that fosters trafficking. In particular, long-term military occupation as well as the presence of "peace keepers" feed the commercial sex industry in these areas and facilitates the sex trafficking of women and girls (Mendelson, 2005; Morris, 2010). Another situation that promotes trafficking is that of natural disaster. Natural disasters can destroy communities in a matter of minutes and create physical and economic insecurity. Children can be separated from their caregivers, making them prime targets for traffickers. Natural disasters not only impact children, they increase adult vulnerability to trafficking as well. The kind of devastation imposed by disasters of this type can create extreme poverty and make it very difficult to meet basic needs. This, for example, may lead to immigration that can lead to victimization at the hands of a trafficker.

Globalization, the Right to Work, and Human Trafficking

Globalization has had an enormous impact on the trade in people, widening the gap between rich and poor and making it easier for traffickers to recruit and move victims. In fact, it can be said that those involved in transnational crime have benefited significantly from globalization. Current global conditions have created increased demand for cheap labor, thereby increasing migration and consequently human trafficking and smuggling (Naim, 2006). Increased supply of individuals vulnerable to exploitation is present because globalization has contributed to an increase in economic disparities between more developed and developing countries. Tourism has also grown because of globalization, which made it easier for consumers of the sex industry to travel and engage in sex tourism.

The right to work is the concept that every human has the right to work and to be fairly compensated. The term was coined by French socialist leader Louis Blanc in the early nineteenth century. The right to work is articulated in the Universal Declaration of Human Rights (United Nations, 1948) and elaborated upon in the International Covenant on Economic, Social and Cultural Rights (1976) (United Nations, 1966). The right to work is also recognized in international human rights law. Article 23.1 of the Universal Declaration of Human Rights states: *"Everyone has the right to work, to free choice of employment, to just and favourable conditions of work and to protection against unemployment."*

Despite Article 23.1 in the Declaration, millions of people around the world work in inhumane conditions for little or no compensation. Corporations from countries with more developed economies intentionally produce goods in countries with fewer resources because it's better for their bottom line. Products that are commonly used, ranging in value from goods such as coffee and chocolate to cell phones and televisions, are too often made by people who are struggling to survive. By utilizing these workers, corporations are exploiting the low cost of labor and lack of environmental and community protections that are characteristic of developing countries. Workers, including children, pay the price by toiling long hours, often in unsafe environments, for wages that barely afford the basic necessities, or in slavery conditions for no compensation at all. The result is corporations and consumers who reap the benefits of this unlawful "employment."

The disproportionate availability of resources worldwide creates conditions of vulnerability to labor exploitation and slavery. Before addressing this issue, it is important to understand the nuances of the different terms involved. The term **migration** is used to describe the movement of people from one country to another. **Immigration** is when a person moves *to* a country and **emigration** is when a person moves *from* a country. The primary reasons for immigration remain constant—immigration is typically fueled by the need to escape poverty, political instability, or warfare. The possibility of finding work that will better enable one to be self-sufficient and meet the basic needs of family members is also a driving force. Human smuggling is one method by which a person may immigrate to a country. According to the US Department of State (2006), **human smuggling** is the facilitation, transportation, attempted transportation, or illegal entry of a person across an international border (see Table 1.1). This usually refers to crossing an international border either secretly, such as crossing at unauthorized locations; or deceptively, such as with the use of falsified or counterfeit documents. Human smuggling is generally a voluntary act, with the person being smuggled paying a significant amount of money to the smuggler. Two common terms in human smuggling are "coyote" and "snakehead" (Kung, 2000; Walters and Davis, 2011). Coyotes and snakeheads perform the same function, which is to smuggle people into the United States. Coyotes transport individuals from Mexico and snakeheads transport people from China. An individual being smuggled may be subjected to unsafe conditions during the smuggling process including physical and sexual violence. It is not uncommon for the smuggled person to be held by the smuggler until her or his debt is paid off by someone (often a family member) in the destination country. It is important to note that at any point in the smuggling process, the person may become a trafficking victim.

Traffickers who actively recruit victims use traditional immigration as a way to conceal their criminal intentions. With the false promise of compensated work in another country, traffickers are more easily able to get people to cooperate with illegal border crossing. For example, a woman may knowingly agree to be smuggled into a country to work in the sex industry or as a nanny, but she may be unaware that the traffickers will keep

Table 1.1 Human Trafficking Compared to Migrant Smuggling

	Human Trafficking	Migrant Smuggling
Action	Recruitment, transportation, transfer, harboring, or receipt of a person by means of threat or use of force, fraud, coercion	Facilitation of illegal entry of a person into a country of which the person is not a citizen or legal resident
Transnational Border Crossing	Not required	Required
Consent	If other elements of definition present, consent not relevant Not relevant for minors	Required
Outcome	Economic exploitation of the individual, which may include sexual exploitation and/or forced labor	Illegal border crossing

all of the money she makes, restrict and control her movement, and subject her to physical and sexual violence. In other instances, an individual may migrate on her or his own, legally or illegally, identify a work opportunity upon arriving in the destination country and become a victim of trafficking due to the illegal practices of an employer.

It has been suggested that more stringent border entry regulations force migrants to use illegal channels more often, which can increase their risk of being exploited (Salt, 2000). Another perspective is that there is a need for additional anti-trafficking legislation and that the enforcement of the laws that are in place is inconsistent across points of entry, thereby reducing the effectiveness of these anti-trafficking laws.

Prevalence and Profits

According to the United Nations Office on Drugs and Crime (2000), human trafficking is the fastest-growing criminal industry in the world and one of the most profitable (Haken, 2011; Interpol, 2002). However, despite its magnitude, there are a variety of reasons why this crime and its included human rights violations are so difficult to quantify. Some reasons include variation in the operational definitions used by researchers, methodological flaws such as those related to sampling techniques, and the difficulty and potential risks involved for researchers wishing to engage in primary versus secondary research. Also, and perhaps most challenging in the quest to obtain accurate statistics on the prevalence and geography of human trafficking, is that traffickers work to keep their crime undetected. Victims are difficult to identify since they often work in businesses or homes or behind the locked doors of a factory. They are closely monitored by the traffickers and often not permitted in close proximity to those who may be of assistance. These and other similar factors make human trafficking particularly difficult to accurately quantify and describe. Therefore, all reports regarding prevalence should be interpreted with caution. What follows are popular estimates in the field today.

- According to the International Labour Organization (ILO, 2012) there are at least 20.9 million people in forced labor (including sexual exploitation) worldwide. United Nations Global Initiative to Fight Human Trafficking (UN.GIFT) estimates that there are 29.8 million people in modern-day slavery (UN.GIFT, 2013).
- Data suggest that women and girls comprise 80 percent of the individuals trafficked across international borders and 55 percent of the total trafficked population (US Department of State, 2010; ILO, 2012).
- Approximately 68 percent of victims are trafficked for forced labor exploitation (ILO, 2012).
- UNICEF estimates that 158 million children between the ages of five and 14 are engaged in child labor. This is equal to one in six children worldwide (UNICEF, 2011).

- The ILO estimates that children comprise 26 percent of the total enslaved population (ILO, 2012).
- In countries with the fewest resources, 29 percent of all children are engaged in child labor that often interferes with their education, robs them of childhood pleasures, and has a negative impact on them physically and psychologically (UNICEF, 2011).

It is similarly as difficult to assess profits as it is to assess forced labor and human trafficking. Globally, it is estimated that annual profits from forced labor are equal to US$150 billion. It is further estimated that of the US$150 billion, 35 percent is generated for Asia and the Pacific; 8 percent is generated for Latin America and the Caribbean; 8.6 percent is generated for Africa; 5.7 percent is generated for the Middle East; and 31.3 percent is generated for developed economies, including the US and the EU (ILO, 2014). The ILO (2014) also estimated that 66 percent of the money made was from forced sexual exploitation, 5.3 percent of the profits were from domestic work and nearly 30 percent of the profits were from non-domestic labor.

The Trafficking Process

The business of human trafficking is carried out by individuals, small, loosely organized criminal networks, or by traditionally organized crime groups. It includes both small "mom-and-pop" type operations, as well as larger well-organized businesses that operate in a competitive international arena. Some involved in trafficking may assist with a single border crossing while others may work in an ongoing manner with a larger trafficking organization. These larger trafficking organizations often function on a more permanent basis and are involved in the entire trafficking enterprise from the recruitment of victims to the selling and reselling of victims to employers. **Organized crime groups** or **criminal organizations** are local, national, or transnational groupings of centralized enterprises with the purpose of engaging in illegal activity for financial gain. **Transnational organized crime** refers to the planning and execution of unlawful business ventures by groups or networks of individuals working in more than one country (Reuter and Petrie, 1995). Those involved in both national and transnational organized crime systematically use violence and corruption to achieve their goals (Albanese, 2004). Transnational organized crime undermines democracy and impedes the social, political, economic, and cultural development of societies around the world (Voronin, 2000). It is multi-faceted and can involve a variety of different illegal activities including drug trafficking, trafficking in firearms, migrant smuggling and human trafficking. In addition to human trafficking being carried out by organized crime groups, it is also carried out by more loosely organized **criminal networks**. These criminal networks are decentralized and less hierarchical, and according to international securities expert Phil Williams, they can be as effective as and more difficult to detect than traditional organized crime groups (Williams, 2001).

The processes through which people are trafficked are varied. Because trafficking is a money-making endeavor for the trafficker, all exchanges are made in an effort to maximize financial gain while minimizing costs and financial loss. Traffickers engage in numerous individual and small group transactions, the characteristics of which are situation-dependent. Common roles traffickers assume in the process are described below; keep in mind that not all roles are relevant for all trafficking situations.

Trafficker Roles

Recruiter: The recruiter identifies, makes contact with and brings the victim into the first phase of the trafficking process. Depending on the situation, the recruiter sells the victim either directly to the employer (e.g., brothel owner) or to the broker. The recruiter does not always know that the person she or he recruited is going to be enslaved. Some common recruitment methods include:

- use of the internet to advertise for employment opportunities, study abroad, or marriage;
- in-person recruitment in public places such as bars, restaurants, and clubs;
- in-person recruitment through community and neighborhood contacts, including families and friends;
- purchase of children from their parents or legal guardians.

Broker (agent): The broker is the middle person between the recruiter and the employer.

Contractor: The contractor oversees all of the exchanges involved in the trafficking of the victim.

Employment agent: The employment agent takes care of securing "employment" for the victim; this sometimes includes making arrangements for identification paperwork such as visas and passports.

Travel agent: The travel agent arranges for the transport of the victim from her or his point of origin to the destination. This can mean arranging for travel within one country or across country borders.

Document forger/thief: The document forger/thief secures identification documents for cross-border travel. In some instances, this may include creating false documents and in others it may mean illegally modifying actual government documents.

Transporter: The transporter actually accompanies the victim on the journey from point of origin to destination. Transportation may be via boat, bus, car, taxi, train, plane, or on foot. Delivery of the victim is made either to the broker or directly to the employer.

Employer (procurer): The employer purchases and then sells or otherwise exploits the human trafficking victim.

Enforcer ("roof" or guard): The enforcer is responsible for ensuring victim compliance, protecting the business and, at times, for ensuring that outstanding debt is paid by the customer (e.g., payment by a john in a sex-trafficking situation).

Pimp: A pimp is a sex trafficker who directly or indirectly controls a person who is prostituted. He or she takes the profit made from the sex act and may or may not dole out a portion of this to the person being prostituted. The notion exists that the pimp provides protection for those being prostituted; however, the pimp himself often presents the most danger to the individual through threats, physical abuse, rape, and the introduction or maintenance of drug use by the person being prostituted.

"Bottom Bitch:" The prostitute who is most trusted by a pimp and will frequently help the pimp with training new women, collecting money from other prostitutes for the pimp, and only having sex with the pimp.

In order for human trafficking to work, the traffickers either have to force or somehow convince victims to leave their homes and to accompany the trafficker to the destination point. While coercion was defined above, what follows are common means of ensuring victim compliance with departing from her or his point of origin:

- abduction or kidnapping;
- purchasing of a child from her or his parents or legal guardians;
- deception through the promise of legitimate employment and/or entry into a country;
- deception about working conditions;
- deception about compensation and other benefits (e.g., school attendance for children);
- deception through a seemingly intimate/romantic relationship (i.e., trafficker pretends to be romantically interested in the victim).

Traffickers will use a combination of methods to control victims. Methods used depend on a variety of factors, including, for example, the personality of the trafficker, the culture of the group in which they are working, the gender and age of the victim, and the behavior of the victim while in the situation. Examples of control methods are:

- violence (including rape and murder) and the threat of violence against the victim and her or his family;
- depravation of agency or the sense of control over self;
- isolation;
- confiscation of identification and/or travel documents;
- religious beliefs and practices (e.g., threat to use voodoo to harm the family member of a victim whose religious beliefs include voodoo).

Also, a commonly employed strategy of control is for traffickers to tell victims that law enforcement and immigration officials are not trustworthy or will treat them harshly if they are discovered. For victims from countries in which the police or other law enforcement are known to be corrupt, this is a very effective method of control. Obstacles to seeking assistance on the part of the victim are many, for example, in many instances of international trafficking, victims are unaware that they have rights and often do not know that contracts they may have signed are not legally binding. Other obstacles to seeking assistance can be related to family loyalty (i.e., desire to protect family from the trafficker), cultural practices, language barriers, and political suppression in countries of origin.

Snapshot of Efforts to End Trafficking

As noted in part by Suchland (2015), the anti-trafficking movement has predominately focused on individual actors (e.g., the trafficker as criminal and the victim as making poor choices). This reduction narrows the scope of consideration of those involved in combatting trafficking and therefore so too the efforts enacted to prevent the problem. In addition, there seems to be more attention paid to the sex trafficking of women and girls than to the labor trafficking of all groups (women, men, and children). According to Suchland (2015) and others in the field, these factors have played a role in obscuring the bigger picture, which if more complete would include analysis of social institutions and global economic and political trends that create and foster conditions of desperation that promote labor and sex trafficking.

With that said, much work has been done, beginning in 2000 by addressing trafficking. Much like work related to other social problems, non-governmental organizations and activists have assumed an integral grassroots role in the fight against human trafficking and have been instrumental in bringing the issue to the attention of governments around the world. At the international level and largely consequent of international agreements reached at the UN, the United Nations Global Initiative to Fight Human Trafficking (UN.GIFT) was initiated in March 2007 to support the global fight on human trafficking.

The Global Initiative is based on the idea that the crime of human trafficking is of such magnitude that it requires an approach to eradication that is implemented globally and by a variety of relevant stakeholders. In order for this to happen according to UN.GIFT, stakeholders must "coordinate efforts already underway, increase knowledge and awareness, provide technical assistance; promote effective rights-based responses; build capacity of state and non-state stakeholders; foster partnerships for joint action; and above all, ensure that everybody takes responsibility for this fight."[2] UN.GIFT sees its role as that of facilitator of coordination and to "create synergies among the anti-trafficking activities of UN agencies, international organizations and other stakeholders to develop the most efficient and cost-effective tools and good practices."[3]

Many small formal and informal groups have worked hard, often with little to no funding to address trafficking. For example, in Uganda some citizens have collaborated with United States based Project to End Human Trafficking (www.endhumantrafficking.org) to raise awareness about risks in that country. Programming has been uniquely tailored to be culturally sensitive to what is effective with regard to spreading awareness (e.g., school-based clubs, posters delivered to 800 church pastors in rural villages, radio announcements) and to reduce vulnerability to trafficking (e.g., skills based training for financial security).

Human Trafficking in the United States

Like most countries with well-developed market economies, the United States plays a role in fueling the international trade of people. Also, as is the case with most if not all countries affected by human trafficking, the United States is faced with the trafficking of its own citizens within country borders. Sex trafficking of women and children, in particular, girls, is the most significant form of domestic trafficking in the United States. Children targeted in these situations by traffickers, who are commonly referred to as "pimps," are most often runaways or homeless youth. The Williams Institute (2012) conducted a study and found that as many as 40 percent of runaways and homeless youth are members of the Lesbian, Gay, Bisexual, and Transgender (LGBT) community. Labor trafficking is also an issue within the United States, however many of these cases involve individuals trafficked into the country to perform a variety of what are characterized as low-paying jobs. An example of labor trafficking of US citizens appears in the textbox below.

At the federal level in the United States, Congress passed the Victims of Trafficking and Violence Protection Act (TVPA) of 2000 (P.L. 106 386), the Trafficking Victims Protection Reauthorization Act of 2003 (H.R. 2620), the Trafficking Victims Protection Reauthorization Act of 2005 (H.R. 972), the Trafficking Victims Protection Reauthorization Act of 2008 (H.R. 7311) and the Trafficking Victims Protection Reauthorization Act of 2013 (H.R. 898). Prior to the passing of the TVPA in 2000, no comprehensive federal law existed to address human trafficking in the United States.

In the United States TVPA severe forms of trafficking in persons are defined as:

(a) Sex trafficking in which a commercial sex act is induced by force, fraud, or coercion, or in which the person induced to perform such act has not attained 18 years of age; or
(b) The recruitment, harboring, transportation, provision or obtaining of a person for labor services, through the use of force, fraud, or

coercion for the purpose of subjection to involuntary servitude, peonage, debt bondage, or slavery.

(8 U.S.C. §1101)

Much like the United Nations trafficking Protocol, the TVPA focuses on the "three Ps" of trafficking to guide anti-slavery efforts: *prevention* of the crime, *prosecution* of the trafficker, and *protection* for victims. Recently, a fourth "P," standing for *"partnerships,"* was added to the framework. Partnerships are intended to take place across all levels of society—local, regional, national, and international—and are to involve both government and civil society organizations. In addition to providing a comprehensive definition of human trafficking, this legislation gave law enforcement tools to enhance the extent to which traffickers are prosecuted and punished. The TVPA also called for the establishment of a global Trafficking in Persons (TIP) Report, which is published annually and the President's Interagency Task Force to Monitor and Combat Trafficking in Persons.

The TIP Report documents and evaluates the anti-trafficking efforts of foreign governments. Countries are ranked in tiers depending on the extent to which they are compliant with minimum standards established by the TVPA. Countries on the lowest tier may be subject to economic sanctions enacted by the United States. While the TIP Report is thought to be a useful tool, it has been criticized for presenting incomplete information, for not including evaluation of the United States and for being biased and "politicized." Three primary concerns are: how the minimum standards are applied; what methods are used to justify tier placements; and how information for the report is collected and analyzed. Recently, efforts have been made to address some of these concerns, the most visible of which is the inclusion of analysis of US efforts in the 2010 publication of the report.

Under the TVPA, the US Department of Health and Human Services can "certify" international human trafficking victims as such in the eyes of the law. After being certified, victims are then qualified for physical and psychological health services, housing, food stamps, educational and vocational programs, as well as support for legal services. Victims of international trafficking may also be granted a T-Visa, which allows them to live and work in the US for up to three years after which application for permanent resident status may be made. Criticisms of the TVPA have included that eligibility requirements for the T-Visa are too rigid and enforcement is deficient, leaving many deserving victims unprotected. Others have noted that there are unnecessary barriers to obtaining the benefits afforded through the TVPA. These include victim identification, difficulty qualifying as a "severe trafficking" victim, and the time it takes to certify a victim. Victims are often left for long periods of time waiting for assistance to meet the most basic of needs such as shelter, food, and clothing. Communities in which grassroots anti-trafficking coalitions are established often step in to provide support at this critical time. The TVPA has been most strongly criticized by victims' rights activists and social service providers for its requirement that victims participate in prosecution of the trafficker prior to releasing funding in support of their basic needs (e.g., shelter, food, clothing, access to healthcare, and counseling). This requirement is tantamount to requiring a rape victim to press charges against her rapist before giving her access to medical attention and counseling.

As of August 2014, all US states have developed laws that address sex and labor trafficking. The distinction now comes with regard to how states institute safe harbor protections, provided access to civil damages and vacating conviction for sex trafficking victims. The Polaris Project, a non-profit agency working against trafficking nationally, has a rating process through which it tracks the presence or absence of ten categories of state statutes they deem essential to a comprehensive anti-trafficking legal framework. While the United States has made progress with regard to the extent to which trafficking is addressed, there is still much to be done.

Notes

1 It was signed by member states of the UN at a conference in Palermo, Italy, on December 15, 2000 and was entered into force on September 29, 2003 (www.unodc.org/unodc/en/treaties/CTOC/index.html).
2 See www.ungift.org/knowledgehub/en/about/index.html.
3 Ibid.

References

Albanese, J. S. (2004). North American organised crime. *Global Crime* 6(1), 8–18.
Bruckert, C., and Parent, C. (2002). *Trafficking in Human Beings and Organized Crime: A Literature Review*. Ottawa, Canada: University of Ottawa, Criminology Department; Research and Evaluation Branch, Community, Contract and Aboriginal Policing Services Directorate, Royal Canadian Mounted Police.
Estes, R. J., and Weiner, N. A. (2002). *The Commercial Sexual Exploitation of Children in the U.S., Canada, and Mexico*. Philadelphia: University of Pennsylvania.
Finkelhor, D., and Ormrod, R. (2004). Prostitution of juveniles: patterns from NIBRS. *OJJDP Juvenile Justice Bulletin*. Washington, DC: OJJDP.
Free the Slaves. (n.d.). About slavery: Slavery today. Retrieved from https://www.freetheslaves.net/about-slavery/slavery-today
Hernandez, T. K. (2001). Sexual harassment and racial disparity: the mutual construction of gender and race. *University of Iowa Journal of Gender, Race & Justice* 4, 183–224.
Human Rights Watch. (2012). World Report: 2012 Events of 2011. Retrieved from https://www.hrw.org/sites/default/files/world_report_download/wr2012.pdf
ILO. (2012). Global estimate of forced labor. International Labor Organization. Retrieved from http://www.ilo.org/sapfl/Informationresources/ILOPublications/WCMS_181953/lang–en/index.htm
ILO. (2014). Profits and poverty: the economics of forced labour. International Labor Organization. Retrieved from http://www.ilo.org/wcmsp5/groups/public/—ed_norm/—declaration/documents/publication/wcms_243391.pdf

Kung, C. J. (2000). Supporting the snakeheads: human smuggling from China and the 1996 amendment to the US statutory definition of "refugee". *Journal of Criminal Law and Criminology*, 90(4), 1271–1316.

Mendelson, S. E. (2005). *Barracks and Brothels: Peacekeepers and Human Trafficking in the Balkans*. Washington, DC: Center for Strategic and International Studies.

Morris, C. (2010). Peacekeeping and the sexual exploitation of women and girls in post-conflict societies: a serious enigma to establishing the rule of law . *Journal of International Peacekeeping*, 14(1–2), 184–212.

Naim, M. (2006). *Illicit*. New York: Anchor Books.

Reuter, P., and Petrie, C. (eds.) (1995). *Transnational Organized Crime: Summary of a Workshop Exit Notice*. Washington, DC: National Academy Press.

Richard, A. O. (1999). *International Trafficking in Women to the United States: A Contemporary Manifestation of Slavery and Organized Crime*. Center for the Study of Intelligence.

Suchland, J. (2015). *Economies of Violence. Transnational Feminism, Postsocialism, and the Politics of Sex Trafficking*. Durham, NC: Duke University Press.

UN General Assembly. (1948). Universal Declaration of Human Rights (217 [III] A). Paris.

UN.GIFT. (2013). Global Slavery Index. United Nations Global Initiative to Fight Human Trafficking. Retrieved from http://www.ungift.org/doc/knowledgehub/resource-centre/2013/GlobalSlaveryIndex_2013_Download_WEB1.pdf

UNICEF. (n.d.). Factsheet: child soldiers. United Nations International Children's Emergency Fund. Retrieved from http://www.unicef.org/emerg/files/child soldiers.pdf

UNICEF. (2011). Child protection from violence, exploitation and abuse. Retrieved from http://www.unicef.org/media/media_45451.html

United Nations (1966). International Covenant on Economic, Social and Cultural Rights. Retrieved from https://www.ohchr.org/en/professionalinterest/pages/cescr.aspxs

United Nations. (1948). Universal Declaration of Human Rights. Available at: http://www.un.org/en/universal-declaration-human-rights/index.html

United Nations. (2000). Protocol to Prevent, Suppress and Punish Trafficking in Persons, especially Women and Children, supplementing the United Nations Convention Against Transnational Organised Crime. Available at: https://www.ohchr.org/en/professionalinterest/pages/protocoltraffickinginpersons.aspx

US Department of State. (2006). The 2006 Trafficking in Persons Report. Retrieved from https://www.state.gov/j/tip/rls/tiprpt/2006

US Department of State. (2010). The 2010 Trafficking in Persons Report. Retrieved from https://www.state.gov/documents/organization/142979.pdf

US Government Accountability Office. (2006). Human Trafficking: Better Data, Strategy, and Reporting Needed to Enhance U.S. Antitrafficking Efforts Abroad. GAO-06 825.

Väyrynen, R. (2003). Regionalism: old and new. *International Studies Review*, 5, 25–51.

Voronin, Y. (2000). Measures to Control Transnational Organized Crime. Retrieved from http://www.ncjrs.gov/pdffiles1/nij/grants/184773.pdf

Walters, J. and Davis, P. H. (2011). Human trafficking, sex tourism, and child exploitation on the southern border. *Journal of Applied Research on Children: Informing Policy for Children at Risk*, 2(1), 1–17.

Williams Institute. (2012). Serving Our Youth: Findings from a National Survey of Service Providers Working with Lesbian, Gay, Bisexual, and Transgender Youth Who Are Homeless or at Risk of Becoming Homeless. University of California Los Angeles. Retrieved from http://williamsinstitute.law.ucla.edu/wp-content/up loads/Durso-Gates-LGBT-Homeless-Youth-Survey-July-2012.pdf

Williams, P. (2001). Transnational criminal networks. *Networks and Netwars: The Future of Terror, Crime, and Militancy*, 1382, 61–97.

Williamson, C., and Cluse-Tolar, T. (2002). Pimp-controlled prostitution still an integral part of street life. *Violence Against Women*, 8(9), 1074–1092.

2 Providing Trauma-Informed Medically Based Healthcare for Survivors of Sex Trafficking[1]

Elizabeth Miller, Katherine W. Bogen and Heather L. McCauley

Introduction

Sex trafficking is a serious human rights concern which confers numerous health impacts on survivors (Oram et al., 2012; Zimmerman et al., 2008). Zimmerman and colleagues' human trafficking process model is a useful framework to understand how multiple exposures and risks influence the health of survivors throughout the trafficking process, which includes recruitment, transit, exploitation, detention, integration, and re-trafficking (Zimmerman et al., 2011). Multiple exposures while trafficked, compounded by the vulnerability of trafficking survivors, result in cumulative, long-lasting harm (Zimmerman et al., 2011). Research on the health impacts of sex trafficking is generally scarce, but evidence is emerging primarily from global settings, including South and Southeast Asia, sub-Saharan Africa, and Eastern Europe. Below, we outline evidence regarding the physical, sexual, and mental health impacts of sex trafficking; describe the pervasive nature of violence victimization throughout the trafficking process; and draw connections between violence exposure and poor health, to inform the provision of trauma-informed healthcare for this underserved population.

Health Impacts of Sex Trafficking

Studies have assessed the prevalence of physical health symptoms of sex trafficking survivors, though these studies do not provide comparisons to non-trafficked counterparts (Oram et al., 2012). For example, a study of 192 sex trafficking survivors recruited from seven European nongovernmental organizations documented persistent headaches, gastrointestinal symptoms, pelvic pain (likely related to undiagnosed sexually transmitted infections, see below), musculoskeletal symptoms (e.g., back pain, fractures) and dermatological symptoms (e.g., rashes, itching, sores), among others (Zimmerman et al., 2008). Sex trafficking is associated with poor mental health, too. In a sample of 120 sex trafficking survivors seeking services from the International Organization for Migration (IOM) Assistance and

Protection Programme in Moldova, more than half met the criteria for any DSM-IV mental disorder, with childhood sexual abuse (AOR (Adjusted Odds Ratio) 4.68, 95% CI (Confidence Interval) 1.04, 20.92) and unmet post-trafficking needs (AOR 1.80, 95% CI 1.28, 2.52) as important risk factors for these poor outcomes (Abas et al., 2013). Additional risk factors for mental disorders include being trafficked for longer durations (Hossain et al., 2010).

There is also evidence, largely collected among women, to indicate that sex trafficking is associated with poor sexual and reproductive health, including unintended pregnancy and sexually transmitted infections. Literature indicates that women who experience sex trafficking and sexual traumas are more likely to experience dissociation during subsequent sexual encounters as well as sexual dysfunction (i.e., being unable to reach orgasm or lacking sexual desire) (Briere and Jordan, 2004; Heise et al., 2002). Among a sample of female sex workers in Thailand, trafficked women were approximately three times more likely to have become pregnant since their entry into sex work (ARR (Adjusted Risk Ratio) 3.09, 95% CI 1.93, 4.95) and to report abortion during their time in sex work (ARR 2.83, 95% CI 1.48, 5.39), compared to women who entered sex work via other mechanisms (Decker et al., 2011). Studies from South and Southeast Asia have documented that sexually transmitted infections, including HIV, are common among survivors of sex trafficking in the region (Falb et al., 2011; McCauley et al., 2010; Silverman et al., 2008; Silverman et al., 2007). One study of 246 survivors in Nepal found that one in three women had positive HIV test results, and those who were HIV positive were more likely than those who were HIV negative to also be diagnosed with syphilis (AOR 1.88, 95% CI 1.17, 3.03) and hepatitis B (AOR 30.0, 95% CI 7.32, 122.7) (Silverman et al., 2008). Sex trafficking confers risk differently for younger compared to older survivors. One study of 287 sex trafficking survivors from Nepal found that those who were trafficked prior to age 15 were at increased risk for HIV (AOR 3.70, 95% CI 1.32, 10.34) compared to women who were trafficked when they were 18 years or older (Silverman et al., 2007). These findings are likely a result of both biological and social mechanisms including an increased biological vulnerability to infection as a result of larger areas of cervical ectopy, inability to refuse sex, difficulty negotiating condom use, and inadequate access to healthcare (Gupta et al., 2009; Venkatesh and Cu-Uvin, 2013).

Violence Victimization as a Mechanism Impacting the Health of Sex Trafficking Survivors

Evidence on the health impacts of sex trafficking within the United States is scarce and generally involves small samples (Goldberg et al., 2017; Muftic and Finn, 2013). However, this research suggests that sex trafficking survivors often have a history of trauma exposure, whether this occurred prior to being trafficked or during the trafficking process. For example, one US study included a retrospective chart review of 41 patients younger than age

18 years who were referred for domestic minor sex trafficking and found that adverse childhood experiences, including child sexual abuse, were common (Goldberg et al., 2017). A recent study of youth in the juvenile justice system in Florida found that youth with a history of human trafficking (most often sex trafficking) were more likely to have experienced childhood sexual abuse (AOR 2.33, 95% CI 1.83, 2.98), emotional neglect (AOR 1.37, 95% CI 1.10, 1.71), physical neglect (AOR 1.55, 95% CI 1.20, 2.01), and come from a home where violence was present (AOR 1.51, 95% CI 1.09, 2.09) (Reid et al., 2016). These findings are important as early exposure to abuse is associated with early substance use, running away from home and homelessness, which are risk factors for sexual exploitation and sex trafficking (Goldenberg et al., 2015; Tyler, 2008; Tyler, 2009).

Research from global settings illustrates pervasive violence exposure throughout the trafficking process. Two studies which surveyed a sample of 800 female sex workers in Thailand found that 25% of women under age 18 (thus meeting the international definition for trafficking) reported experiencing physical violence in the week before the survey, compared to 14.6% of the total sample (Decker et al., 2010). Moreover, women who were sex trafficked (defined as being forced or coerced into sex work or being younger than 18 years old) were more likely to experience sexual violence at initiation to sex work (Adjusted Risk Ratio (ARR) 2.29, 95% Confidence Interval (CI) 1.11, 4.72), and recent workplace violence or mistreatment (ARR 1.38, 95% CI 1.13, 1.67) (Decker et al., 2011). Sexual violence at initiation or early in the trafficking process (Parcesepe et al., 2016; Silverman et al., 2011), and recent physical or sexual violence regardless of duration in sex work (George and Sabarwal, 2013; Gupta et al., 2011) was also found among samples of female sex workers in India and Kenya (George and Sabarwal, 2013; Gupta et al., 2011; Parcesepe et al., 2016; Silverman et al., 2011). Sex trafficking survivors experience violence perpetrated by recruiters (i.e., traffickers), brothel owners, and clients (Sarkar et al., 2008). Violence experienced at initiation is often perpetrated by brothel owners to instill fear and compliance. Violence perpetrated by clients may include manipulation of or refusal to use condoms, physical threats, and sexual assault and harassment (Ratinthorn et al., 2009).

How does violence increase risk for poor health among survivors? In addition to obvious physical health implications (e.g., fractures) that result from physical violence, persistent fear and stress from violence victimization may result in chronic health conditions (Campbell, 2002). Another mechanism linking violence and poor health, specifically sexual and reproductive health, includes the inability of survivors of violence (including trafficking) to assert sexual agency and negotiate condom use with their sex partners (Goldenberg et al., 2015; Gupta et al., 2009; Urada et al, 2012). For example, a study of more than 1,800 female sex workers in Karnataka, India found that forced prostitution in the presence of additional sexual violence increased the odds of being HIV-infected more than ten times compared to forced prostitution in the absence of additional sexual violence (AOR 11.13, 95% CI 2.41, 51.40) (Wirth et al., 2013). These findings suggest that sexual violence while trading sex made it difficult to enact harm reduction behaviors (i.e., condom use, STI testing). Finally, mental health difficulties are common among survivors of sexual violence victimization more broadly, and sex trafficking, specifically. For example, a study of 204 survivors of sex trafficking who were seeking post-trafficking services in seven European countries found that exposure to sexual violence was associated with higher levels of post-traumatic stress disorder (PTSD) (AOR 5.6, 95% CI 1.3, 25.4), illustrating how powerful sexual violence is with regard to mental health (Hossain et al., 2010).

Collectively, these findings highlight the numerous health risks experienced by survivors of sex trafficking, but also the critical importance of addressing exposure to trauma in the provision of healthcare for this marginalized population. Healthcare providers are uniquely equipped to not only recognize signs and symptoms of sex trafficking among patients, but also to support agency for survivors and provide compassionate, comprehensive care. First, we present a trauma-informed approach towards assessment and care (in lieu of disclosure-based screening), followed by an outline of best practices for providing trauma-informed care for sex trafficking survivors after they have been identified.

Trauma-Informed Approach in Assessment and Care of Survivors of Sex Trafficking: Preparing a Practice

Regaining a sense of safety, dignity, and control (including over one's own body) is critical for supporting trafficked persons as they begin the steps towards healing and recovery. Healthcare providers not only serve as a critical source of information and gateway to services, they can also foster a sense of security and caring. Patients should always be encouraged to seek information, question their options, and assert their choices. Care practices should emphasize client confidentiality, safety, information sharing, informed consent, shared decision making, and autonomy. Healthcare providers should help protect patients from present and future harm by ensuring that their services and staff are sensitive to the vulnerabilities of trafficked persons and that referral options are safe, appropriate and convenient.

A trauma informed approach in a clinical practice means that all clinicians and staff recognize that patients seeking care often have histories of exposure to violence and may currently be in abusive relationships and unsafe situations, and that those experiences of trauma impact health and care seeking behaviors (Elliott et al., 2005). Preparing a clinical practice to identify and care for trafficked persons requires development of policies and protocols related to intimate partner violence and sexual assault, staff and clinician training on rationale for and how to implement these protocols, development of collaborative partnerships with victim service agencies and trauma-focused treatment providers, and staff supports for secondary trauma. The Substance Abuse and Mental Health Services Administration (SAMSHA) provides one guiding definition for trauma informed care (Substance Abuse and Mental Health Services Administration, 2014):

> A program, organization, or system that is trauma-informed realizes the widespread impact of trauma and understands potential paths for recovery; recognizes the signs and symptoms of trauma in clients, families, staff, and others involved with the system; and responds by fully integrating knowledge about trauma into policies, procedures, and practices, and seeks to actively resist re-traumatization.

Reactions to traumatic experiences, the presenting symptoms in the clinical setting, and how patients talk about what happened vary considerably among trafficked persons. This means that there is no simple "right way" to approach all trafficked persons.

All care should be:

- adapted to the individual's needs;
- supportive and should avoid judgmental statements or actions;
- integrated and holistic—treating the trafficked person as a whole person (not just a list of clinical symptoms);
- empowering—ensuring that the rights of the trafficked person to information, privacy, bodily integrity, and participation in decision-making are respected and promoted
- promoting healing and recovery through implementing a patient-centered treatment plan

Hypervigilance around being examined, mistrust of healthcare providers, anxiety about sitting in a waiting room full of other people, and fear of medical procedures may all be related to abuses experienced while being trafficked, often compounded by the experiences of abuse prior to trafficking.

For providers who may only see these patients for brief clinical encounters, a non-judgmental, comforting approach helps to reinforce for the patient that no one deserves to be hurt, and everyone deserves to be treated with respect. Disclosure about the details of what happened to them is not the goal of the clinical encounter.

Seeing the Clues, Spotting "Red Flags"

Although there is no one set of specific symptoms or signs from which providers can know for sure that a person has been trafficked, there are some common features associated with trafficking, which taken together, may indicate that a patient may have been trafficked. Key characteristics may include trauma symptoms, injuries associated with abuse, vague somatic symptoms, and chronic pain that might suggest that a person has been trafficked. Having a "partner" or "family member" who refuses to leave the patient for their clinical assessment is a significant clue that exploitation and controlling behaviors may be occurring. In addition to exploring the possibility of intimate partner violence, providers should keep the possibility of sex trafficking in mind.

It is not uncommon for a person who has been trafficked to not be aware that trafficking is a crime and that they are a victim. Many trafficked persons will not have heard of the crime of "trafficking" and consider the exploitation or abuse that occurred to be a matter of "bad luck," a result of "poor judgment," or a series of poor choices that they made. Thus, the trauma-informed universal education approach described above helps to create a setting that promotes increased trust and supports patient-centered care.

Health providers who have the opportunity to work for more extended periods with trafficked persons (i.e., in partnership with behavioral health), a trauma-informed approach can serve to build trust with clients who over time may become more open to sharing their stories and discussing how the abuse may be impacting their health (Chang et al., 2005). Empowering clients throughout the clinical encounter supports recovery and reduces the possibility of re-traumatization (Clark and Power, 2005; Salasin, 2005), as illustrated by the *Women, Co-occurring Disorders and Violence Study* which demonstrated that trauma-informed services that can result in improved physical and mental health outcomes for women (Huntington et al., 2005; Morrissey et al., 2005). Medical and mental health needs are also addressed in an integrated fashion, recognizing the intersection of mental and physical problems for trafficked persons.

Related to trauma-informed care is the concept of **patient-centered care**—care that places patients centrally in the decision-making process throughout all stages of the clinical encounter. For trafficked persons, lack of control in the context of unpredictable abusive behaviors is common. Thus, encouraging patients' participation in decision-making throughout the clinical encounter is critical to ensuring that the clinical setting does not inadvertently re-traumatize patients who have been trafficked or result in a violation of their rights. This involves training not only healthcare providers, but front-desk staff and medical assistants as well, to provide empathic attention. Shared decision making should occur at all steps of the encounter including development of the treatment plan. Patients are more likely to adhere to prescribed treatment and be an active participant in their own care when given the opportunity to participate actively in the development of the treatment plan.

Clear communication with patients regarding what will happen during the exam before it happens is critical to keep the patient informed and empower him or her. Use of verbal, visual, and written tools (being attuned to low literacy) can help communicate informed consent. Providers should reiterate the voluntary nature of the clinical history and exam as well as receipt of services; provide information both verbally and in writing; offer multiple opportunities for patients to ask questions. The right to refuse should be reiterated at regular and appropriate stages during complicated, lengthy or stressful procedures.

Creating a Clinical "Safe Space"

A supportive and safe environment includes having posters, brochures and messages in the clinical space that discuss privacy, patient rights, and confidentiality, and also provide key information about trafficking, including hotline numbers. Posters with concrete examples of trafficking communicates that the clinic staff care about and are familiar with this issue. Educational brochures (preferably palm-sized, discrete cards that can be hidden) provide information about sexual violence, relationship abuse, and sexual exploitation with questions for patients to consider which lay the groundwork for a conversation with the provider. The materials used should be multicultural and reflect a diversity of relationships and gender expression.

Always strive to do no harm—inadvertent disclosures of trafficking history, breaches of confidentiality, judgmental comments and probing unnecessarily or in an insensitive manner for details about abuse by staff and providers, all contribute to mistrust and fears that many trafficked persons may have about the healthcare system. Providers can minimize the potential for re-traumatizing trafficked persons by having well-trained personnel and clear protocols for supporting patients through acute and ongoing care. For example, showing patients how their records will remain in password-protected computer files and discussing the limits of maintaining privacy (records can be subpoenaed) helps to build trust. Patients should be made aware of limits of confidentiality prior to any delivery of clinical services, such as required reporting for suicidality or homicidal ideation. Especially for minors, providers should know their mandatory requirements for reporting child abuse.

At all times, access to a well-integrated network of resources to support survivors is essential. All providers should be familiar with established protocols within their clinics for contacting local community-based advocacy organizations to address needs such as food, housing, shelter, education, legal aid and job skills development.

Clinical Assessment

Ensure Private Space for Conducting Health Assessment

In addition to emphasizing patient-centered care, privacy, confidentiality, and informed consent, healthcare providers should ensure that the history and exam occur with the patient alone (i.e., with health provider and chaperone when necessary, but no accompanying persons). While some patients may state that they want their "partner" or family member to stay, it is critically important to have time with the patient, who may be scared to ask the accompanying party to leave the room. You may need to state that it is the clinic's policy to see all patients individually and in private at some point during the visit, to afford everyone the same kind of privacy.

Goals for the clinical encounter:

- Create a safe space for the patient where the care is individualized, supportive, non-judgmental, and integrated.
- Conduct a comprehensive health assessment as this clinical encounter may be the only contact the trafficked person has with the healthcare system (i.e., individual may be in detention, in transit). This includes a thorough and systematic review of symptoms, careful "head to toe" exam, and appropriate laboratory testing, recognizing that trafficked persons may present with conditions that are co-morbid with other complex and chronic disorders.
- Focus the clinical encounter as much as possible on those medical problems identified by the patient.
- If possible, receive training in mental health assessment and/or have access to a mental health provider to offer detailed assessment necessary to identify specific mental health diagnoses and treatment needs. The impact of traumatic experiences on patients' symptoms, adherence to treatment, and outcomes cannot be overstated.
- Ensure that a consistent mechanism exists for patients to have results of any testing done shared with them and to receive ongoing care (including preventive care).
- Confirm that patients are connected to resources and services to address multiple needs, including food, shelter, legal advocacy, mental health support, education and job skills development, all critical to the health and well-being of trafficked persons.

Disorders Co-Occur: Comprehensive Health Assessment Is Necessary

While patients may present with specific symptoms as the focus of the clinical encounter, healthcare providers are responsible for conducting a *comprehensive medical and mental health assessment*. The likelihood of co-occurring conditions is high. Knowledge of the multiple health problems that trafficked persons face may assist in taking a systematic approach to the care of these patients with often complex medical problems. Depending on the context of trafficking (including homelessness, addiction), trafficked persons (men, women, and children) will have experienced a range of abuse, violence, and other health risks. For example, a child exploited sexually will also likely have experienced physical abuse, poor nutrition, and sleep deprivation. Careful "head-to-toe" assessments should also be developmentally appropriate. Examinations of children should be conducted, when at all possible, by a provider comfortable with the care of abused children, including forensic examination.

Poor Health Status Is Often Present Prior to And Exacerbated by Trafficking

Trafficked persons are likely to have poor health status even prior to being trafficked, as factors such as poverty and exploitation that increase susceptibility for being trafficked also predict baseline poor health (Beyrer, 2004). Patients may have other active medical problems (e.g., asthma, diabetes, anemia) that are likely to have been exacerbated in the context of trafficking. If a patient presents with a condition that has gone untreated for a long time, such lack of treatment could be a signal that the patient is a trafficked person. Living in unstable housing conditions, poor nutrition, restricted lifestyles, and limited access to healthcare all contribute to poor health and greater acuity and severity of presentation.

Physical and Mental Health Symptoms Are Intertwined

Trafficked persons may present with a wide-range of symptoms that should be carefully assessed in a thorough, systematic review of symptoms at the time of taking a detailed medical history. Somatic symptoms without a clear organic cause are not uncommon, but require thorough assessment to ensure that underlying organic causes are not missed. Physical and mental health symptoms are often intertwined, in particular during the acute period while still in or immediately after leaving a trafficking situation. The constellation of symptoms that trafficked persons present with often intersect with and are exacerbated by post-traumatic reactions. Specifically, somatic and behavioral symptoms related to a history of trauma may include re-experiencing traumatic events, hypervigilance, hyperarousal, irritability and hostility, lack of motivation, poor concentration, chronic headaches, dizziness, sleep disorders, memory problems, chronic fatigue, anorexia, and chronic pain. These post-traumatic symptoms contribute to the overall poor health status of trafficked persons.

Conduct Patient-Centered Physical Exam

Conduct a careful, complete physical exam from head to toe. All physical injuries must be documented, and when appropriate, photo documentation included as well. As is the case with all victims of violence and torture, providers should review the physical exam prior to having the patient undress into a gown, and explain each step of the exam throughout the process, always giving the patient the option to refuse at any point. Patients may not always share all of their complaints nor respond to questions honestly out of fear, mistrust, or shame. Providers must remain vigilant to look for signs of other medical conditions that were not addressed in the medical history. Finally, the physical exam may trigger flashbacks for some patients. This may include the patient "zoning out" such that they appear to be in a different place, stop responding to questions, and hyperventilate or have near-syncope. Stating up front that the exam may remind the patient of prior victimization can be helpful, as is constantly checking with the patient throughout the exam. For example, some trafficked persons may have been exploited through pornography, so particular care should be taken if it is necessary to photograph lesions.

Conduct a Thorough, Systematic Review of Symptoms

While vague somatic concerns, chronic pain, and fatigue may not have an underlying organic cause, the healthcare provider conducting the initial medical assessment must have a high index of suspicion for organic conditions and resist the urge for premature closure of the patient encounter prior to considering the range of possible diagnoses. This means avoiding quick conclusions about the patient's complaints, without conducting a thorough evaluation of presenting symptoms. Providers should expect a vague and unclear history in the context of the trauma the patient has experienced—forgetting details and poor memory are not uncommon.

In addition to the standard review of symptoms, the following includes some additional history questions to consider in the assessment.

Head/Eyes/Ears/Nose/Throat:

- Any history of head trauma?
- Exposure to loud noises?
- Any pharyngeal trauma (lacerations, tears) from forced oral sex?
- Dental or gingival pain?
- Any visual changes? Sudden or gradual?

Neck:

- Any history of strangulation?

Cardiovascular:

- Any trauma to the chest?

Respiratory:

- Any exposure to chemicals, fumes, asbestos (other occupational exposures)?

- Possible exposure to TB? (living conditions? number of people sharing one bedroom? ventilation?)

Gastrointestinal:

- Abdominal trauma?
- Chronic diarrhea? Constipation? (some of these symptoms may be related to mental health in addition to poor nutrition)

Genitourinary:

- Sexual trauma (in addition to forced sex) that includes foreign objects?
- Enuresis or encopresis (a potential result of sexual abuse)?

Musculoskeletal:

- Repetitive and non-repetitive work-related injuries?
- Fractures? (also consider vitamin D deficiency)
- History of physical abuse such as burns? Contractures?

Neurological/Behavioral:

- Seizure activity (may also need to consider pseudo-seizures)?
- Sleep disorders (inability to fall asleep, frequent awakenings, nightmares)?
- Any history of head trauma?

Nutrition:
- Any nutritional deficiencies (assess food intake, content)?
- Disordered eating (e.g., anorexia or bulimic behaviors)?

Head Injury

Among the most common symptoms that trafficked persons report is chronic headaches. Many survivors describe multiple head traumas associated with loss of consciousness, stories suggestive of concussion, and post-concussion syndromes. With chronic headaches, the question of need for neuro-imaging arises. Head imaging is appropriate when history and exam suggest an intracranial process. However, a careful history (inquiring about migraine characteristics—aura, unilateral pain, nausea, photophobia, phonophobia—visual changes, seizure activity, loss of coordination, imbalance) and thorough neurological exam are generally sufficient to rule out significant underlying pathology such as chronic subdural hematomas.

Seizure Disorders, Pseudo-Seizures, and Dissociation

In addition to non-specific symptoms of headaches and dizziness, trafficked persons also report experiences of "passing out," not remembering things, and falling. In particular, in light of the potential traumatic head injuries that some patients may have experienced, a thorough history and neurological examination are critically important. Specifically, asymmetries in exam (e.g., "mini-strokes" related to strangulation), ataxia (e.g., loss of balance, disordered gait), and proprioceptive dysfunction may indicate a serious underlying cause. More often, however, the overall neurologic examination is normal, without evidence of deficits, but the patient continues to have near-syncope or actual falling, sometimes with what appears to be seizure activity. The apparent dissociative states and pseudo-seizures should first be evaluated for organic causes before assuming these are post-traumatic reactions.

Nutritional Deficiencies

Trafficked persons have often had their movement highly restricted and access to food constrained. Access to fresh produce, adequate protein and mineral intake, and exposure to the sun (for vitamin D) are often severely limited. Histories of substance abuse (often co-occurring with other clinical problems) compound the problem of poor nutrition. Thus, close attention to a detailed history of nutritional intake as well as physical exam looking for evidence of nutritional deficiencies (e.g., gum disease, tongue and skin changes) are necessary. Laboratory testing should include at minimum a complete blood cell count (with mean corpuscular volume); when available, iron, total iron binding capacity, B12, folic acid, calcium, phosphorus, and vitamin 25-OH D levels may help guide treatment.

Sexual and Reproductive Health

The intimate nature of sexual and reproductive health for the trafficked man, woman, or child, especially if sexually exploited, cannot be overstated. The examination of the reproductive system can be difficult and possibly re-traumatizing for the trafficked person. Having a normal reproductive life including a family and children is an extremely important concern of many trafficked persons, particularly those who have been sexually exploited. As with women, sexual exploitation or abuse of men and boys may be highly stigmatizing. Health providers must be supportive of all persons who have experienced such abuse.

Trafficked persons (especially younger adolescent patients) sometimes have little knowledge about human anatomy and physiology. For example, they may not know how antibiotics or contraception works, or how much damage a sexually transmitted infection can do their bodies, or that some of them are incurable. Therefore, explanations about medical problems and procedures need to remain very basic.

Despite education and explanation by health providers about necessary tests and treatments, trafficked persons may choose not to pursue sexual and reproductive health services. Trauma-informed care recognizes the tension between beneficence and patient autonomy in the long-term care and development of empowerment for the survivor. To be able to have some control over what happens to their bodies can be an empowering experience for trafficked people.

Examination

Conduct the medical examination only with the trafficked person's consent and with a same-gender examiner or chaperone, if needed. It should be compassionate, confidential, systematic, and complete, following a protocol that is explained before and during the exam. It is important to inform the patient what you are doing as you are doing it. Reassure the trafficked person that they are in control of the pace of the examination and that they have the right to refuse any aspect of the examination. Explain that the findings are confidential, but be honest about which results must or may be reported to comply with legal obligations. Due to sexual abuse or dangerous abortions, trafficked women and girls may suffer from vaginal and perineal tears as well as other external and internal injuries. Therefore, a complete pelvic examination should be conducted. Care should be taken to reduce as much pain and discomfort as possible. Men and boys may also suffer trauma from sexual abuse; a complete genital and anal examination is necessary to assess for lesions and tears. Providers should explain the rationale for these detailed examinations and seek the patient's permission. Patients can also provide guidance on how they would like the exam to proceed (e.g., provider explains every step, or patient listens to music during exam).

Contraception, Pregnancy Testing, and STI Testing

Trafficked persons should be provided with information regarding contraception options. Selection should take into account their desire for pregnancy, prevention of sexually transmitted infections, as well as their ability to continue use of a preferred contraceptive in their current situation. Counseling should include discussions of emergency contraception. Pregnancy testing and options counseling (if a pregnancy is diagnosed) should be made available to all women of reproductive age. Finally, providers must identify where HIV counseling, testing, and treatment can be obtained in a safe and confidential setting. Comprehensive access to HIV prevention, treatment, care and support is essential. Post-exposure prophylaxis for HIV must be considered for all who have had high-risk exposure within the prior 72 hours. When treating sexually transmitted infections, providers must recognize that trafficked persons may have been infected with a drug-resistant strain, or may have developed a drug-resistant strain through inappropriate treatment, and may not respond to first line antibiotics. Where possible, providers must provide follow-up visits to ensure effective treatment.

Preventive Care, Immunizations, and Presumptive Care

While the acuity of the physical and mental health needs for trafficked persons are often overwhelming, this approach offers providers a systematic way to approach patients with complex medical problems. Because of the multitude of acute concerns, preventive care may be overlooked. This can include blood pressure screening, eye exams, immunizations, and cancer screening (testicular, cervical, as well as breast and colorectal for older patients). As this health assessment may be the only clinical encounter for a trafficked person (i.e., the individual may be in transit), consider offering comprehensive preventive care if resources exist for this. However, a protocol should be in place for patients to receive results and be directed to follow-up care as needed.

The question of presumptive care, or the treatment of diseases without test results, is a controversial area in the care of trafficked persons. If it is unlikely that the trafficked person can be contacted after the initial visit to discuss test results, some providers will opt to treat patients presumptively for common diseases such as Chlamydia, in particular if the treatment costs less than the laboratory test. Consider having policies and procedures in place to determine under what circumstances such presumptive care would be delivered, if at all.

The healthcare system holds a unique position in serving as a safe place for trafficked persons. Trafficked persons are often referred to health providers by assistance organisations or police, as part of a protection plan provided to individuals who have been identified as victims of trafficking. However, there may be times when healthcare providers care for a patient who shows signs of being trafficked, abused, or exploited, but the individual has not been formally identified as such. The trafficked person may be seeking care after she or he is free of the trafficking situation or while still trapped in these circumstances.

This second type of encounter may happen in various settings, from a general clinic setting including private practice; care provision for individuals in an immigration detention, reception facility or prison; to outreach services for sex workers or refugee populations. In each case, it is important for you to safely assess the whole situation and decide on appropriate response options. Although trafficked persons caught in the trafficking situation are generally kept away from assistance organizations and settings, given the nature of the abuse and exploitation, it is not unusual for trafficked persons to sustain injuries or become ill, limiting their usefulness, decreasing profitability. Both because of the need for medical attention and because traffickers may consider health providers to be less of a threat (compared to other service providers), medical care might be sought for trafficked persons.

Forensic Exam

If the medical assessment may possibly be used for prosecution, and in particular, if evidence collection is necessary to prove assault (especially rape), a specially trained health provider should carry out a forensic exam. Providers examining children, in particular, should have additional training in child abuse evaluations, including strategies for history-taking from a child, proper techniques for visualization, and documentation. Counsel the survivor about taking evidence for criminal prosecution. It is essential to know in advance where to refer victims of sexual violence safely and assure the trafficked person that information will only be released to the authorities with their consent.

Conclusion

Victims of sex trafficking often experience multiple and compounding health effects, though symptoms may not clearly indicate that such patients are experiencing trafficking. Healthcare providers must remain vigilant regarding the provision of trauma-informed, patient-centered, comprehensive care, while maintaining awareness of resources for survivors of sex trafficking in their area. There are many small steps—such as placing posters regarding human trafficking and identifying the clinic as a resource for survivors—that providers can take to help their patients feel safe. Additionally, providers should be strategic regarding provision of care in private (i.e., ensuring that individuals accompanying the patient to their appointment are not present in the room while providers take medical history or complete an exam), and should ensure that they clearly communicate all parts of their exam to patients.

The compounding health impacts of sex trafficking on victims may cause patients to present with a wide array of health challenges, which may not seem to be connected or may not make sense to the provider. With these "red flags," providers should ask open-ended questions of the patient, try to gather as much information possible regarding living and working conditions, and establish whether or not the patient has available resources to ensure continuity of care. Though sex trafficking is a complex challenge for healthcare providers, clinicians and care providers are uniquely equipped to access and assist this vulnerable populations. Further, it is in the collective community interest to pay special attention to the prevention of sex trafficking and treatment of victims—doing so may feasibly have an impact on community-level health (such as the prevalence of HIV and unwanted/underage pregnancies). It is important that clinics prioritize the health and safety of this highly vulnerable population. Establishing procedures and policies that will allow clinics to effectively and efficiently assess for sex trafficking is a vital component of care in the community and is tied to continued improvement in local and national health systems.

Note

1 Sections of this chapter have been adapted from the following report for which Elizabeth Miller was a co-author: *United Nations Global Initiative to Fight Human Trafficking, International Organization for Migration. Caring for Trafficked Persons: Guidance for Health Providers*, 2009.

References

Abas, M., Ostrovschi, N. V., Prince, M., Gorceag, V. I., Trigub, C., and Oram, S. (2013). Risk factors for mental disorders in women survivors of human trafficking: a historical cohort study. *BMC Psychiatry*, 13(1), 204. doi:10.1186/1471-244x-13-204

Beyrer, C. (2004). Is trafficking a health issue? *The Lancet*, 363, 564.

Briere, J., and Jordan, C. E. (2004). Violence against women: outcome complexity and implications for assessment and treatment. *Journal of Interpersonal Violence*, 19(11), 1252–1276.

Campbell, J. C. (2002). Health consequences of intimate partner violence. *The Lancet*, 359(9314), 1331–1336. doi:10.1016/S0140-6736(02)08336-08338

Chang, J. C., Decker, M. R., Moracco, K. E., Martin, S. L., Petersen, R., and Frasier, P. Y. (2005). Asking about intimate partner violence: advice from female survivors to health care providers. *Patient Education and Counseling*, 59(2), 141–147. doi:10.1016/j.pec.2004.10.008

Clark, H. W., and Power, A. K. (2005). Women, co-occurring disorders, and violence study: a case for trauma-informed care. *Journal of Substance Abuse Treatment*, 28(2), 145–146. doi:10.1016/j.jsat.2005.01.002

Decker, M. R., McCauley, H. L., Phuengsamran, D., Janyam, S., Seage, G. R., and Silverman, J. G. (2010). Violence victimization, sexual risk and STI symptoms among a national sample of FSWs in Thailand. *Sexually Transmitted Infections*, 86(3), 236–240.

Decker, M. R., McCauley, H. L., Phuengsamran, D., Janyam, S., and Silverman, J. G. (2011). Sex trafficking, sexual risk, sexually transmitted infection and reproductive health among female sex workers in Thailand. *Journal of Epidemiology and Community Health*, 65, 334–339.

Elliott, D. E., Bjelajac, P., Fallot, R. D., Markoff, L. S., and Reed, B. G. (2005). Trauma-informed or trauma-denied: principles and implementation of trauma-infomred services for women. *Journal of Community Psychology*, 33(4), 461–477.

Falb, K. L., McCauley, H. L., Decker, M. R., Sabarwal, S., Gupta, J., and Silverman, J. G. (2011). Trafficking mechanisms and HIV status among sex-trafficking survivors in Calcutta, India. *International Journal of Gynecology & Obstetrics*, 113(1), 86–87. doi:10.1016/j.ijgo.2010.11.009

George, A., and Sabarwal, S. (2013). Sex trafficking, physical and sexual violence, and HIV risk among young female sex workers in Andhra Pradesh, India. *International Journal of Gynecology & Obstetrics*, 120(2), 119–123. doi:10.1016/j.ijgo.2012.08.019

Goldberg, A. P., Moore, J. L., Houck, C., Kaplan, D. M., and Barron, C. E. (2017). Domestic minor sex trafficking patients: a retrospective analysis of medical presentation. *Journal of Pediatric and Adolescent Gynecology*, 30(1), 109–115. doi:10.1016/j.jpag.2016.08.010

Goldenberg, S. M., Silverman, J. G., Engstrom, D., Bojorquez-Chapela, I., Usita, P., Rolon, M. L., and Strathdee, S. A. (2015). Exploring the context of trafficking and adolescent sex industry involvement in Tijuana, Mexico: consequences for HIV risk and prevention. *Violence Against Women*, 21(4), 478–499.

Gupta, J., Raj, A., Decker, M. R., Reed, E., and Silverman, J. G. (2009). HIV vulnerabilities of sex-trafficked Indian women and girls. *International Journal of Gynecology & Obstetrics*, 107(1), 30–34. doi:10.1016/j.ijgo.2009.06.009

Gupta, J., Reed, E., Kershaw, T., and Blankenship, K. M. (2011). History of sex trafficking, recent experiences of violence, and HIV vulnerability among female sex workers in coastal Andhra Pradesh, India. *International Journal of Gynecology & Obstetrics*, 114(2), 101–105. doi:10.1016/j.ijgo.2011.03.005

Heise, L., Ellsberg, M., and Gottmoeller, M. (2002). A global overview of gender-based violence. *International Journal of Gynecology & Obstetrics*, 78(S1), S5–S14.

Hossain, M., Zimmerman, C., Abas, M., Light, M., and Watts, C. (2010). The relationship of trauma to mental disorders among trafficked and sexually exploited girls and women. *American Journal of Public Health*, 100(12), 2442–2449. doi:10.2105/AJPH.2009.173229

Huntington, N., Moses, D. J., and Veysey, B. M. (2005). Developing and implementing a comprehensive approach to serving women with co-occurring disorders and histories of trauma. *Journal of Community Psychology*, 33(4), 395–410.

McCauley, H. L., Decker, M. R., and Silverman, J. G. (2010). Trafficking experiences and violence victimization of sex-trafficked young women in Cambodia. *International Journal of Gynecology & Obstetrics*, 110(3), 266–267. doi:10.1016/j.ijgo.2010.04.016

Morrissey, J. P., Jackson, E. W., Ellis, A. R., Amaro, H., Brown, V. B., and Najavits, L. M. (2005). Twelve-month outcomes of trauma-informed interventions for women with co-occurring disorders. *Psychiatric Services*, 56(10), 1213–1222.

Muftic, L. R., and Finn, M. A. (2013). Health outcomes among women trafficked for sex in the United States: a closer look. *Journal of Interpersonal Violence*, 28(9), 1859–1885.

Oram, S., Stockl, H., Busza, J., Howard, L. M., and Zimmerman, C. (2012). Prevalence and risk of violence and the physical, mental and sexual health problems associated with human trafficking: systematic review. *PLoS Medicine*, 9(5), e1001224.

Parcesepe, A. M., L'Engle, K. L., Martin, S. L., Green, S., Suchindran, C., and Mwarogo, P. (2016). Early sex work initiation and violence against female sex workers in Mombasa, Kenya. *Journal of Urban Health*, 93(6), 1010–1026. doi:10.1007/s11524-016-0073-6

Ratinthorn, A., Meleis, A., and Sindhu, S. (2009). Trapped in a circle of threats: violence against sex workers in Thailand. *Health Care for Women International*, 30, 249–269.

Reid, J. A., Baglivio, M. T., Piquero, A. R., Greenwald, M. A., and Epps, N. (2016). Human trafficking of minors and childhood adversity in Florida. *American Journal of Public Health*, 107(2), 306–311. doi:10.2105/AJPH.2016.303564

Salasin, S. E. (2005). Evolution of women's trauma-integrated services at the substance abuse and mental health services administration. *Journal of Community Psychology*, 33(4), 379–393.

Sarkar, K., Bal, B., Mukherjee, R., Chakraborty, S., Saha, S., Ghosh, A., and Parsons, S. (2008). Sex-trafficking, violence, negotiating skill, and HIV infection in brothel-based sex workers of Eastern India, adjoining Nepal, Bhutan, and Bangladesh. *Journal of Health, Population and Nutrition*, 26(2), 223–231.

Silverman, J. G., Decker, M. R., Gupta, J., Maheshwari, A., Willis, B. M., and Raj, A. (2007). HIV prevalence and predictors of infection in sex-trafficked nepalese girls and women. *Journal of the American Medical Association*, 298(5), 536–542.

Silverman, J. G., Decker, M. R., Gupta, J., Dharmadhikari, A., Seage, G. R., and Raj, A. (2008). Syphilis and hepatitis B co-infection among HIV-infected, sex-trafficked women and girls, Nepal. *Emerging Infectious Diseases*, 14(6), 932–934.

Silverman, J. G., Raj, A., Cheng, D. M., Decker, M. R., Coleman, S., Bridden, C., Samet, J. H., et al. (2011). Sex trafficking and initiation-related violence, alcohol use, and HIV risk among HIV-infected female sex workers in Mumbai, India. *Journal of Infectious Diseases*, 204, S1229–1234.

Substance Abuse and Mental Health Services Administration. (2014). *SAMHSA's Concept of Trauma and Guidance for a Trauma-Informed Approach.* Rockville, MD: Substance Abuse and Mental Health Services Administration.

Tyler, K. A. (2008). A comparison of risk factors for sexual victimization among gay, lesbian, bisexual and heterosexual homeless young adults. *Violence and Victims*, 23(5), 586–602.

Tyler, K. A. (2009). Risk factors for trading sex among homeless young adults. *Archives of Sexual Behavior*, 38(2), 290–297. doi:10.1007/s10508-007-9201-4

Urada, L. A., Morisky, D. E., Pimentel-Simbulan, N., Silverman, J. G., and Strathdee, S. A. (2012). Condom negotiations among female sex workes in the Philippines: environmental influences. *PLoS One*, 7(3), e33282.

Venkatesh, K. K., and Cu-Uvin, S. (2013). Assessing the relationship between cervical ectopy and HIV susceptibility: implications for HIV prevention in women. *American Journal of Reproductive Immunology*, 69(s1), 68–73.

Wirth, K. E., Tchetgen, E. J., Silverman, J. G., and Murray, M. B. (2013). How does sex trafficking increase the risk of HIV infection? An observational study from Southern India. *American Journal of Epidemiology*, 177(3), 232–241.

Zimmerman, C., Hossain, M., Yun, K., Gajdadziev, V., Guzun, N., Tchomarova, M., Watts, C., et al. (2008). The health of trafficked women: a survey of women entering posttrafficking services in Europe. *American Journal of Public Health*, 98(1), 55–59. doi:10.2105/AJPH.2006.108357

Zimmerman, C., Hossain, M., and Watts, C. (2011). Human trafficking and health: a conceptual model to inform policy, intervention and research. *Social Science & Medicine*, 73(2), 327–335. doi:10.1016/j.socscimed.2011.05.028

3 The Adult Trafficking Survivor and Post-Traumatic Stress Disorder

Veronica M. Lugris, Mary C. Burke and Leah Russell Flaherty

Trauma is defined as an experience that threatens one's sense of safety and security, and may or may not involve physical harm. Generally, trauma is experienced as either a single or a repeating event that overwhelms an individual's coping mechanisms and interferes with one's ability to integrate and make sense of emotions and thoughts related to the experience. According to the *Diagnostic and Statistical Manual of Mental Disorders 5* (APA, 2013), a traumatic event is one that involves "exposure to actual or threatened death, serious injury, or sexual violence" (p. 271). In order to meet diagnostic criteria a person does not necessarily have to have experienced the event themselves, they may have witnessed the event, learned about it having happened to a close family member or friend, or they may have repeated or extreme exposure through media to the trauma. A wide variety of events can be characterized as traumatic. Examples include naturally occurring or human-made catastrophic events such as dangerous storms and war or interpersonal violence such as intimate partner violence, rape, and emotional or physical abuse. Trafficking victims are among those individuals for whom captivity and threatened death, serious injury, and/or sexual violence are repeated which increases their risk of developing PTSD.

Particularly vulnerable to PTSD are trafficking victims who experience severe physical and sexual assaults. Given that 70 percent of trafficking victims are trafficked for sexual exploitation and sexual assault is a traumatic experience, these victims are likely to experience PTSD or post traumatic stress symptoms (PTSS). Furthermore, 80 percent of trafficking victims are women and girls, and research suggests that women are more vulnerable to PTSD than men (Seedat et al., 2005) and that PTSD symptoms last longer in women than in men (Breslau et al., 1998).

The distinction between PTSS and PTSD is an important one. To warrant a diagnosis of PTSD one must meet full criteria as specified by the *Diagnostic and Statistical Manual of Mental Disorders 5* (APA, 2013). If one experiences symptoms of PTSD that are subthreshold this is referred to as PTSS or "partial PTSD." The symptom criteria for PTSD are presented in four clusters. These clusters are: intrusion, avoidance, negative alterations in cognition or mood, and heightened arousal. In order to meet full criteria for PTSD a person must present with each of these symptoms.

Intrusion symptoms include memories of the event which are involuntary, intrusive, and distressing. Distressing dreams, dissociative reactions, distress at exposure to triggers of the event, and physiological reactions to trauma cues are also included in this cluster. Avoidance is the next symptom set. This is characterized by efforts to avoid thoughts or feelings associated with the trauma and/or efforts to avoid external reminders that activate memories of the event.

Negative alterations in cognition or mood is a symptom cluster that was recently added for the DSM-5. This refers to a broad range of symptoms including an inability to remember aspects of the event, exaggerated negative beliefs about oneself, others, or the world, distorted cognitions of guilt, negative emotional state, anhedonia, feelings of detachment, and inability to experience positive emotions.

The final cluster, hyperarousal or hyper-reactivity, is evidenced by irritability, recklessness, exaggerated startle response, problems with concentration, and sleep disturbance.

To meet a PTSD diagnosis, the duration of the four latter criteria must persist more than one month, and in some cases may last throughout a lifespan, causing significant distress or impairment in social, occupational, or other areas of functioning. Complicating early and accurate diagnosis is the fact that individuals may not exhibit PTSD for months or years following the traumatic event, only to be triggered by a situation that resembles the original trauma.

A recent diagnostic addition to the DSM-5 is PTSD for Children Six Years and Younger. This diagnosis was added to appreciate the fact that children often have a different sequelae of psychological trauma than adults. The main differences in these diagnoses are: (1) traumatic experience cannot include media exposure; (2) intrusive memories may not appear distressing, may in fact be expressed through play; (3) content of dreams though frightening may appear to be unrelated to traumatic event; (4) the avoidance cluster and the negative cognitions cluster have been collapsed into one category.

Often a person diagnosed with PTSD also meets criteria for other diagnoses, including mood and anxiety disorders, alcohol or substance abuse and dependence, or personality disorders, potentially complicating treatment (Alexander et al., 2005; Zimmerman et al., 2006; Zimmerman, 2003; Raymond et al., 2002).

The Complexity of Human Trafficking and PTSD

Herman (1992) suggests that current PTSD criteria fails to consider the complexity of symptoms present in individuals exposed to prolonged violence, such as domestic abuse, sexual abuse, and torture, all commonly seen in trafficking victims. Herman proposes an alternative formulation that takes into account somatization, dissociation, and pathological changes in identity.

The state of the science reflects a trend toward a greater understanding of the complexity of trauma and the DSM-5 has begun to capture these more complicated traumatic reactions with specifiers under the PTSD diagnosis of dissociative symptoms. Survivors of more complex trauma, such as trafficking victims are also at risk for self-destructive and risk-taking behaviors as well as re-victimization (Courtois, 2004).

It is important to consider that current PTSD diagnostic criteria reflects Western culture and worldview, limiting our understanding of the impact of cultural influences on the experience of trauma, specifically with regard to trafficking victims from non-Western societies. Culture is a significant variable, given that there are approximately 15–20 million in bonded labor in India, Pakistan, Bangladesh, and Nepal and the remaining (of the estimated 27 million) are primarily in South East Asia, northern and western Africa, and parts of North and South America (Bales, 2012). Furthermore, countries of origin are primarily in south Asia, South East Asia, Latin America and the Caribbean, former Soviet republics, eastern Europe, and Africa, while countries of destination primarily include United States, Japan, Canada, and many countries in western Europe, emphasizing the need for culturally sensitive approaches to working with traumatized trafficking survivors in our sphere, if not elsewhere in the world.

Strong family or social support networks can mitigate the risks of PTSD in trafficking victims. But while the Trafficking Victims Protection Act makes clear that all the risk factors for severe PTSD are present in the human trafficking experience, the mitigating factors that might help prevent the long-term mental health consequences, such as family and social supports, are generally absent.

Neurobiological Correlates of PTSD

Over the past two decades, neuroscience has begun to uncover the neurobiological changes that correlate with symptoms of traumatic stress disorders. Under normal circumstances, the human brain has evolved to effectively assess different stimuli, discriminate what is truly life threatening, and respond quickly. While threat activates autonomic nervous system (ANS), exposure to more extreme forms of threat, such as that found in human trafficking, significantly impacts individuals' ability to modulate sympathetic and parasympathetic nervous systems in the ANS, failing to organize an effective response to threat. Instead of a fight or flight response, immobilization ensues (Van der Kolk, 2006). A clear example of this is the conditioned behavioral response of immobilization that follows inescapable shock in laboratory animals.

The traumatization of trafficking victims takes place in a context of repetitive and unrelenting boundary violations, and loss of agency, self-regulation, and social support. Such conditions lead traumatized trafficking victims to develop a mechanistic compliance or resigned submission not unlike the response demonstrated in laboratory animal subjects, even in situations where one might expect them to react differently.

Neurobiological findings show that trauma entails a fundamental dysregulation of arousal modulation at the brain stem level. Traumatized victims suffer from baseline autonomic hyperarousal and lower resting heart rate compared to controls, suggesting that they have increased sympathetic and decreased parasympathetic tone (Cohen et al., 2002; Sahar et al., 2001). These biological changes can have a long-lasting impact on a traumatized trafficking victim's personality, such as losing the ability to regulate emotions or manage even small amounts of stress. They may exhibit chronic states of irritability or anger. For some, dissociation may become the primary way of coping and they may be unable to account for significant periods of time. Victims may also become "dissociated" from their emotions so as to seem emotionally numb.

Many traumatized victims become chronically overwhelmed by their emotions and are unable to use their affective states as guides to adaptive action. They frequently fail to identify their feelings and may freeze at the moment of responding (Van der Kolk, 2006). When they try to attend to their internal process, they often report becoming overwhelmed by intrusive imagery and distressing physical and emotional feelings triggered by their traumatic experiences. Traumatized victims also tend to struggle with a clear sense of self and often report negative body image, potentially leading them to ignore physical concerns. Thus, a lack of emotional attunement may cause traumatized victims to neglect their needs and/or the needs of others.

Biological changes in the cortical regions of the brain may cause loss of cognitive abilities, so that a traumatized trafficking victim may experience difficulty remembering, organizing, planning, or thinking. Alternatively, a constant emotional state of numbness may lead to depression, lack of energy and a sense of hopelessness. One of the most robust findings of neuro imaging studies of traumatized people is that, under stress, the higher brain areas involved in "executive functioning" (i.e., planning for the future, anticipating the consequences of one's actions, and inhibiting inappropriate responses) become less active (Markowitsch, 2000; Shin et al., 2001).

Neurological studies of trauma survivors show changes in cognitive abilities, such as preferential use of the right hemisphere; inhibition of left frontal cortical areas of the brain; activation of the limbic area; and diminished hippocampus volume. There is also a wide literature showing dysregulation in various neurotransmitter and neurohormonal systems, including the hypothalamic pituitary axis, catecholamines, serotonin, and opioid systems (Van der Kolk, 2006).

Reminders of traumatic experiences activate brain regions that support intense emotions and decrease activation in the central nervous system (CNS) regions involved in integrating sensory input with motor output, modulating physiological arousal, and communicating experience into words. Traumatized research participants show cerebral blood flow increases in the right medial or bitofrontal cortex, insula, amygdala, and anterior temporal pole, and in a relative deactivation in the left anterior prefrontal cortex, specifically in Broca's area, the expressive speech center in the brain, the area necessary to communicate what one is thinking and feeling (Hull, 2002; Lanius et al., 2001; Lindauer et al., 2004; Rauch et al., 1996).

Neuropsychology and neuroimaging research reports findings that traumatized individuals have problems with sustained attention and working memory, which causes difficulty performing tasks with focused concentration, and with being fully engaged in the present. This is most likely the result of a dysfunction of frontal–subcortical circuitry, and deficits in corticothalamic integration (Vasterling et al., 1998; Clark et al., 2003). Such dysregulation helps to explain how traumatized trafficking victims may either lash out or appeared stunned in the context of minor challenges, leaving witnesses to question the validity of victims' responses.

Specifically, neuroimaging studies of people with PTSD have found decreased activation of the medial prefrontal cortex (mPFC) (Markowitsch et al., 2000; Shin et al., 2001; Devinsky et al., 1995). The medial prefrontal comprises anterior cingulate cortex (ACC) and medial parts of the orbito frontal prefrontal cortices. The ACC specifically has consistently been implicated in PTSD. The ACC plays a role in the experiential aspects of emotion, as well as in the integration of emotion and cognition.

The mPFC plays a role in the extinction of conditioned fear responses by exerting inhibitory influences over the limbic system, thereby regulating the generalization of fearful behavior, by attenuating peripheral sympathetic and hormonal responses to stress, and in the regulation of the stress hormone cortisol by suppressing the stress response mediated by the HPA. The fact that the mPFC can directly influence emotional arousal has enormous clinical significance, since it suggests that activation of intero ceptive awareness can enhance control over emotions and allow traumatized victims to overcome their conditioned immobilization (Van der Kolk, 2006).

A dearth exists in the literature that might determine the longitudinal impact of trauma after successful treatment. Research has found positive changes in the anterior cingulate and amygdala of patients with PTSD after a successful response to CBT. Future research may uncover the potential for psychotherapy to positively affect neurobiology post-trauma.

Treatment Considerations

Ethnicity can impact the way individuals seek assistance, identify their problems, consider psychological difficulties, experience their trauma, and understand recovery. Many cultures do not distinguish psychological, emotional, and spiritual reactions from physical ones. Just as therapy can be commonplace in Western culture, individuals from other cultures may turn to folk healing or other forms of treatment in support of psychological wellness (Williamson et al., 2008).

It is recommended that treatment be individualized to focus on the traumatized trafficking survivor's needs and capabilities, all the while considering safety and affect regulation as foundational to the work. Part of creating safety and a sense of self-determination includes informed patient consent, the assessment of motivation for treatment, clarification of treatment expectations, education about the therapy process in ways that are demystifying, and communication of a sense of hope.

Initial sessions typically assess for prior traumatic experiences, co-morbid symptoms, and availability of resources. When inquiring about prior traumas, it is important to not assume that disclosure will be forthcoming, even when there is a history of trauma present. Some traumatized trafficking survivors may only disclose later, as trust develops in the therapy relationship.

Trauma that is acknowledged can be assessed as part of a battery of psychological tests that include validated measures of PTSD, such as the Clinician-Administered PTSD Scale (CAPS; Blake et al., 1996), the Impact of Event Scale—Revised (IES–R; Weiss and Marmar, 1997), the Detailed Assessment of Posttraumatic States (DAPS; Briere, 2001), and the Posttraumatic Stress Diagnostic Scale (PDS) (Foa, 1995). These tools can help guide the therapist in identifying the traumatized trafficking survivor's preferred psychological defenses, ability to self-regulate, and relational capacities. Two other recommended instruments offer information that is useful in assessing more complex trauma, such as that found in trafficking victims. They are the Trauma Symptom Inventory (TSI), which assesses domains of the self and relations with others (Briere, 1995; Briere et al., 1995), and the Structured Interview for Disorders of Extreme Stress (SIDES), developed for the DSM–IV field trial (Pelcovitz et al., 1997; Zlotnick and Pearlstein, 1997). Also helpful are the Inventory of Altered Self Capacities (IASC) (Briere, 2000b), which assesses difficulties in relatedness, identity, and affect regulation, the Cognitive Distortion Scales (CDS) (Briere, 2000a) and the Trauma and Attachment Belief Scale (Pearlman, 2003), both of which assess cognitions. Measures of dissociation include: the Dissociative Experiences Scale (DES) (Bernstein and Putnam, 1986; Carlson and Putnam, 1993), which can be enhanced by the Multiscale Dissociation Inventory (MDI) (Briere, 2002a) and the Somatoform Dissociation Scale (SDQ-20) (Nuenhuis, 2000), and the Structured Clinical Interview for DSM–IV Dissociation Disorders (SCID-D) (Steinberg, 1994).

Regardless of whether or not treatment includes psychological testing, it is paramount from the beginning for the therapist to emphasize safety in the therapy relationship. Part of this includes teaching traumatized trafficking patients ways in which they may exercise self-determination during sessions and ways to contain emotions that may spill over following sessions.

Neurobiological findings suggest that it may be useful for traumatized trafficking survivors to learn to regulate their physiological arousal through techniques such as mindfulness training (Lazar et al., 2005). Mindfulness training allows the traumatized trafficking patient to become a careful observer of one's inner experience, and to notice one's breath, gestures, thoughts, feelings, bodily sensations, and impulses that arise.

Traumatized trafficking individuals need to experience that it is safe to have feelings and sensations. If they learn to attend to their inner experience, traumatized trafficking victims can appreciate that bodily experiences are always in flux and they, themselves, can exert greater agency in their present experiences.

By learning to attend to nontraumatic stimuli in the present, traumatized trafficking individuals can learn to release themselves from reliving their past traumas and they can practice re-engaging their ability to protect themselves. Thus, the therapist helps the traumatized trafficking survivor to gain control over extreme affective responses that may seem out of place, self-destructive thoughts and behaviors, addictions, and dissociative episodes.

While self-attunement is a fundamental building block in physiological self-regulation, interpersonal trauma also often results in a fear of intimacy. Engaging a traumatized trafficking individual in a therapy relationship may trigger shame and memories of betrayal. On the other hand, a strong working alliance of empathic attunement can provide opportunities to resolve past attachments and improve self and relational capacities. Furthermore, connecting affectively with traumatic memories in the context of a supportive therapeutic relationship helps to provide resolution (Fosha, 2003; Neborsky, 2003; Schore, 2003a, b; Solomon and Siegel, 2003). The goal is not to trigger the emergence of new memories, although that is a possibility when the trauma is addressed more directly (Gold and Brown, 1997). Part of connecting affectively with traumatic memories includes grief work that creates space for the traumatized patient to mourn losses associated with the experience. The goal is to emerge from the therapeutic experience with decreased PTSD and co-morbid symptoms, increased self-attunement and self-regulatory skills, improved self-care, a greater sense of agency, adaptive interpersonal capacities, and a sense of hope and planning for the future.

Evidence-based techniques founded on research that shows them to be effective are recommended, although this does not mean that other treatment modalities may not be effective, just simply less studied due to the complexity of variables involved. Examples of evidence-based techniques that have been shown to be effective with traumatized populations include cognitive-behavioral therapy (CBT) (Rauch and Cahill, 2003; Ursano et al., 2004), cognitive-processing therapy (CPT) (Resick and Schnicke, 1992), and attention to trauma-based cognitions can help decrease cognitive symptomatology related to a negative sense of self (Jehu et al., 1985; Roth and Batson, 1997).

CBT combines cognitive and behavioral approaches to change dysfunctional thoughts, feelings, and behaviors through techniques such as exposure therapy, thought stopping, and breathing regulation. Exposure therapy entails confronting a specific source of anxiety through progressively intense exposure until habituation is reached. Exposure therapy can take place in imaginal or in vivo formats. Thought stopping and breathing regulation are self-explanatory.

CPT is based around the concept of understanding how trauma impacts a client's life. CPT aims to help clients overcome the self-blame, changes in belief systems, overgeneralizations, and distortions that occur as a result of trauma. Before processing the trauma in depth the client is taught to label emotions and like CBT, to recognize the connections between events, thoughts, and feelings. The three major goals of CPT are to remember and accept the trauma without avoidance of memories or emotions, to allow natural emotions to be experienced in totality, and to work toward more balanced beliefs as opposed to insincere maladaptive emotions (Resick, Monson, and Chard, 2017). Importantly, the therapist works to teach the clients to question thoughts and assumptions related to the trauma so that they can act as their own therapist after termination.

Eye movement desensitization and reprocessing (EMDR) (Shapiro and Solomon, 1995) is another empirically validated treatment for trauma survivors that uses rapid eye movement to induce bilateral simulation to decrease traumatic imagery and negative emotions (Bradley et al., 2005; Rauch and Cahill, 2003; Ursano et al., 2004).

CBT has been found to have long-term effectiveness 8–14 years following treatment in patients with co-morbid anxiety (McIntosh et al., 2004), while a combination of CBT and interpersonal therapy that focuses on the correlation between relationships and mood has been found to be effective for co-morbid depression (Karasu et al., 2000; McIntosh et al., 2004; Weersing et al., 2006).

CBT, motivational enhancement therapy, behavioral therapy, 12-step groups, and interpersonal therapy are evidence-based treatment for co-morbid substance-related disorders. In addition, self-help books, brief inter ventions, case management, group, marital, and family therapy can also help (Kleber et al., 2006).

Motivational enhancement therapy uses motivation to form decisions and plans for change (Miller, 2003a, b). Twelve-step groups make use of group support under the rubric of acceptance of a higher power to help with long-term recovery (Nowinski, 2003). Treatment that focuses on managing substance abuse or dependence without addressing the underlying trauma will have less successful outcomes and patients are more likely to relapse (Alexander et al., 2005).

Despite existing research on the psychological effects of trauma, more evidence-based research is needed on trafficking populations. Many non-Western cultures have healing traditions that activate and use physical movement and breath, such as yoga, chi qong, and tai chi all of which claim to regulate emotional and physiological states.In terms of pharmacological treatments, there is evidence to suggest that selective serotonin re-uptake inhibitors (SSRIs) can work in conjunction with psychotherapy to improve PTSD and comorbid symptoms related to anxiety and mood disorders

(Seedat et al., 2005; Ursano et al., 2004; Weersing et al., 2006). The Veterans Affairs Clinical Practice Guidelines echo the recommendation of SSRIs for the treatment of PTSD and as an alternative for those who do not respond well to SSRIs they recommend TCAs or MAOIs under the care of a health care professional and in concert with psychotherapy.

Diagnosis of PTSD in children has been less studied than in adults (Pfefferbaum, 1997). Research on younger sexually abused children shows CBT to be more effective than other approaches (Putnam, 2003; Ramchandani and Jones, 2003). Psychological treatment should consider that sexually abused children often have long-term symptoms and/or later onset, and they may not benefit from long-term therapy (Putnam, 2003; Ramchandani and Jones, 2003). Importantly, a review of research on children receiving psychotherapy post-trauma found improvements across all forms of therapy (including CBT, exposure-based, psychodynamic, narrative, supportive counseling, and EMDR) were greater than control in reducing PTSD symptoms (Gillies et al., 2013).

If we are to have successful outcomes, it is just as important to understand what does not work as it is to understand what does work in treating traumatized trafficking individuals. One example of what has been shown to be counter-therapeutic and potentially increase PTSD is psychological debriefing shortly after the traumatic event (Ursano et al., 2004).

Regardless of the technique(s) selected, the pace and intensity of treatment should match the client's capabilities. Briere (2002b) has cautioned therapists about the need to work within what he calls the "therapeutic window," or the client's ability to feel without repeating familiar destructive behaviors such as dissociation, self-injury, alcohol/substance abuse, and suicidality.

Treatment is not formulaic, meaning it needs to take into account the needs of the individual and the techniques described should be selected taking this individuality into consideration. For some it may require more sessions than for others; still for others, they may only complete part of the work. The option to return to therapy when needed is also advisable as transitions and life changes and stressors may trigger prior traumas, albeit at a likely decreased level of symptomatology. Finally, termination (i.e., ending) can potentially trigger feelings of grief, fear, and abandonment. Thus, it is best when termination can be collaborative and clearly demarcated and processed.

References

Alexander, K. W., Quas, J. A., Goodman, G. S., Ghetti, S., Edelstein, R. S., Redlich, A. D., Cordon, I. M., and Jones, D. P. (2005). Traumatic impact predicts long-term memory for documented child sexual abuse. *Psychological Science*, 16(1), 33–40. Available at: https://www.ncbi.nlm.nih.gov/pubmed/15660849

APA. (2013). *Diagnostic and Statistical Manual of Mental Disorders* (5th edn.). Washington, DC: American Psychiatric Association.

Bales, K. (2012). *Disposable People: New Slavery in the Global Economy* (3rd edn.) Berkley and Los Angeles: University of California Press.

Bernstein, E., and Putnam, F. W. (1986). Development, reliability and validity of a dissociation scale. *The J Nerv Ment Dis*, 174(12), 727–735.

Blake, D. D., Weathers, F. W., Nagy, L. M., Kaloupek, D. G., Klauminzer, G., Charney, D. S., and Keane, T. (1996). *Clinician Administered PTSD Scale for DSM-IV: Current and Lifetime Diagnostic Version*. Boston, MA: National Center for Posttraumatic stress disorder, Behavioral Science Division, VA Medical Center.

Breslau, N., Kessler, R. C., Chilcoat, H. D., Schultz, L. R., Davis, G. C., and Andreski, P. (1998). Trauma and posttraumatic stress disorder in the Community. The 1996 Detroit area survey of trauma. *Archives of General Psychiatry*, 55(7), 626–632. doi:10.1001/archpsyc.55.7.626

Briere, J. (1995). *Trauma Symptom Inventory (TSI)*. Odessa, FL: Psychological Assessment Resources.

Briere, J. (2000). *Cognitive Distortions Scale (CDS) Professional Manual*. Odessa, FL: Psychological Assessment Resources.

Briere, J. (2001). *DAPS—Detailed Assessment of Posttraumatic Stress Professional Manual*. Odessa, FL: Psychological Assessment Resources.

Briere, J. (2002). *Multiscale Dissociation Inventory (MDI) Professional Manual*. Odessa, FL: Psychological Assessment Resources.

Briere, John, and Runtz, Marsha (2002). The inventory of altered self-capacities (IASC). *Assessment*, 9(3), 230–239.

Briere, J., Elliott, D. M., Harris, K., and Cotman, A. (1995). Trauma Symptom Inventory: Psychometrics and association with childhood and adult victimization in clinical samples. *Journal of Interpersonal Violence*, 10, 387–401.

Carlson, Eve, and W. Putnam, Frank. (1993). An Update on the Dissociative Experiences Scale. Dissociation: Progress in the dissociative disorders. *Dissociation*, 6(1), 16–27.

Clark, C. R., McFarlane, A. C., Morris, P., Weber, D. L., Sonkkilla, C., Shaw, M., Marcina, J., Tochon-Danguy, H. J., and Egan, G. F. (2003). Cerebral function in posttraumatic stress disorder during verbal working memory updating: a positron emission tomography study. *Biological Psychiatry*, 53(6), 474–481.

Cohen, J. A., Perel, J. M., Debellis, J. M., Friedman, M. J., and Putnam, F. W. (2002). Treating traumatized children: clinical implications of the psychobiology of posttraumatic stress disorder. *Trauma, Violence, & Abuse*, 3(2), 91–108. Available at: http://journals.sagepub.com/doi/abs/10.1177/15248380020032001?journalCode=tvaa

Courtois, C. A. (2004). Complex trauma, complex reactions: assessment and treatment. *Psychotherapy: Theory, Research, Practice, Training*, 41, 412–425.

Devinsky, O., Morrell, M. J., and Vogt, B. A. (1995). Contributions of anterior cingulate to behavior. *Brain*, 118, 279–306.

Felmingham, K., Kemp, A., Williams, L., Das, P., Hughes, G., Peduto, A., and Bryant, R. (2007). Changes in anterior cingulate and amygdala after cognitive behavior therapy of posttraumatic stress disorder. *Psychological Science*, 18(2), 127–129.

Foa, E. B. (1995). *PDS (Posttraumatic Stress Diagnostic Scale) Manual*. Minneapolis, MN: National Computer Systems.

Fosha, D. (2003). Dyadic regulation and experiential work with emotion and relatedness in trauma and disorganised attachment. In M. F. Solomon, and D. J. Siegel (eds.), *Healing Trauma: Attachment, Mind, Body, and Brain* (pp. 221–281). New York: W.W. Norton & Co.

Gillies, D., Taylor, F., Gray, C., O'Brien, L., and D'Abrew, N. (2013). Psychological therapies for the treatment of post-traumatic stress disorder in children and adolescents (review). *Evidence-Based Child Health: A Cochrane Review Journal*, 8(3), 1004–1116.

Gold, S. N., and Brown, L. S. (1997). Therapeutic responses to delayed recall: Beyond recovered memory. *Psychotherapy: Theory, Research, Practice, Training*, 34(2), 182–191.

Herman, J. L. (1992). Complex PTSD: a syndrome in survivors of prolonged and repeated trauma. *Journal of Traumatic Stress*, 5(3). Available at: https://onlinelibrary. wiley.com/doi/abs/10.1002/jts.2490050305

Hull, A. (2002). Neuroimaging findings in post-traumatic stress disorder: Systematic review. *British Journal of Psychiatry*, 181(2), 102–110. doi:10.1192/bjp.181.2.102

Jehu, D., Gazan, M., and Klassen, C. (1985). Common therapeutic targets among women who were sexually abused in childhood. *Journal of Social Work and Human Sexuality*, 3(2–3), 25–45.

Karasu, T. B., Gelenberg, A., Merriam, A., and Wang, P. (2000). *Practice Guideline for the Treatment of Patients with Major Depressive Disorder* (2nd edn.). Washington, DC: American Psychiatric Association. doi:10.1176/appi. books.9780890423363.48690

Kilpatrick, D. G. (2000). The Mental Health Impact of Rape. National Violence Against Women Prevention Research Center. Retrieved from https://www. musc.edu/vawprevention/research/mentalimpact.shtml

Kleber, H. D., Weiss, R. D., AntonJr., R. F., George, T. P., Greenfield, S. F., Kosten, T. R., et al. (2006). *Practice Guideline for the Treatment of Patients with Substance Use Disorders* (2nd edn.). Arlington, VA: American Psychiatric Association.

Lanius, R. A., Williamson, P.C., Densmore, M., Boksman, K., Gupta, M. A., Neufeld, R. W., Gati, J. S., and MenonR. S. (2001). Neural correlates of traumatic memories in Posttraumatic Stress Disorder: A functional MRI investigation. *American Journal of Psychiatry*, 158(11), 1920–1922.

Lazar, S. W., Kerr, C. E., Wasserman, R. H., Gray, J. R., Douglas, N., Treadway, M. T., et al. (2005). Meditation experience is associated with increased cortical thickness. *Neuroreport*, 16(17), 1893–1897.

Lindauer, R. J. L., Booij, J., Habraken, J. B. A., Uylings, H. B. M., Ol□, M., Carlier, I. V. E, Den Heeten, G., Van Eck-Smit, B. L. F., and Gersons, B. P. R. (2004). Cerebral blood flow changes during script-driven imagery in police o□cers with posttraumatic stress disorder. *Biological Psychiatry*, 56(11), 853–861. Retrieved from https://www.bio logicalpsychiatryjournal.com/article/S0006-3223(04)00854–00856/fulltext

Markowitsch, H. J. (2000). Repressed memories. In E. Tulving (ed.), *Memory, Consciousness, and the Brain* (pp. 319–330). Philadelphia, PA: Psychology Press.

McIntosh, A., Cohen, A., Turnbull, N., Esmonde, L., Dennis, P., Eatock, J., et al. (2004). *Clinical Guidelines and Evidence Review for Panic Disorder and Generalised Anxiety Disorder*. Sheffield: University of Sheffield/London: National Collaborating Centre for Primary Care.

Miller, W. R. (2003a). Enhancing motivation for change. In R. K. Hester and W. R. Miller (eds.), *Handbook of Alcoholism Treatment Approaches: Effective Alternatives* (pp. 131–151) (3rd edn.). Boston, MA: Allyn & Bacon.

Miller, W. R. (2003b). On motivational interviewing. *Monitor on Psychology*, 34(10), 1–14.

Monson, C. M., and Chard, K. M. (2014). *Cognitive Processing Therapy: Veteran/ Military Version: Therapist and Patient Materials Manual*. Washington, DC: Department of Veterans Affairs.

Neborsky, R. A. (2003). Clinical model for the comprehensive treatment of trauma using an affect experiencing-attachment theory approach. In M. F. Solomon and D. J. Siegel (eds.), *Healing Trauma: Attachment, Mind, Body and Brain* (pp. 282–321). New York: Norton.

Nijenhuis, E. R. S. (2000) Somatoform dissociation: major symptoms of dissociative disorders. *Journal of Trauma & Dissociation*, 1(4), 7–29.

Nowinski, J. (2003). *Twelve Step Facilitation with Ce Test.* Center City, MN: Hazelden Publishing.

Pearlman, L. A. (2003). *Trauma and Attachment Belief Scale (TABS).* Los Angeles, CA: Western Psychological Services.

Pelcovitz, D., Van der Kolk, B.A., Roth, S., Mandel, F., Kaplan, S., and Resick, P. (1997). Development of a criteria set and a structured interview for disorders of extreme stress (SIDES). *Journal of Traumatic Stress*, 10(1), 3–16.

Pfefferbaum, B. (1997). Posttraumatic stress disorder in children: A review of the past 10 years. *Journal of the American Academy of Child and Adolescent Psychiatry*, 36(11), 1503–1511.

Putnam, F. W. (2003). Ten-year research update review: Child sexual abuse. *Journal of the American Academy of Child and Adolescent Psychiatry*, 42(3), 269–278.

Ramchandani, Paul, and Jones, David P. H. (2004). Treating psychological symptoms in sexually abused children—From research findings to service provision. *The Br J Psychiatry: The Journal of Mental Science*, 183(6), 484–490.

Rauch, S. A. M., and Cahill, S. P. (2003). Treatment and prevention of posttraumatic stress disorder. *Primary Psychiatry*, 10(8), 60–65.

Rauch, S. L., van der Kolk, B. A., Fisler, R. E., Alpert, N. M., Orr, S. P., Savage, C. R., Fischman, A. J., Jenike, M. A., and Pitman, R. K. (1996). A symptom provocation study of posttraumatic stress disorder using positron emission tomography and script-driven imagery. *Archives of General Psychiatry*, 53(5), 380–387. doi:10.1001/archpsyc.1996.01830050014003

Raymond, J. G., D'Cunha, J., Dzuhayatin, S. R., Hynes, H. P., Rodriguez, Z. R., and Santos, A. (2002). *A Comparative Study of Women Trafficked in the Migration Process: Patterns, Profiles, and Health Consequences of Sexual Exploitation in Five Countries (Indonesia, the Philippines, Thailand, Venezuela, and the United States).* New York: Coalition Against Trafficking Women International.

Resick, P. A., and Schnicke, M. K. (1992). Cognitive processing therapy for sexual assault victims. *Journal of Consulting and Clinical Psychology*, 60(5), 748.

Resick, P. A., Monson, C. M., and Chard, K. M. (2017). *Cognitive Processing Therapy for PTSD: A Comprehensive Manual.* New York: The Guilford Press.

Roth, S. R., and Batson, R. (1997). *Naming the Shadows: A New Approach to Individual and Group Psychotherapy for Adult Survivors of Childhood Incest.* New York: Free Press.

Rothbaum, B. O., Foa, E. B., Riggs, D. S., Murdock, T., and Walsh, W. (1992). A prospective examination of post-traumatic stress disorder in rape victims. *Journal of Traumatic Stress*, 5, 455–475. doi:10.1002/jts.2490050309

Sahar, T., Shalev, A. Y., and Porges, S. W. (2001). Vagal modulation of responses to mental challenge in posttraumatic stress disorder. *Biological Psychiatry*, 49(7), 637–643. Available at: https://www.ncbi.nlm.nih.gov/pubmed/11297721

Schore, A. (2003a). *Affect Regulation & the Repair of the Self.* New York: Norton.

Schore, A. (2003b). *Affect Dysregulation & Disorders of the Self.* New York: Norton.

Seedat, S., Stein, D., and Carey, P. (2005). Post-traumatic stress disorder in women: epidemiological and treatment issues. *CNS Drugs*, 19(5), 411–427.

Shapiro, F., and Solomon, R. M. (1995). *Eye Movement Desensitization and Reprocessing*. Hoboken, NJ: John Wiley & Sons, Inc.

Shin, L. M., Whalen, P. J., Pitman, R. K., Bush, G., Macklin, M. L., Lasko, N. B., Orr, S. P., McInerney, S. C., and Rauch, S. L. (2001). An fMRI study of anterior cingulate function in posttraumatic stress disorder. *Biological Psychiatry*, 50, 932–942. Available at: https://www.ncbi.nlm.nih.gov/pubmed/11750889

Solomon, M. F., and Siegel, D. J. (eds.). (2003). *Healing Trauma: Attachment, Trauma, the Brain and the Mind*. New York: Norton.

Steinberg, M. (1994). *Interviewer's Guide to the Structured Clinical Interview for DSM-IV Dissociative Disorders (SCID-D)* (rev. edn.). Arlington, VA: American Psychiatric Association.

Ursano, R. J., Bell, C., Eth, S., et al. (2004) Practice guideline for the treatment of patients with acute stress disorder and posttraumatic stress disorder. *American Journal of Psychiatry*, 161(11), 3–31.

Van der Kolk, B. A. (2006). Clinical implications of neuroscience research in PTSD. *Ann N Y Acad Sci*, 1071(1), 277–293.

Vasterling, J. J., Brailey, K., Constans, J. I., and Sutker, P. B. (1998). Attention and memory dysfunction in posttraumatic stress disorder. *Neuropsychology*, 12(1), 125–133. doi:10.1037/0894-4105.12.1.125

Weersing, V. R., Iyengar, S., Kolko, D. J., Birmaher, B., and Brent, D. A. (2006). Effectiveness of cognitive-behavioral therapy for adolescent depression: a benchmarking investigation. *Behavior Therapy*, 37(1), 36–48.

Weiss, D. S., and Marmar, C. R. (1997). The impact of event scale—revised. In: J. P. Wilson and T. M. Keane (eds.), *Assessing Psychological Trauma and PTSD* (pp. 399–411). New York: Guilford Press.

Williamson, D. M., Abe, K., Bean, C., Ferré, C., Henderson, Z., and Lackritz, E. (2008). Report from the CDC: Current research in preterm birth. *Journal of Women's Health*, 17(10), 1545–1549.

Zimmerman, C. (2003). *The Health Risks and Consequences of Trafficking in Women and Adolescents: Findings from a European Study*. London: London School of Hygiene & Trop Med.

Zimmerman, C., Hossain, M., Yun, K., Roche, B., Morison, L., and Watts, C. (2006). *Stolen Smiles: A Summary Report on the Physical and Psychological Health Consequences of Women and Adolescents Trafficked in Europe*. London: London School of Hygiene & Trop Med. Retrieved from: https://aspe.hhs.gov/report/evidence-based-mental-health-treatment-victims-human-trafficking

Zlotnick, C., and Pearlstein, T. (1997). Validation of the structured interview for disorders of extreme stress. *Comprehensive Psychiatry*, 38(4), 243–247.

Zlotnick, C., Franklin, C. L., and Zimmerman, M. (2002). Does 'subthreshold' posttraumatic stress disorder have any clinical relevance? *Comprehensive Psychiatry*, 43(6), 413–419.

4 Trafficking of Children and Adolescents

Conceptualization and Evidence-Based Treatment

Katie A. McIntyre

Human trafficking, often described as modern day slavery, was estimated to impact 40.3 million victims worldwide in 2016 alone (ILO, 2017). This total was comprised of both forced labor as well as forced marriage, which are estimated to total 24.9 million victims and 15.4 million victims respectively. Of the overall victims of human trafficking, a disproportionate 71% were women and girls (28.7 million). It is further estimated that of the total victims of human trafficking in 2016, 25% were children, including 5.7 million children in forced marriages. Children also comprised 21% of the total victims of commercial sex trafficking, 18% of those trafficked for forced labor overall, and 7% of those subjected to state-sponsored forced labor (ILO, 2017). UNICEF (2018) estimates that these rates are even higher among the world's poorest countries, wherein they report that roughly 25% of all children in these countries are subjected to child labor, either paid or unpaid, which has been deemed "detrimental to their health and development."

While these statistics are alarming, it is important to recognize that they are likely an under-estimate (Farrell, 2014). Additionally, though it is clear that trafficking occurs within the borders of the United States, there is currently no reliable or standardized process for measuring this activity (Farrell, 2014). Past estimates pertaining to trafficking in the US have focused on cases brought forth for prosecution or those brought into the country illegally, as opposed to ongoing activity within the country (Farrell, 2014).

Child Maltreatment and Human Trafficking

Human trafficking represents one discrete condition in which child abuse and neglect can occur. In order to fully appreciate the potential impact of human trafficking on a child or adolescent, it is essential to first have an understanding of child maltreatment in a general sense. In response to a call for uniform definitions of child maltreatment, the Center for Disease Control and National Center for Injury Prevention and Control proposed that child maltreatment be defined as an "act or series of acts of commission or omission by a parent or other caregiver that results in harm, potential for harm, or threat of harm to a child" (Leeb et al., 2008, p. 11). In this regard, acts of commission would encompass physical, sexual, and psychological abuse and pertain to a willful act of an authority figure onto the child. Acts of omission, in contrast, relate to the absence of action to the detriment of the child. These offenses span physical, emotional, medical, and educational neglect as well as exposure to violence and inadequate supervision.

Within the context of human trafficking, it is quite likely that children and adolescents incur a variety of these abuses over an extended period of time. This repeated exposure to maltreatment is referred to as complex trauma and is often characterized by severe trauma-related symptomology across several domains of functioning (Cohen et al., 2012). According to the Victims of Trafficking and Violence Protection Act of 2000 (TVPA), the illegal practice of human trafficking includes both sex trafficking wherein the individual is "induced by force, fraud, or coercion" to perform a commercial sex act, instances when the individual performing the sex act is under the age of 18 years and "the recruitment, harboring, transportation, provision, or obtaining of a person for labor or services, through the use of force, fraud, or coercion for the purpose of subjection to involuntary servitude, peonage, debt bondage, or slavery" (US Department of State, 2000). The Trafficking in Persons Report (US Department of State, 2017) elaborates further to specify the forms of trafficking most likely to impact children and adolescents, including child sex trafficking, forced child labor and the unlawful recruitment and use of child soldiers. Of note, the victim does not have to be physically transported in order for the encounter to qualify as human trafficking, thereby opening the door to all forms of cyber abuse.

With regard to forced child labor specifically, in contrast to lawful work conditions for minors, the distinction is often that the child is unable to leave, the performed work does not financially benefit the child or child's family, and often the child is in the custody of a non-family member (US Department of State, 2017). Additionally, there is often considerable overlap between these forms of trafficking wherein the child or adolescent may be forced to perform labor tasks, contribute to the armed forces, and engage in sex acts with adults, particularly within the context of child soldiering (US Department of State, 2017). Once under the regime of traffickers, victims can be exposed to unsanitary conditions, hazardous working conditions, long work hours, physical abuse, and lack of access to medical care, leading to increased rates of sexually transmitted disease, as well as the ramifications of these living conditions on physical and mental health globally (US Department of State, 2017).

In terms of recruitment, these children may have been forcibly abducted by traffickers or unknowingly volunteered by their families of origin. With regard to the latter, the promise of financial security and educational opportunity can often lead destitute parents to trust the care of their children to unrelated adults who seem to be trustworthy. Traffickers may even have a favorable reputation among the community based on the assumption that they have secured work for other members of the community. In this regard, traffickers may explain lack of communication between these individuals and their families as a legitimate consequence of the arrangement. It is important to recognize that this process of entrusting one's children to unrelated adults is often an act of desperation on the part of the parent in seeking a better life for the child. In fact, in some areas, adults and minors alike place themselves on waiting lists for work opportunities that they believe will culminate in a better life, only to find once they have been cut off from all social supports at home that they have been sold into modern-day slavery.

Trauma–Related Disorders among Children and Adolescents

With the publication of the *Diagnostic and Statistical Manual of Mental Disorders,* 5th edition (DSM-5) (APA, 2013), diagnoses precipitated by exposure to trauma were placed in a separate subsection entitled Trauma- and Stressor-Related Disorders. This reorganization of the DSM-5 highlights the importance of conceptualizing trauma-related symptoms as a reaction to trauma explicitly, a framework that can provide diagnostic clarity when differentiating trauma-related diagnoses from other possible explanations for the presenting concerns. According to the DSM-5, in order for a stressful experience to qualify as a traumatic stressor for diagnostic purposes, the individual must have been exposed to or threatened with "death, serious injury or sexual violence" which can include direct exposure, bearing witness to the event, and learning of the event second-hand from a loved one. For children under the age of six years, this definition extends further to include harm that has befallen a parent or caregiver. With these environmental conditions in mind, children may respond with wide-ranging symptomology depending on developmental level, the severity of traumatic exposure, genetic pre-disposition, and protective factors both historically and currently (Cohen et al., 2006).

Assessment of Trauma–Related Symptomology

For the purpose of comprehensive diagnostic intake for children and adolescents with known or suspected history of trauma, Cohen et al. (2012) recommend explicitly assessing traumatic exposure and trauma-related outcomes (i.e. degree of impairment across multiple domains) in addition to a standard comprehensive diagnostic evaluation. In this regard, objective assessments may be indicated due to the sensitive nature of these discussions, as a thorough understanding of the extent of trauma is vital for a clinician to effectively implement trauma-related care. These instruments may include both parent- and self-report symptom checklists as well as semi-structured interviews. By posing targeted, direct questions to patients and caregivers, the clinician is more likely to receive a complete description of the trauma, though clinicians must be sensitive to the difficulty that caregivers in particular have in discussing the traumatic experiences of their children. In circumstances when the caregiver appears to be holding back information due to the presence of the child, it may be necessary to readdress this topic in a future parent consultation session. Clinicians may alternatively opt to set aside a portion of the diagnostic evaluation to speak with both the caregiver and the child separately, though within the context of history of trauma, it is important to consider the comfort level of the child in separating from the caregiver during the initial appointment.

Clinicians must further be sensitive to the unknowing misattribution of symptoms by caregivers. For instance, if a child who was isolated and sexually abused during a large family event, that child may present with externalizing behavioral concerns when in a crowd. Without knowledge of the contextual factors surrounding the abuse, a clinician may not directly attribute these acting-out behaviors as a reaction to a trauma trigger and may instead inappropriately diagnose behaviorally oriented co-morbidities. In doing so, the clinician would be unnecessarily complicating the recommended treatment plan and runs the risk of shifting parent focus away from the impact of the trauma. As is always the case in diagnostic interviews, it is the responsibility of the patient and family to provide a description of what they observe, while it is the clinician's responsibility to integrate this information into a clear and meaningful conceptualization of the presenting concerns.

As mentioned previously, presenting symptomology following trauma may vary substantially but generally falls into four broad categories of affective, behavioral, cognitive, and psychobiological concerns (Cohen et al., 2006). Affective symptoms may include difficulty regulating emotions either within specific contexts or globally, as well as prominent fear, anxiety, depression, and anger. While these emotional reactions may very well be understandable given the nature of traumatic exposure, targeted treatment is warranted due to the disruptive influence of these powerful emotions on current functioning and future development. With regard to behavioral manifestations of trauma, children and adolescents may avoid situations or even cognitions that remind them of the traumatic experience as a means to self-protect, inadvertently reinforcing ongoing fear. Particularly within the context of complex trauma beginning in early childhood, they may demonstrate difficulty fostering and maintaining healthy attachment with caregivers, as we will observe with respect to reactive attachment disorder and disinhibited social engagement disorder. Cognitive symptoms associated with traumatic exposure are typically the child or adolescent's attempt to make sense of the events that have occurred and are often contributory to the affective dysregulation that is simultaneously observed. In this regard, children and adolescents may develop dysfunctional beliefs about their own identities as well as expectations for others in their lives. For example, a child who was physically abused may develop the core belief of being unworthy of love and protection, whereas a child who is sexually abused may believe that others will not value them in the absence of a sexual relationship. While these are two isolated examples of cognitive distortions among abused children, they illustrate the devastating impact that cognitive symptoms can have on the child or adolescent's future development if left untreated. Lastly, psychobiological symptoms would include the physiological manifestations such as heightened startle response and hypervigilance as well as clear neuro-biological implications of history of trauma among children and adolescents.

Structural neuroanatomic changes following childhood trauma have been observed, including decreased hippocampal volume and activity, increased activation of the amygdala, reduced volume in the prefrontal cortex and anterior cingulate, and decreased medial prefrontal activation (Sherin and Nemeroff, 2011). With this in mind, it is perhaps unsurprising that maltreated children are at increased likelihood of impaired academic performance, lower IQ, and difficulties with both working memory and executive functioning (Getz, 2014). These risks are further confounded if history of traumatic brain injury is endorsed (Getz, 2014). Bremner (2006) summarizes that children with PTSD present with the "behavioral manifestation of stress-induced changes in brain structure and function ... [including] acute and chronic changes in neurochemical systems and specific brain regions which result in long-term changes in brain 'circuits' involved in the stress response." Given these concerns, a seasoned clinician would incorporate a discussion of educational performance into the diagnostic evaluation and make appropriate referrals for further psychoeducational testing and school-based supports when clinically indicated.

Differentiating between Trauma–Related Diagnoses

According to the DSM-5, there are five trauma or stressor-related diagnoses: 1) PTSD; 2) acute stress disorder; 3i) reactive attachment disorder (RAD); 4) disinhibited social engagement disorder; and 5) adjustment disorder (APA, 2013). Adjustment disorder is reserved for reactions to a stressor that typically does not meet criteria for a trauma and includes presenting symptomology that is typically less severe in comparison to other diagnoses in this category. For that reason, this chapter will focus on the other four trauma-related diagnoses which are more likely to emerge from the context of human trafficking.

Acute stress disorder and post-traumatic stress disorder are the diagnostic terms describing similar, specific symptom clusters emerging following exposure to trauma. In both cases, patients must have endorsed an experience meeting criteria for a trauma and subsequently developed symptoms of intrusion, avoidance, negative alterations in cognition or mood, and alterations in arousal and reactivity. The symptom threshold varies depending on diagnosis. In the case of PTSD, separate diagnostic criteria are also outlined in the DSM-5 for those under the age of six years. The primary differentiator between these two diagnoses relates to the duration of symptoms. Those with acute stress disorder evidence clinically significant symptoms between three days to one month with symptoms often presenting immediately following the trauma, whereas individuals with PTSD must have symptoms for a minimum of one month.

Of note, a reaction consistent with acute stress disorder is a powerful predictor of future PTSD (Alisic et al., 2011). Additional predictors of long-term post-traumatic stress among children include endorsement of depression, anxiety and parental post-traumatic stress (Alisic et al., 2011). While female gender, severity of injury, duration of hospitalization and elevated heart rate shortly after hospitalization were also statistically significant predictors of long-term post-traumatic stress, a meta-analysis by Alisic et al. (2011) found the effect sizes to be relatively small.

As mentioned previously, additional diagnostic considerations for children exposed to trauma in early childhood specifically include reactive attachment and disinhibited social engagement disorder. These diagnoses are explored in cases when the child is presenting with a dysfunctional relationship to caregivers and represent two opposing ends of this continuum. The common thread between RAD and disinhibited social engagement disorder is a "pattern of extremes of insufficient care" as evidenced by either caregivers persistently neglecting basic emotional needs, frequent change in primary caregivers, or rearing in an unusual setting with limited opportunities to developp secure attachment, wherein this absence of attachment is deemed responsible for the presenting concerns (APA, 2013). From there, children may demonstrate a pattern of withdrawing from caregivers and adults while having minimal social reciprocity, restricted affect, and unexplained negative reactions to caregivers during benign interactions as is the hallmark of RAD. On the contrary, other children without secure attachments may become indiscriminate in their attempts to gain favor with adults. These children are at increased risk of revictimization due to their tendency to approach, act familiar (verbally and physically), and go willingly with unfamiliar adults, all without checking with familiar adults or caregivers. This presentation is consistent with disinhibited social engagement disorder.

Trauma-Informed Case Conceptualization

Guided by information obtained during the comprehensive clinical interview and subsequent diagnostic clarity, the trauma-focused clinician should begin to develop a theoretically grounded case conceptualization of the patient's presenting concerns. Regardless of theoretical orientation, there are some factors that should be thoughtfully considered prior to embarking on treatment. Some have been mentioned previously, such as evaluating for the potential need for academic supports given the cognitive impact on trauma. It is also helpful to consider developmental theory to ascertain the degree of departure from anticipated developmental norms given the child or adolescent's age and level of cognitive functioning. In that regard, patients deemed to have clinically significant developmental delay may require adaptations to the treatment protocol to accommodate these differences.

To guide the conceptualization process as it pertains to trauma-related care specifically, Cohen et al. (2006) developed the acronym CRAFTS representing difficulties in the areas of Cognitive, Relationship, Affective, Family, Traumatic behavior, and Somatic problems. While many of these factors overlap considerably with the symptom clusters discussed previously and were designed as targeted areas of problems, it is important to note that the conceptualization should focus not only on areas of concern but also protective factors and strengths. For example, the clinician may notice that a child reporting inadequate social relationships with peers (Relationship) may have a strong support system at home (Family), or that an adolescent who evidences significant affective dysregulation (Affective) and physiological (Somatic) symptoms is quite intelligent (Cognitive) and therefore more likely to excel with cognitive-based strategies. It is a great disservice to patients when these strengths and protective factors go unrecognized as these strengths can serve as the foundation for early success in treatment when incorporated appropriately.

Once clinicians are comfortable with their understanding of patient difficulties across all of the CRAFTS domains and strengths have been identified, they are encouraged to take the extra step of fitting these concerns into the framework of their theoretical orientation. This information will then guide the approach to treatment to insure maximum benefit for the patient. Of note, the chosen theoretical orientation of the clinician may lead the provider to emphasize certain concerns but should not eliminate others. For instance, a relational or interpersonal therapist may take additional care to ensure that the relationship and family concerns are thoroughly addressed, utilizing this relationship as a crucial protective factor through increasing social support. Meanwhile, a systems-focused clinician may invest additional time in building up school-based supports with a similar rationale. This is not to say that the interpersonal therapist would not communicate with the school or that the systems-focused therapist would not work with the parent. Rather, the difference is nuanced relating to the explanatory power of these interventions for the overall conceptualization.

While little information is available pertaining to the clinical case conceptualization of trafficking victims specifically, two theoretical orientations, socioeconomic theory and feminist theory, have consistently emerged in the existing literature (Cecchet and Thoburn, 2014). Socioeconomic theory emphasizes the vulnerability of disenfranchised individuals in unstable economies and the close relationship between these illegal activities in communities with low socioeconomic status and the amount of pressure placed on potential victims (Cecchet and Thoburn, 2014). Meanwhile, feminist theory adds that women and children are disproportionately impacted as vulnerable populations, a concern that is significantly exacerbated in instances of co-occurring racism (Cecchet and Thoburn, 2014). Cecchet and Thoburn (2014) further recommend the use of ecological systems theory in examining the multifaceted experience of victims of human trafficking which incorporates the relevant systemic considerations of classism, sexism, and racism while tying each systemic influence equally and directly to the holistic impact on the individual.

Evidence-Based Treatment Approaches

In 2017, the Society of Clinical Child and Adolescent Psychology (Division 53 of the American Psychological Association) published the most recent analysis of evidence-based treatments for children and adolescents impacted by trauma (Dorsey et al., 2017). This was an update to the previous literature review published by Silverman et al. (2008) which examined publications dated 1993–2007. Research was not limited to randomized controlled trials (RCT) alone to better account for the entirety of the literature base (Dorsey et al., 2017). Studies were grouped by theoretical approach, service type, such as individual or group counseling, and whether the sessions included parent engagement or were focused on the child alone. Following an investigation into methodological rigor of available research, each group was assigned a level of support. Across both review articles, these levels were characterized as well established, probably efficacious, possibly efficacious, experimental, and questionable efficacy. The following recommendations for treatment will reflect the most up-to-date literature review in clinical child and adolescent psychology (Dorsey et al., 2017). These findings were consistent with the previous analysis of the literature base (Silverman et al., 2008) and included an additional 37 studies for review (Dorsey et al., 2017).

Well-Established Treatment Modalities

For Dorsey et al. (2017), this highest level of support requires stringent adherence to a variety of qualifications. In order to meet criteria for a well-established treatment, these modalities must have demonstrated statistically significant superiority over other active treatments/placebo, or equivalence to an already well-established treatment. This empirical support must have been observed by two or more independent research teams and should be evidenced among studies meeting the following criteria for research method: randomized controlled design; manualized treatment as an independent variable; clear inclusion criteria for the population being studied; reliable and valid outcomes assessments; and appropriate analysis of data.

Cognitive behavioral therapy (CBT). According to Dorsey et al. (2017), the treatment modality with the greatest empirical support for children and adolescent with post-traumatic stress utilizes a cognitive behavioral approach and may consist of individual CBT with parent involvement, individual CBT focused on the patient alone, and group CBT focused on patients alone. Of these, trauma-focused CBT (TF-CBT) specifically was the most widely studied and well-supported format of CBT (Dorsey et al, 2017).

Traditionally, the TF-CBT therapist will divide hour-long treatment sessions into parallel individual and parent consultation components while working towards a conjoint session with the child and parent towards the end of treatment (Cohen et al., 2006; Dorsey et al, 2017). Treatment spans 10–12 sessions and follow the acronym PRACTICE which is defined as

Psychoeducation and parenting skills, Relaxation, Affective identification/regulation/expression, Cognitive coping strategies, Trauma narrative, In vivo exposure, Conjoint session, and Enhancing safety (Cohen et al., 2006). Other individual CBT formats that incorporate parent involvement incorporate most aspects of PRACTICE while differing in the implementation of parent education/consultation (Dorsey et al., 2017). Further, a variety of adaptations to TF-CBT have been studied including a brief version consisting of only eight sessions. Overall, the empirical support for this treatment family has been described by Dorsey et al. as having a large supportive literature base which is methodologically rigorous and contains large sample sizes. The available studies do focus mostly on the implementation of varieties of TF-CBT to the detriment of other CBT formats.

Similarly, individual CBT for trauma is supported by studies that mostly follow the TF-CBT format, though without the parent component. Overall, this modality was reported to take slightly longer on average (12–14 sessions). Brief formats have also been examined with positive results. Studies utilizing other formats of individual CBT beyond TF-CBT were also studied and found to be efficacious with long term gains identified by those who assessed this. Of note, most studies did include relatively small sample sizes.

Group CBT for post-traumatic stress among children and adolescents without parent involvement has also received strong support. Treatment typically consists of ten sessions though this may extend to up to 20 sessions. Group CBT is often implemented in school settings. Greater empirical support exists for middle- and high-school students in comparison to elementary students, though two studies have been conducted in this population with similar findings. Common elements include psychoeducation and cognitive strategies with relaxation. Some formats included imaginal trauma exposure though other studies demonstrated efficacy without this aspect.

Probably Efficacious Treatment Modalities

Empirical support necessary for a level of probably efficacious includes either two experiments demonstrating that the treatment is statistically superior to a wait-list control group or studies meeting the threshold as well established that only come from a single research lab. All of the methods criteria outlined previously are also required.

Group CBT with parent involvement. In comparison to treatment modalities previously discussed, group CBT with parent involvement focuses on physical abuse explicitly and includes targeted interventions for this form of trauma such as ongoing commitment to non-violence. Treatment tends to be long both per session and overall. Typically, patients and parents engage in two-hour sessions during which parents and children meet separately with occasional combined activities for roughly 16 sessions. Studies have been relatively small and have only included short-term follow-up on outcomes.

Eye movement desensitization and reprocessing therapy (EMDR). EMDR includes many components of CBT previously discussed with the addition of "simultaneous bilateral sensory input" via eye movement (Dorsey et al., 2017, p. 322). Despite demonstrated efficacy in a couple of studies as superior to no treatment control and equivalence to CBT, the overlap of CBT skills with EMDR-specific techniques complicated the analysis of outcomes.

Possibly Efficacious

A treatment deemed possibly efficacious may have one RCT demonstrating statistically significant improvement over a wait-list or no treatment control group meeting all of the methods criteria. Alternatively, modalities demonstrating statistically significant efficacy in two or more studies that do not utilize RCT design but otherwise meet all methods-related criteria.

Individual integrated therapy for complex trauma. This eclectic approach combines various theoretical orientations (attachment, developmental, family-systems, and CBT) with an emphasis on affective regulation, interpersonal skills, and risky behaviors. Treatment may or may not include parents though their participation was described as preferable. Three studies including one RCT comprise this literature base with mixed results when comparing to other treatment modalities, though patients evidenced positive outcomes. Some methodological concerns were noted for one of the studies.

Group mind–body skills. This approach to group therapy consisted of mindfulness strategies, relaxation skills, meditation, imagery, and biofeedback. The evidence base consists of two studies (one RCT) among children affected by war. There was some evidence for efficacy, though outcomes were not maintained at follow-up.

Experimental

These treatment approaches have never been subjected to RCT or have been examined in one or more studies but were not able to meet criteria for possibly efficacious.

Individual client-centered play therapy. This treatment approach was examined in one RCT with no evidence of benefit. However, a modified version of TF-CBT was also not efficacious in this study, though this intervention is otherwise well-supported in the literature base.

Individual mind–body skills. This approach is relaxation-based with a meditative component and was studied in one RCT. In that study, this approach achieved similar outcomes to an individual CBT treatment condition with these gains being maintained at follow-up.

Individual psychoanalysis. This treatment modality was examined in one small study with adolescents during which imagery and visualization were also emphasized. Statistically significant benefits were observed across a variety of symptoms (dissociative, anxiety, depression, anger, and PTSS). No treatment benefit was observed for sexual concerns in that study.

Questionable Efficacy

These treatment modalities have been examined with no observable benefit or less effectiveness than other treatments available or no-treatment controls.

Group creative expressive with CBT. Group creative expressive therapy with CBT incorporates games, drama and music and traditional CBT components. Two large RCTs examined this approach in a school/classroom setting. These studies were unable to demonstrate efficacy.

Overview of Treatment Considerations

Given this comprehensive recent analysis by Dorsey et al. in conjunction with the previous analysis by Silverman et al., it is clear that the most well-studied approach to treatment consists of CBT in a wide variety of formats. It is up to the commitment of the current and future researchers to continue evaluating established approaches and explore future directions for the future of trauma-based treatment among children and adolescents.

Case Studies

With knowledge of the impact of trauma on children and adolescents, case conceptualizations and treatment guidelines, students are recommended to apply these concepts to the following case vignettes.

Vignette 1

Jane is a 14-year-old African girl who had recently been taken into custody by US law enforcement following several months as a victim of human trafficking. She was turned over to Child Protective Services (CPS) and assigned to foster care. The extent of her abuse is unknown at this time. Currently, she presents with observable hypervigilance and quick startle response. When adults approach her, she is visibly shaken and recoils. Her foster parents have brought her to treatment both at the recommendation of child protective services as well as genuine concern for her wellbeing. During the intake assessment, Jane is closed off initially. There are no obvious communication concerns as Jane speaks English relatively well. Her foster mother is present but has no information about her history. You ask to speak with Jane alone and come to learn that she was originally born in a small village in Africa. Jane recounts a general overview of her experience to date, appearing nervous throughout. She reports that in her village, she had no access to formal education. Her parents were described as loving and sought out an opportunity for her to attend boarding school. The individuals who claimed to run the school were thought to be respectable among families in her village and had reportedly placed other teenagers at schools abroad in the past. You find out that a condition of her attendance at this school was limited opportunity to communicate with her parents. As far as Jane is aware, her biological parents are not expecting to hear from her and believe she is away at school. The details of Jane's travel to the United States are unclear. She is reluctant to describe her abductors or any specific aspects of her time with them.

Vignette 2

Howard is a 7-year-old Caucasian male, originally from California. He had been taken into Child Protective Services (CPS) when his mother was apprehended for prostitution. Howard immediately hugs you upon arrival. He is presenting for evaluation with his foster parents who have expressed concern that Howard is overly affectionate, which is making them feel uncomfortable. They are reluctant to provide details in front of him though they whisper that they are worried that he has been touched inappropriately. They have also noticed various healed lacerations on his body and suspect that he has had some broken bones that have not healed properly. None of this is visible with his clothes on in your office. Throughout the evaluation, Howard also frequently asks questions about his mother, such as whether you know her, how long she will be away this time, and when he will be able to see her. He also asked if he will be staying with you for a while. Overall, his presentation suggests a happy child. When asking targeted questions about his past, Howard provides surface-level responses such as that he "knows a lot of people" or "goes to a bunch of schools." When you ask about his relationship with his mother, he seems less open. Foster parents have limited information about Howard's past as his mother has not been cooperative with CPS inquiries. The only history available is that Howard was with his mother at the time of her arrest, sitting in a nearby car. Foster parents also believe that his biological mother tested positive for various illicit substances including opioids once she was brought into custody. Howard's past academic enrollment is unclear due to frequent transfers and chronic absenteeism across a variety of schools. Currently, he is enrolled in an elementary school near his foster parents' home. Teachers have been describing him as inattentive and impulsive.

★Please note that the cases presented above are fictional in nature and compiled from the stories of several children and adolescents who have experienced various types of abuse resulting in post-traumatic stress.

References

Alisic, E., Jongmans, M. J., Wesel, F. V., and Kleber, R. J. (2011). Building child trauma theory from longitudinal studies: a meta-analysis. *Clinical Psychology Review*, 31(5), 736–747. doi:10.1016/j.cpr.2011.03.001

APA. (2013). *Diagnostic and Statistical Manual of Mental Disorders*, 5th edn. Arlington, VA: American Psychiatric Association.

Bremner, J. D. (2006). Traumatic stress: effects on the brain. *Dialogues in Clinical Neuroscience*, 8(4), 445–461.

Cecchet, S. J., and Thoburn, J. (2014). The psychological experience of child and adolescent sex trafficking in the United States: trauma and resilience in survivors. *Psychological Trauma: Theory, Research, Practice, and Policy*, 6(5), 482–493. doi:10.1037/a0035763

Cohen, J. A., Mannarino, A. P., and Deblinger, E. (2006). *Treating Trauma and Traumatic Grief in Children and Adolescents*. New York: The Guilford Press.

Cohen, J. A., Mannarino, A. P., and Deblinger, E. (eds.). (2012). *Trauma-Focused CBT for Children and Adolescents: Treatment Applications*. New York: The Guilford Press.

Dorsey, S., McLaughlin, K. A., Kerns, S. E., Harrison, J. P., Lambert, H. K., Briggs, E. C., ... Amaya-Jackson, L. (2017). Evidence base update for psychosocial treatments for children and adolescents exposed to traumatic events. *Journal of Clinical Child & Adolescent Psychology*, 46(3), 303–330. doi:10.1080/15374416.2016.1220309

Farrell, A. (2014). Human trafficking (issues in measurement). *The Encyclopedia of Criminology and Criminal Justice*, 1–5. doi:10.1002/9781118517383.wbeccj404

Getz, G. (2014). *Applied Biological Psychology*. New York: Springer Publishing Company.

ILO. (2017). Global Estimates of Modern Slavery. International Labour Organization and Walk Free Foundation. Retrieved from http://www.alliance87.org/global_estimates_of_modern_slavery-forced_labour_and_forced_marriage.pdf

Leeb, R. T., Paulozzi, L. J., Melanson, C., Simon, T. R., and Arias, I. (2008). Child Maltreatment Surveillance: Uniform Definitions for Public Health and Recommended Data Elements, version 1.0. Retrieved from Center for Disease Control and Prevention, National Center for Injury Prevention and Control website: https://www.cdc.gov/violenceprevention/pdf/CM_Surveillance-a.pdf

Sherin, J. E., and Nemeroff, C. B. (2011). Post-traumatic stress disorder: the neurobiological impact of psychological trauma. *Dialogues in Clinical Neuroscience*, 13(3), 263–278.

Silverman, W. K., Ortiz, C. D., Viswesvaran, C., Burns, B. J., Kolko, D. J., Putnam, F. W., and Amaya-Jackson, L. (2008). Evidence-based psychosocial treatments for children and adolescents exposed to traumatic events. *Journal of Clinical Child & Adolescent Psychology*, 37(1), 156–183. doi:10.1080/15374410701818293

UNICEF. (2018). UNICEF Data: monitoring the situation of children and women. Retrieved from https://data.unicef.org/topic/child-protection/child-labour/#

US Department of State. (2000). Victims of Trafficking and Violence Protection Act of 2000. October 23. Retrieved from https://www.state.gov/j/tip/laws/61124.htm

US Department of State. (2017). Trafficking in Persons Report. June. Retrieved from https://www.state.gov/documents/organization/271339.pdf

5 Psychological Treatment

Reflections on a Psychoanalytic Perspective to Work with Human Trafficking

Paola M. Contreras

The author discusses a range of psychoanalytic theories and philosophies that relate to the dynamics of human trafficking. The chapter is an initial attempt to situate human trafficking in the intrapsychic and intersubjective space. The author starts with a review of the history of psychoanalysis and its challenges to respond to social issues. Next, she draws on Hegel's Master–Slave dialectic to outline the perpetration dynamics of human trafficking today. She closes with reflections on how she has used a combined intersubjective and liberation psychology perspective to engage with individuals who have experienced exploitation. Case examples of sex trafficking and trafficking for manual labor highlight concepts throughout the chapter.

Reflections on Human Trafficking and Psychoanalysis

Freud's 19th-century explorations into women's psyches revealed the intimate connection between sexual trauma and neurosis (Freud, 1896). A discovery that lacked the shine, the El Dorado, that the rising physician sought to acquire, as it implied that respectable family men were not so (Herman, 2015). Dismayed by the public's rejection of his pronouncement, Freud omitted reports of incest in his following case presentations claiming later that "discretion" had led him to suppress this information. Within a year, Freud had mostly abandoned the so called "seduction theory". In its place, he advanced a theory of fantasized sexual trauma that led to the fundamental concept of psychoanalysis, the unconscious (Freud, 1905a). The social price was steep though as countless people, mostly women and girls, continued to be abused. Over-time, women and girls succumbed to the idea that oppression is a given of the female experience. A feeling reinforced at every point in history where a powerful person (usually a man) has again, as Freud did once, turned their back on the aggrieved.

If Freud's cease on real trauma as the main contributor to neurosis helped him rise among the scholarly class in his time, after his death his theory received broad criticism from contemporary trauma theorists (Herman, 2015; McCullough, 2001; Masson, 1984; McNally, 2003). A tension that siloed psychoanalysis further away from the trauma field that, in my opinion, has been a loss for psychoanalysts and trauma therapists. The only hope for the atonement of psychoanalysis is to address Freud's misstep by taking up the path that he abandoned. I think Freud would want boldness where he fell short. Because as contemporary Freudian theorists have noted (Gay, 1988; Verhaeghe, 1998), Freud remained conflicted and never completely abandoned the sexual trauma theory. He settled his demur, to a degree, by noting that discovery of the seduction theory bore the unconscious where it is impossible to distinguish between reality and fantasy. A significant yet unsatisfying point that provided limited direction to the subsequent generations of psychoanalysts whose patients continued to report sexual traumas and other pertinent social issues.

Today is a different time. A time when careers can rise rather than flounder, as one could in Freud's day, in the pursuit of social justice. Yet one question that originated with Freud's struggles for recognition continues to haunt his heirs: Can psychoanalysts still be psychoanalysts travelling the unpolished path of responding to social issues? Or, in Freud's turning away from sexual traumas did psychoanalysis become the theory of the unconscious forever divorced from the social issues that surround it? A question that I believe psychoanalysts can answer only if willing to travel the path of social issues with the same unwavering and determined commitment that Freud used on his path to the unconscious.

Dora, a young woman that Freud treated, is relevant to the history of human trafficking and psychoanalysis (Freud, 1905b). As my colleague, psychologist Jane Keat (2017), put forward in her persuasive discussion of a version of this paper that I presented at the Boston Psychoanalytic Institute and Society, Freud's rendition of his work with Dora was a famous case of sexual exploitation. Again, and again Freud dismissed Dora's reports that her father was giving her in exchange to Frau K so that he could continue an affair with Frau K's wife. Freud could not believe Dora's report and also help her explore the unconscious aspects of her strife. To explore the unconscious, he opted to dismiss the young woman's conscious and real-life struggles, a decision that eventually led to a failed treatment.

In this chapter, I will attempt to share how I have remained committed to issues of social justice amidst my psychoanalytic training. A position that many psychoanalysts abide by today by attending to both the social and contextual and the unconscious. My motive is clear, I want to demonstrate that it is possible to walk down the path of social justice using psychoanalytic principles to illuminate the way. And spotlight that it is an approach that not only works but also cultivates and enlivens psychoanalytic and psychotherapy practice for patients and clinicians, especially when the presenting problems derive from experiences of extreme traumas.

Communicating reflections on my work with human trafficking as a psychoanalytic psychotherapist is also a pursuit to join the burgeoning publications that describe psychoanalytic concepts, which relate to working with trafficked persons. Kleinschmidt's (2009), *Keeping Mother Alive: Psychotherapy with a Teenage Mother Following Human Trafficking*, describes the benefits of psychoanalytic treatment for extreme traumas. Similarly, Bennett-Murphy's (2012) article, *Haunted: Treatment of a Child Survivor of Human Trafficking*, highlights the deep impacts directly tied to the relational disruptions, secrecy, and loss of home that characterize cases of human trafficking.

I will start the chapter by describing the human trafficking experience. Next, I will discuss thoughts on the unconscious and working with trauma. Following, I will provide an overview of how my identity as a psycho-analyst committed to issues of social justice has consolidated throughout my training, and the theories I have used to frame my work. Next, aspiring towards an intrapsychic framing of human trafficking, first I discuss the contested issue of choice and human trafficking from a psychoanalytic per-spective, followed by a section on the psychological and historical, and then on the philosophical. To close, I discuss issues of power in psychoanalytic culture that mirror dynamics of human trafficking. Throughout the chapter I offer brief case examples of my clinical work with survivors of sex traf-ficking and trafficking for manual labor, as well as examples from the media.

Human Trafficking

Human trafficking is a relational trauma characterized by a trafficker's use of coercion to exploit another for the trafficker's financial benefit. A social issue that has gained increasing attention in the United States since Congress passed the Trafficking Victims Protection Act (TVPA) in 2000. Human trafficking hides in the most developed cities around the world impacting thousands of people (UN, 2014).

It constitutes one of the fastest growing crimes globally and an extreme form of human rights abuse, especially of women and children (UN, 2014). In the United States, at least 15,000 people are trafficked from another country into US territory every year (US Department of State, 2016). Within the United States, children and adolescents in the foster care system with running away behaviors are at highest risk for trafficking. Trafficking victims are hard to identify and often referred to as a "hidden population" (Hepburn and Simon, 2013; Herman, 2003).

The trafficking scenario follows a path that goes something like this: A trafficker makes a false promise of a job that does not exist, or feigns that s/he loves the trafficked person. Armed with a sophisticated set of physical and psychological coercion tactics, traffickers then force others into sexual, domestic, or manual labor from which they profit financially (UN, 2014). Trafficking is difficult to identify because trafficker's tactics are often subtle and perpetrated within the intimacy of relationships. Additionally, extreme social prejudice towards trafficked people also appears to push victims into isolation (Contreras et al., 2017; Logan et al., 2009; Silver et al., 2015).

In 2015, the American Psychoanalytic Association (APsaA) published a position statement on human trafficking. It highlights that trafficking victims are often targeted at critical developmental stages and suffer severe psychological disorders as a consequence of the abuse and humiliation that traffickers perpetrate on them. APsaA called for programs and policy makers to work with psychoanalysts and psychoanalytic psychotherapists who have the skill set to develop comprehensive long term, relationship-based psychotherapy for victims of exploitation.

Providers report that the relational issues and psychological disorders that result from human trafficking and other forms of subjugation often feel unmanageable, and psychoanalytic theories with attention to transference and countertransference (the internal mechanics of relationships) can address these issues. Victims of human trafficking can also become "traumatically attached" to their trafficker (Harris, 2014; Hargreaves-Cormany et al., 2016). A dynamic that suggests, as I discussed in another paper (Contreras, 2018), an interaction between the trafficker's ruse, the victim's attachment patterns, and a combination of contextual, social, and historical factors including demand for paid sex and cheap labor, and societal stigma towards trafficked people (e. g., those in the sex trade, undocumented immigrants and runaway youth that fall prey to traffickers).

The Unconscious and Working with Trauma

Freud's focus on fantasy life contained the seeds of psychoanalytic listening that generated the many forms of listening that psychoanalysts of different theoretical orientations practice today. A relevant point to working with complex trauma, which requires deep listeners that can hear the implicit and meta communications of pains that dwell in the intrapsychic structures of the mind. Related to this last point, Halberstadt-Freud (1996) notes that Freud's focus on the unconscious helped explain complex symptoms that were characteristic of hysteria, symptoms such as splitting and dissociation that have resurfaced and become contemporary clinical issues.

While mental health researchers have developed Evidence Based Treatments (EBTs) to address symptoms that derive from exposure to trauma, practitioners continue to face mounting challenges with victims of extreme traumas like human trafficking. Namely, the states that emerge after body symptoms abate—the complex relational and identity issues, shame, mistrust, deep states of displeasure, and other intrapsychic rooted vicissitudes that defy the evidence-based interventions (Contreras et al., 2017). Psychoanalysis has the theories to understand the complex states that arise in the transference with people afflicted by the consequences of extreme relational traumas.

A patient[1] who survived multiple experiences of sex trafficking who I have been working with for over five years voiced in a crucial moment of her treatment, "Nothing will ever take the pain away. I read through my list of pleasurable activities in the DBT group. I told the group that running a mile had helped me cut myself less this week. I feel like cutting my body when I'm here with you though. I wonder what that's about?" I let a shared silence underscore her question and after a moment I said, "I also wonder what that's about, that you feel like cutting when you're here with me, let's think about it. What comes to mind?"

My response heeded the deep listening that my psychoanalytic training has encouraged. Note that I say deep listening, which is not the caricature of the objective an impassive psychoanalyst sitting behind the couch waiting for the moment to pounce on the patient with a clever inter- pretation. No. Deep listening requires hard work by ridding one's self of any preconception about the patient as Bion (1983) prescribed. Without preconception, the analyst listens and waits for a pattern to emerge. "I realize that I feel more scared and confused the more time I spend with you," the patient I talked about earlier continued hence revealing a pat- tern that we could explore further. See I could have moved in a beha- vioral direction with her and helped her develop a plan to address the sudden urge to cut in the session. I am sure it would have been helpful as I strongly believe that direct tending to the body and its symptoms is just as important as attention to the mind and the unconscious. However, she was a patient who knew her problematic behaviors well and had several strategies and plans that she had developed in her group sessions.

In our work, I understood that my patient needed my full presence to invite her to explore her burgeoning curiosity about us and how we related in the therapy and what it stirred up for her. I am describing a con- temporary intersubjective approach with two subjects relating (the patient and the analyst) and working towards co-creating meanings (as opposed to the analyst always interpreting the patient). Later in that same session my patient said, "I just had a thought that you could cut me, like cut my body. That would be painful." I responded, "That would be painful, that after all this time that we've worked together and after all the energy and trust that you put into this space and me, that I would cut you off suddenly. That would be painful. Maybe this is what you were feeling when you said that you feel more confused the more time we spend together."

What else does it mean to be a psychoanalyst that works with extreme traumas? How have I come to this work and more important is the ques- tion, how have I remained committed to continue to travel the path of social justice and still be a psychoanalyst?

Liberation Psychology, Intersubjectivity, and Resistance of Power Structures

A detour is pertinent here into what I refer to as the emancipating qualities of psychoanalysis. Colleagues often ask me how being someone deeply committed to issues of social justice did I develop an interest in psycho- analysis, which some view as being distant from social issues for many of the reasons I explained earlier in this chapter regarding the origins of psycho- analysis. I explain myself as follows.

I completed my first psychology degree in a Guatemalan Jesuit University where Martin-Baró's (1986) liberation psychology principles informed part of my training. Liberation psychology derives mainly from the tenets of liberation theology. It is an ethical philosophy that advocated for the un-silencing of the oppressed and marginalized populations of Latin America. Liberation theorists posited that the power and privilege of academia, education, and research could become a platform for the voices of the oppressed classes. It is beyond the scope of this paper to provide a thorough review of liberation psychology and its associated theories, such as Freire's (1970) Critical Pedagogy and Fals-Borda's (1991) participatory action research. Suffice to say for now that liberation psychology is a practice that involves positioning one's self as being inextricably connected to other selves. From that connection between self and other selves, the liberation psychologist is tasked with generating actions in collaboration with communities that emancipate the oppressed and marginalized.

In addition to liberation psychology, my Guatemalan university's psychology department offered Lacanian and Freudian seminars. The links between these seemingly disconnected perspectives, liberation psychology, and psychoanalysis, became apparent the more I practiced. Participation in psychoanalytic seminars and my own psychoanalysis taught me that, as much as I could understand, even personally empathize with the external horrors the communities I worked with faced (I was a psychology trainee in Guatemala towards the end of the country's 36-year civil war, and practiced with organizations that attended communities ravaged by Genocide and other atrocities), I also learned that the path to emancipation from the sequelaes of trauma required me to work from a position where I did not define others by their traumas. For a general review of some of the ideas I am putting forth here, I invite the reader to refer to Hollander (2001) and Gaztambide (2015, 2016), who have comprehensively outlined the influence of liberation psychology in Latin American psychoanalysis.

The Indigenous Australian activist, Lilla Watson's (1985) famous quote "If you have come here to help me, you are wasting your time. But if you have come here because your liberation is bound up with mine, then let us work together" reflects the spirit of liberation psychology well. The "together" of Watson's phrase represents the link that I see between a liberation psychology stance and psychoanalytic intersubjective practice. The sought ideal from both the liberation psychology and intersubjective perspective is, in a sense, emancipation.

The path to a psychoanalytic practice concerned with the ideal of liberation is probably best expressed by Foucault's notion that the road towards liberation is in the act of combating power structures through "resistance, not liberation" (Teo, 2015, p. 246). Because psychoanalysis can only resist power structures; complete freedom is impossible because of the instituted boundaries and power differentials, which are inherent for fundamental treatment processes to unfold, such as transference. As Yeatman

(2015) delineates, Jessica Benjamin's intersubjective, two-person relational positioning (you and me instead of, me over you) offered a stance that, if not entirely liberating, freed-up psychoanalytic practice. Unlike the lofty emancipatory ideals of liberation psychology, psychoanalysis may need to settle for something less exciting to continue being psychoanalysis.

Yeatman goes on to explain that the traditional one-person conception of freedom constitutes a limiting patriarchal position where the world exists only for self-assertion and where "freedom is confused with domination" (2015, p. 5). Yeatman further notes that one of Benjamin's main contributions to psychoanalysis was discussing the challenges of subject-to-subject relating. She states, "[Benjamin] presupposes that [subject-to-subject relating] can come into play only if an ethical commitment to intersubjectivity has become socially and culturally intelligible. [Benjamin] also presupposes that it is in the practice of this commitment that we learn what it demands of us" (2015, p. 6).

What power structures does psychoanalysis need to resist when it is considering extreme traumas such as human trafficking? The first line of resistance, I think, is towards the tendency in the mental health field to pathologize trauma, almost in an impulsive manner. Many of my patients have suffered unfathomable forms of victimization, but do those experiences, in essence, make them victims or survivors? To apply the label of "victim" or "survivor" (which I also use) surely makes sense in courtrooms and sometimes in health care billing systems, but in the privacy of the analytic or psychotherapy practice, clinicians ought to resist these labels, and also validate the patient's resistance to these same labels. The intersubjective task then becomes to engage in meaningful work with others as equals, while still recognizing the existing and irreconcilable power differentials present in the analytic space.

If I believe that a part of my unconscious includes an intimate place unscathed even by the worst of my traumas, from where the essence of my subjectivity operates. A place where despite the external violations I remain free, then I believe the same goes for my patients. Hence, a radical position that moves away from the victim and survivor construct to seek the unconscious positioning of traumas, as Freud did when he moved away from the seduction theory, continues to be necessary. Working to understand, or "metabolize" as Bion (2013) proposed, the complex mind and body states that surface to resist the overpowering and placating consequences that can follow all forms of trauma remains an important psychoanalytic task.

An unconscious understanding of human trafficking and subjugation does not need to negate the existence of real human trafficking. Instead, the task of locating subjugation in the unconscious strives to recognize the complexity of human trafficking. It recognizes that people afflicted by trafficking continue to have an unconscious during victimization. And that to treat the whole person who has suffered an experience of victimization, one needs to attend to the body and also the mind that holds the unconscious.

Defining Human Trafficking and the Issue of Choice

Common questions about trafficking include: How are people trafficked? How is this crime and human rights violation possible? The assumption is that all trafficked people are abducted, beaten into submission and then locked away. The common imagined human trafficking scenario is that it is an underground phenomenon. Part of what sustains this myth is the picture the media has painted about human trafficking; of extreme cases involving abduction and seclusion (Gulati, 2010). Such cases do exist but do not reflect the typical trafficking cases psychotherapists in the United States are likely to see in their practice.

The over-representation of trafficking cases fraught with extreme forms of violence has also contributed to the excessive portrayal of trafficked people as weak and helpless. While all trafficked people have experienced varying degrees of marginalization that created vulnerability to trafficking, Tummala-Narra et al. (2012) caution on the common assumptions about the term human trafficking:

> [The term human trafficking] can often obscure the actual context of the human experience, the circumstances that result in people's vulnerability to being abused and exploited, choices that people may have made that resulted in harmful outcomes, the effects of poverty and the complexity of the familial, social and political environment that shape a person's life trajectory.
>
> (Tummala-Narra et al., 2012, p. 22)

Polarized discourse on trafficking also often depicts trafficked people as completely deprived of choice when trafficked. The concern is that recognizing any degree of choice on the part of the trafficked person is synonymous with a less good victim, a point that one study's findings substantiated well with college students and their perception of victims of exploitation (Silver et al., 2015). Most of the college students that participated in the study identified US prostituted women as less worthy than foreign victims of sex trafficking, even when the vignettes that described the victimization of each group was nearly indistinguishable. One of the authors' hypothesis is that the college students held polarized views based on their values, ideals, and family morals; that US women had chosen to participate in prostitution, while the foreign women were victims who had no choice and coerced into prostitution. Therefore, both sides of this discourse, good and bad victims, can potentially strip people with experiences of trafficking of all their power, rights, and dignity. The victim construct of human trafficking has also contributed to the creation of governmental efforts to "rescue" women and to anti-trafficking movements often marked by morals and biases.

Further complicating the issue of a trafficked person's agency or choice is a split that exists regarding sex trafficking, or human trafficking for sexual exploitation. Groups that support the sex worker model believe that prostitution, a term often used synonymously with sex trafficking, should be recognized as legitimate and potentially empowering work (Elrod, 2015). Sex worker advocates oppose human trafficking discourse arguing that it labels all activities in the sex industry as exploitative, thus further stigmatizing prostitution.

For this paper, I use the terms human trafficking, sex trafficking, and labor trafficking to represents people coerced into any work activity, irrespective of their awareness or not of the coercion. Or who, at the very least, feel dubious or conflicted about their involvement in the work they perform(ed). I justify this position because those are the people who self-refer to treatment, or who other providers refer to my practice. Deborah Castillo (2012), who interviewed trafficked women from Tijuana, Mexico and discussed the sex worker model, merits direct quote here, she observed that:

> Regardless of other factors, the [trafficked and prostituted] people we surveyed and interviewed express an understanding that to live means to work and that the work they are doing is precisely work, not organized labor, not a career path. They know that their bodies are made marginal or invisible and their voices go unheard. At the same time, while their lives may seem unimaginably harsh to many of us, in their stories they often present themselves as rational actors, making the best choices they can from among limited options for themselves and their families.
>
> (Castillo, 2012, p. 835)

There is a need to highlight the complex nature of human trafficking as an exploitative relationship that many people enter knowing they will encounter some difficulties, which should not be confused with a person's consent to being exploited. Psychoanalysis has much to contribute to challenge the stigmatizing portrayal of the trafficked person completely devoid of choice. For instance, the practice in today's clinic of subjecting patients to assume the victim or survivor position. Verhaeghe (1998) deconstructs the issue well, he states that "Either one considers the patient as a mere victim or an external agent, which means that he or she is entitled to help and support; or one considers the patient not solely as a victim but someone with an impact of his or her own, even with a limited form of choice" (1998, p. 96).

From the perspective of subjectivity and hence intersubjectivity, "responsibility" is complexly defined and overdetermined. Teo (2015) describes that subjectivity includes the "possibilities of a concrete individual's mental life, from the first-person standpoint, in the conduct of everyday life. From a critical perspective, subjectivity is contextually embedded in the world, cultural-historical, socioeconomic, active, embodied, and in flux" (2015, p. 246).

In Freud's formulation of neurosis, some degree of unconscious choice is always present. Again, I am referring here strictly to unconscious choice and not to conscious choice, which would mistakenly suggest that people agree

to their victimization. Clinicians that strictly follow the victim/survivor rationale may inadvertently facilitate a stuck treatment. Because even in traumatic
events that denied the person of conscious choice, at the level of the unconscious, choice remains present. If trauma forecloses the possibility of acknowl-
edging the person's unconscious, then the fatalistic conclusion might be that
"The patient has become what s/he had to become, [a victim], due to his/her
traumatic experiences" (Verhaeghe, 1998, p. 96).

If there was no choice on the part of the patient (again, I am referring to the
intrapsychic positioning of the patient), then there is nothing to psychoanalyze.
And if the process of making the unconscious conscious is central to psychoanalytic practice, implicit is the intrapsychic position where one's subjectivity is, to
varying degrees, always a factor to understand and make meaning of. Further,
from this intrapsychic position, there is always a place for unconscious responsibility. Dealt with empathically and compassionately, awareness of how one is
unconsciously responsible can become a liberating rather than a shaming
experience.

Another patient that I worked with who was sex trafficked by a much
older "boyfriend" in her early adolescence expressed an issue of unconscious
responsibility well. That is, she understood that something else in her had
pushed her further into her experience of trafficking keeping her trapped
for nearly five years. While trying to make sense of her experiences in one
of her sessions we had the following exchange:

PATIENT: I knew all along, at pretty much every moment that I could have
left, that if I stayed, he was going to mistreat me. I really wanted to
leave but something else in me, something stronger than the me that
could leave, didn't let me leave for a long time. The part of me that
didn't let me leave felt that everything that was happening with him
kind of made sense. He was very loving sometimes and I held on to
those moments hoping that more would follow. Those loving
moments are what helped me push through the fear and stay. I'm sure I
would have died there if I hadn't left.
ME: You did leave.
PATIENT: I did but now I feel stuck, trapped, everywhere.
ME: You often feel trapped here too.
PATIENT: Almost always but it's getting better.
ME: Are you feeling trapped right now?
PATIENT: Yes, by the smells in here, I liked how it smelled when I walked
in and now it's overwhelming my head and I feel like I can't escape it.

Human Trafficking the Historical and Psychological

To begin to develop an unconscious representation of human trafficking a
historical and psychological understanding is pertinent. Slavery scholars
characterize trafficking by a rather invisible power relation that was also

present in the slavery of the past. Orlando Patterson (1982) described this power relationship with three facets: the social, which is enacted via a threat to control the other person; the psychological, namely in the form of persuasion to influence and change the person's perception of his/her situation; and the cultural, the process whereby the slave owner successfully transforms the person's obedience into a sense of duty. In modern day trafficking, this power relation is often subtle that is, it cannot be seen with the naked eye and, it is only upon deeper exploration that one may identify human trafficking.

A lure phase exists in human trafficking, which distinguishes it from US slavery of the past when Africans were abducted and forcibly transported to the US. The lure phase, then, substituted abduction in modern day trafficking. It is an insidious form of psychological coercion where the trafficker avoids the use of physical violence. It is the moment when the trafficker stages an ideal scenario for the victim—a well-paid job or the potential for a loving relationship, a "boyfriend" or "partner" who will care for her/him (UN, 2014). In reality, most of the time traffickers do not force people into exploitative situations by using violence. Trafficked people often appear to willfully travel and live with their traffickers in a manner that would suggest free will and choice. Only after the trafficker has gained the trafficked person's trust does the trafficker typically escalate coercive tactics and use physical and sexual violence (Contreras et al., 2016). The typical cycle is similar to narratives of domestic violence; acts of kindness and caring alternated with physical violence and psychological coercion. The result is a trafficked person who struggles to break free from the trafficker's exploitation.

An important question that is challenging the anti-trafficking field today is: Why is it so often hard for the trafficked person to break away from their trafficker? Riddling the answer are various complexities including the psychological coercion that human traffickers use on their victims (Contreras et al., 2016; Hargreaves-Cormany et al., 2016). Sex trafficked girls and boys, formerly referred to as "child prostitutes" and placed in juvenile detention are increasingly recognized as "victims"—here the victim status is welcomed and needed. Trafficked children are provided with health and social services.

For adults involved in the sex industry, even if coercion is clear, gaining victim status is more complex partly due to some of the ideas supported by the sex worker model that I noted earlier in this paper. Societal bias typically assumes that an adult involved in the commercial sex industry is culpable, guilty of prostitution (which is still considered a crime in most US states) until proven a victim of human trafficking (Halter, 2010; Herman, 2003; Maynard, 2002). Therefore, many trafficked people, feeling lost in a social reality that stigmatizes their experience, run back to their traffickers—often several times before they can exit or escape (Baker et al., 2010).

Other factors that contribute to people returning to their traffickers include extensive trauma histories that existed before trafficking, primarily experiences of sexual abuse and domestic violence that pushed people out of their homes and into the foster care systems or the streets, making them vulnerable to traffickers (Reid 2011; Ribando Seelke, 2015). Runaway youth in the United States are a population highly vulnerable to human trafficking (US Department of State, 2016). Demand for sex buying and cheap labor include other factors that also proliferate human trafficking (Shively et al., 2012).

How then is human trafficking fundamentally different from the slavery of the past in the United States? A psychosocial-historical outline (Contreras, 2018) recognizes that the "chains" of slavery, once tethered to a slave's body, now deprive freedom of the psyche by locking parts of the person's mind. Modern day traffickers—unlike slave owners of past centuries—do not need shackles to transport their victims overseas or to move them between US cities to exploit them.

Traffickers today use a person's relationship needs as a lure into the exploitation that characterizes human trafficking. To this point, one study identified high levels of psychopathy among male and female traffickers (Hargreaves-Cormany et al., 2016). The authors categorized traffickers as either "aggressive/antisocial" or "charismatic/manipulative." Violent charismatic/manipulative traffickers posed the greatest threat to the victim and society. This group often combines caring behaviors with the use of physical violence to control the victim, and in some cases, the use of physical force may be completely absent. Additionally, the author surmises that this type of trafficker is likely to possess high levels of intelligence, especially social skills that facilitate perpetration and evasion of law enforcement.

The United Nations (UN, 2014) notes that human trafficking hides in the most developed cities around the world, impacting thousands of people. Sarah's story, featured in the Boston Globe, highlights many of the issues discussed thus far. At age 16 she was forced to leave her abusive home and taken in by a "boyfriend" who convinced her to prostitute. She met him on Berkeley Street in Boston. Sarah escaped her trafficker once the violence turned unbearable—bruises, broken teeth, and broken bones that landed her in the hospital. She became the first juvenile witness in a case against a group of East Coast traffickers that moved girls between Maine to Florida. While her physical wounds healed, she continued to struggle with feelings of shame and guilt that were further compounded by societal stigma and ostracism. When the Boston Globe published her story, she was in social work school and frustrated that her academic program dismissed her on the grounds of her prostitution charges—because it made school officials "uncomfortable." Partly to blame were contradictions between federal and state laws. Had Sarah been an immigrant, the US's Federal trafficking law would have protected her, but as a US citizen, the state of Massachusetts prosecuted her for prostitution. Fortunately, Massachusetts legislature changed since 2011 after trafficking protections went into effect, but these came too late for women like Sarah.

For several years now, I have consulted to immigration and law enforcement agents who are baffled by the stories of individuals, like Sarah, who remained under a trafficker's control for years even while living in an open-door residence. More challenging to comprehend is how people stay in a "trafficked state of mind," even after realizing they have been tricked, coerced, or otherwise? From here on, I will attempt to discuss one way to answer this question from psychoanalytic and philosophical theories.

Human Trafficking and the Intrapsychic

In Freud's discerning 1931–1932 response to Einstein's "Why war?" question, he noted that "in principle" human beings had an instinctive craving for violence, thus highlighting that killing an enemy had little to do with survival. An alternative scenario to killing was the possibility of enslaving an enemy, which Freud explained as follows:

> another consideration may be set off against this will to kill: the possibility of using an enemy for servile tasks if his spirit be broken and his life spared. Here violence finds an outlet not in slaughter but in subjugation. Hence springs the practice of giving quarter; but the victor, having from now on to reckon with the craving for revenge that rankles in his victim, forfeits to some extent his personal security.
>
> (Einstein and Freud, 1933)

Freud established that aggression could find an outlet in subjugation, a process that Hegel before Freud had deconstructed in the Master–Slave dialectic. Hegel's philosophy has been used by many post-Freudian psychoanalytic and intersubjective theorists between the 1970s and late 1990s (Macdonald, 2011), including Paul Ricoeur, Lacan, Julia Kristeva, Jessica Benjamin, Slavoj Žižek, and Andre Green to explain multiple scenarios that unfold in the intersubjective space. Hegel's Master–Slave dialectic is also useful to highlight some of the dynamics that occur in the trafficking situation.

Lacan (1977) designated psychoanalysis as the theory that explains the birth of subjectivity, which takes place in the societal sphere. Social interactions generate sociocultural representations—say human trafficking—that he called the Other. For Lacan, Other is present from the beginning of life, ineludible, intrinsically tied and expressed through language and as such constitutional in intrapsychic development.

And Hegel's Master–Slave dialectic, Lacan pointed out "provided the ultimate theory of the proper function of aggression in human ontology, seeming to prophesy the iron law of our time. From the conflict of the Master and Slave, he deduced the entire subjective and objective progress of our history" (1977, p. 26). Now I will discuss a case to bridge fully into Hegel's dialectic.

Tanya's Modern–Day Slavery Experience

Tanya was a 22-year-old woman from Chiapas, Mexico whom I evaluated for immigration purposes. The man who trafficked Tanya met her while she worked in her family's food stand located on the side of a road frequented by tourists. Her father was a farmer, and the family struggled to survive. She had faced experiences of both sexual and physical abuse, yet remained determined to study and work hard to in her words, "make something of myself." Tanya had an alcoholic and abusive father, a depressed and battered mother, and a life of poverty compounded by the Chiapas internal conflict that had gripped Mexico in the 1980s. Not much was in her favor, yet she never stopped dreaming that she would find a way out.

Tanya was 16 years old when she met her trafficker. She said,

> He saw me and noticed how hard I worked and then he told me that I should be doing something bigger. He said that he could give me a job that would open my opportunities. He spoke about things that I had dreamed about.

Tanya was indeed a hard worker. When her father refused to pay for her education beyond the sixth grade, she worked long hours during school vacations and made enough money to continue to finance her schooling. Tanya left Mexico with the consent of her family. Mr. R, her trafficker, promised he would care for her. Mr. R., a native of Mexico and a college graduate, and his wife, a US citizen of Irish ancestry and a professional in the medical field, had told Tanya that she would babysit during the day and that they would pay for her to take evening English classes. They also offered her US legal permanent residency and possibly a college education.

Tanya faced a very different reality from what Mr. R and his wife had promised. When she arrived at Mr. R's home, she was forced to labor for 16 hours a day without pay, she was bullied by the children and forbidden from relating to the neighbors. On her first night in the US, Mr. R showed Tanya the barren basement room with a mattress sprawled over the floor where she would sleep. A stark contrast to the well-appointed rooms in the rest of the home that included an empty guest room. Mr. R started to rape Tanya two weeks after her arrival; she lived under these terrible conditions for two years.

Hegel and the Enslaved Mind

Hegel's (1977)[2] Master–Slave dialectic explains the acquisition of self-consciousness, which takes place in a primal moment and place that is before any human community existed and where—for the first time—two individuals encountered one another. Up until this time, each had thought of their selves as supreme and unique. With this encounter, each is faced with an image of another individual that is quite similar and hence threatening to his unique and supreme position. If these people acknowledged each other as individuals of the same order, they would forcibly need to abandon their identities. A process requiring each to hold back the innate desire that both have to be recognized as supreme. In Hegel's myth, neither is willing to recognize the other and cede their claim to supremacy.

Tanya described her first encounter with Mr. R with scenarios relatable to Hegel's primal encounter. She said, "I remember that Mr. R asked me what a smart and beautiful girl like me was doing selling food on the side of a poor Mexican road. He reminded me of everything I had always wanted to be." In other words, he presented her with a challenge, something to fight for. Tanya, who worked hard for everything, had waited for this moment of recognition. As for Mr. R, despite his wealth and success in the US, Tanya described him as someone who yearned to be recognized by his community. She said, "He spent extended periods in Mexico, he helped with the funds to build one of the local churches, and he was always inviting people to come back to the US with him." Mr. R likely also felt challenged and envious of this young Mexican girl's drive to succeed despite her numerous limitations, a feat he may have once faced himself.

In the second part of Hegel's myth, each person attempts to assert their unique self by trying to destroy the other. Hegel denominated this second part of the myth as the primal fight to death, which can conclude in one of two manners. In the first, neither individual gives up their claim for supremacy, and one eventually kills the other. The second is that one of the individuals—hoping for survival—submits to the other recognizing the winner's supremacy and agrees to live under his/her control. Tanya's choices were to let Mr. R's offer pass and see her dreams perish or to submit to his desire. Her future in Mexico was "bleak." She said, "college was impossible, I'd have to marry someone soon and pray that he was not abusive or an alcoholic," the fate of many of her friends. To say no to Mr. R was equivalent to renouncing her dreams and face an unsatisfying life—a psychological death of sorts. Hence, Tanya accepted Mr. R's offer and submitted.

There is an interesting twist in Hegel's Master–Slave dialectic. The only recognition that the Master accepts is one that comes from an equal and the Slave—now subjected to the Master's supremacy—is stripped of the equality needed for a meaningful recognition. Here the Master moves into a position of constant self-reference from where he demands recognition, which he devalues the moment the Slave gives it. Instead of killing the Slave, the Master strives to dominate completely and puts the Slave to work—to produce objects that the Master can consume. The demands that the Master has for the Slave are ones that supersede anything that the Master had been accustomed to.

Mr. R became obsessed with the cleanliness of the house and made Tanya perform senseless tasks such as scrubbing all the floors every day. Mr. R would only eat Mexican food that Tanya prepared. Favoring the Slave in these tasks is the exercise of suspending her desire, which she uses to work, alter nature, and create. Whereas the Master lives in a state of pure self-reference, the Slave meanwhile has learned to govern desire by postponing it. Over time, the Master increasingly feels dependent on the Slave's work to satiate his desire and paradoxically a part of him also becomes enslaved. Emerson's (1917) words are pertinent here, "If you put a chain around the neck of a slave, the other end fastens itself around your own" (p. 417). A dialectical process is now born where the Slave also controls the Master advancing one step beyond in the Master–Slave dynamic.

Tanya had lived in Mr. R's home for two years. During this time, she was often left alone, hence the possibility of escape had always been present, yet she stayed. She said that one day she thought she had had enough. She explained it like this, "I snapped out of it, I was living in hell and I chose to stop taking it. I left, and I never looked back." In Hegel, the Master–Slave myth ends when the Master perishes in self-reference, while the Slave rises to govern nature and thus her fear of death, which was what had led her to submit in the primal confrontation, has diminished. It is from this repeated suspension and deferral of desire that Hegel believes that human community was born.

Concluding Thoughts

The dynamics that make slavery possible in all its forms, including human trafficking manifest across various configurations of relating. Countless examples exist, and human trafficking is but one—think of the individual and power relationships with institutions, communities, and with other individuals. Think of institutions and their power relationships with other institutions. Also pertinent are institutions and their relationships to countries, or even the relationships that exist between countries—think more and less powerful nations.

Pre-existing vulnerabilities to human trafficking for US persons include histories of sexual abuse, witnessing domestic violence, and involvement in the foster care system, all representing different forms of subjugation and dominance (Contreras et al., 2016). An unconscious theory of subjugation poses some questions for the psychoanalytic field that are already present in intersubjective theories. Namely, the inherent power differentials between patient and psychoanalyst; while these power differentials are necessary for practice, they can also elicit dominance and submission states in the transference. An issue outlined by Benjamin (2004) in the "doer and done to" dynamics that she also referenced in Hegel's Master and Slave dialectic.

Other important factors to consider about human trafficking from an intersubjective perspective are the needs and vulnerabilities of psychoanalysts and psychotherapists. In trafficking, the trafficker exploits the needs and vulnerabilities of the victim. Therefore, careful consideration to needs and vulnerabilities of both the patient with a history of human trafficking and the therapist are of utmost importance. As one of Goldner's (2016) studies demonstrated, the analyst's needs influence the analyst–patient bond. Also of note is Shaw's (2014) formulation of the traumatized narcissistic psychoanalyst as one who is prone to abolish the complimentary relational dynamic required for an intersubjective encounter. The traumatized narcissist can only allow unilateral recognition toward him or herself, a dynamic that, as Shaw reminds, can also be repeated in psychoanalytic training relationships. In fact, power differentials exist across the entire mental health training system and also manifest in multiple ways in psychotherapy practice (Raubolt, 2006).

The important point here is that if the institutions, organizations, and the people who belong to these, do not begin to understand their particular position as Masters or Slaves, then how can psychoanalysts engage ethically with others who have suffered from the effects of those very dynamics? In my psychotherapy therapy work with people who have experienced human trafficking, there is always a moment where I must relinquish some of my power and transition into a position of "not knowing." In a sense, if I am working towards equality within the psychotherapy space that is burdened by power differentials, I need to be willing to occupy, with the patient, the space of Slave. Stated more simply, my work needs to move away from the impositions inherent in the act of diagnosing, prescribing, and interpreting, and move towards being with, working with, and everything that the act of making sense together entails (Buirski and Haglund, 2010). It is from this intrapsychic position, of Slaves working together, that the limiting Master discourse can be both reclaimed and tempered. The task becomes then to resist the subjugation through the productive and non-exploitative work that psychoanalysis can generate under the right conditions.

I find it fitting now to close with Kojève, from his lectures on Hegel, a quote that has often inspired my anti-trafficking work:

> The complete, absolutely free [person], definitively and completely satisfied by what s/he is, the [person] who is perfected and completed in and by this satisfaction, will be the Slave who has "overcome" his Slavery. If idle Mastery is an impasse, laborious Slavery, in contrast, is the source of all human, social, historical progress. History is the history of the working slave.
>
> (Kojève, 1980, p. 20)

Notes

1 All case examples have been de-identified to protect confidentiality.
2 Kojève's (1980) interpretation and review of Hegel's Phenomenology of Spirit has also guided me to compare human trafficking and the Master–Slave dialectic.

References

APsa Association (2015). Position Statement on Human Trafficking, Retrieved from http://www.apsa.org/sites/default/files/Position%20Statement%20on%20Human%20Trafficking.pdf

Baker, L. M., Dalla, R. L., and Williamson, C. (2010). Exiting prostitution:A integrated model. *Violence Against Women* 16(5): 579–600.

Benjamin, J. (2004) Beyond doer and done-to: an intersubjective view of thirdness. *Psychoanalytic Quarterly* 73(1): 5–46.

Bennett-Murphy, L. M. (2012) Haunted: treatment of a child survivor of human trafficking. *Journal of Infant, Child, and Adolescent Psychotherapy*, 11(2), 133–148. doi:10.1080/15289168.2012.673413

Bion, W. R. (1983). *Attention and Interpretation*. Lanham, MD: Rowman & Littlefield Publishers.

Bion, W. R. (2013). The psycho-analytic study of thinking. *The Psychoanalytic Quarterly*, 82, 301–310. doi:10.1002/j.2167-4086.2013.00030.x

Buirski, P., and Haglund, P. (2010). *Making Sense Together: The Intersubjective Approach to Psychotherapy*. Lanham, MD: Rowman & Littlefield Publishers.

Castillo, D.A. (2012). On the line: work and choice. *The Modern Language Association of America* 127(4): 835–844.

Contreras, P. M. (2018). Human trafficking of women and girls in the United States: toward an evolving psychosocial-historical definition. In C. B. Travis, J. W. White, A. Rutherford, W. S. Williams, S. L. Cook, K. F. Wyche, *et al.* (eds.), *APA Handbook of the Psychology of Women: Perspectives on Women's Private and Public Lives* (pp. 175–193). Washington, DC: American Psychological Association. doi:10.1037/0000060-010

Contreras, P. M., Kallivayalil, D., and Herman, J. L. (2016). Psychotherapy in the aftermath of human trafficking: working through the consequences of coercion. *Women and Therapy* 40(1–2): 31–54.

Contreras, P. M., Kallivayalil, D., and Herman, J. L. (2017). Psychotherapy in the aftermath of human trafficking: working through the consequences of psychological coercion. *Women & Therapy*, 40(1–2), 31–54, doi:10.1080/02703149.2016.1205908

Einstein, A., and Freud, S. (1933). Why war? In A. Kaes, M. Jay, and E. Dimendberg (eds.), *The Weimar Republic Sourcebook*. Los Angeles: University of California Press.

Elrod, J. (2015). Filling the gap: refining sex trafficking legislation to address the problem of pimping. *Vanderbilt Law Review* 68(3): 961–996.

Emerson, R.W. (1917). Ralph Waldo Emerson. In A.G. Newcomer, A.E. Andrews, and H.J. Hall (eds.), *Three Centuries of American Poetry and Prose*. New York: Scott, Foresman and Company.

Fals-Borda, O. (1991). Some basic ingredients. In O. Fals-Borda and M. Anisur Rahman (eds.), *Action and Knowledge, Breaking the Monopoly with Participatory Action-Research* (pp. 3–12). New York: The Apex Press.

Freire, P. (1970). Cultural action and conscientization. *Harvard Educational Review* 40(3): 452–477.

Freud, S. (1905a). *Three Essays on the Theory of Sexuality*, Standard Edition, Vol. 7, trans. J. Strachey (London: Hogarth Press, 1962).

Freud, S. (1905b). *Fragment of an Analysis of a Case of Hysteria*, Standard Edition, Vol. 7, trans. J. Strachey (London: Hogarth Press, 1962).

Freud, S. (1896). *The Aetiology of Hysteria*. Standard Edition, Vol. 3, trans. J. Strachey (London: Hogarth Press, 1962).

Gay, P. (1988). *Freud: A Life for Our Time*. New York: W. W. Norton and Co.

Gaztambide, D. (2015). A preferential option for the repressed: psychoanalysis through the eyes of liberation theology. *Psychoanalytic Dialogues* 25(6): 700–713.

Goldner, L. (2016). Therapists' self-perception, attachment, and relationship: The role of selfobject needs. *Psychoanalytic Psychology* 33(4): 535–553. doi:10.1037/pap0000049

Gulati, G. J. (2010). News frames and story triggers in the media's coverage of human trafficking. *Human Rights Review* 12: 363–379.

Halberstadt-Freud, H.C. (1996). Studies on hysteria: One hundred years on: a century of psychoanalysis. *International Journal of Psychoanalysis* 77: 983–994.

Halter, S. (2010). Police conceptualizations of girls involved in prostitution in six U. S. cities: Child sexual exploitation victims or delinquents? *Child Maltreatment* 15(2): 152–160.

Hargreaves-Cormany, H. A., Patterson, T. D., and Muirhead, Y. E. (2016). A typology of offenders engaging in the sex trafficking of juveniles (STJ): implications for risk assessment. *Aggression and Violent Behavior* 30: 40–47.

Harris, A. (2014). Human trafficking: exploring inaction through a psychoanalytic lens, *Quarterly Magazine of The Psychoanalytic Association*, 48(3), 1–35. Available at: http://www.apsa.org/sites/default/files/TAP%202014%20vol48no3.pdf

Hegel, G.W.F. (1977). *Phenomenology of Spirit*. New York: Oxford University Press.

Hepburn, S., and Simon, R. J. (2013). *Human Trafficking around the World: Hidden in Plain Sight*. New York: Columbia University Press.

Herman, J.L. (2015). *Trauma and Recovery: The Aftermath of Violence—From Domestic Abuse to Political Terror*. New York: Basic Books.

Herman, J.L. (2003). Hidden in plain sight: clinical reflections on prostitution. *Journal of Trauma Practice* 2(3–4):1–13.

Hollander, N.C. (2001) *Love in a Time of Hate*. New York: Other Press.

Keat, J. (2017). Unpublished discussion on paper titled, "Reflections on human trafficking and psychoanalysis", delivered at the Boston Psychoanalytic Institute and Society in Newton, MA for Member's Meeting on October 2, 2017.

Kleinschmidt, L. (2009). Keeping mother alive: psychotherapy with a teenage mother following human trafficking. *Journal of Child Psychotherapy*, 35(3), 262–275. doi:10.1080/00754170903234416

Kojève, A. (1980). *Introduction to the Reading of Hegel: Lectures on the Phenomenology of Spirit*. Ithaca, NY: Cornell University Press.

Lacan, J. (1977). *Ecrits*. New York: W. W. Norton.

Logan, T., Walker, R., and Hunt, G. (2009). Understanding human trafficking in the United States. *Trauma, Violence, and Abuse* 10(1): 3–30.

Macdonald, H. (2011). Hegel, psychoanalysis and intersubjectivity. *Philosophy Compass* 6(7): 448–458.

Masson, J. M. (1984). *The Assault on Truth: Freud's Suppression of the Seduction Theory*. New York: Farrar, Straus, and Giroux.

Maynard, W.R. (2002). Human trafficking "under the sentencing guidelines". *Federal Sentencing Reporter* 14(5): 316–318.

McCullough, M. L. (2001). Freud's seduction theory and its rehabilitation: a saga of one mistake after another. *Review of General Psychology* 5(1): 3–22.

McKim, J. B. (2010). A former teenage prostitute struggles to move on. *Boston Globe*, October 10, at A1. Retrieved from http://www.boston.com/business/arti cles/2010/10/10/a_former_teenage_prostitute_struggles_to_move_on/?page=4

McNally, R.J. (2003). *Remembering Trauma.* Cambridge, MA: Harvard University Press.

Martín-Baró, I. (1986). Hacia una psicología de la liberación. [Toward a psychology of liberation]. *Boletín de Psicología* [Bulletin of Psychology] 22: 219–231.

Patterson, O. (1982). *Slavery and Social Death: A Comparative Study.* London: Harvard University Press.

Patterson, O. (2012). Trafficking, gender, and slavery: past and present. In J. Allain (ed.), *The Legal Understanding of Slavery: From the Historical to the Contemporary.* Oxford: Oxford University Press.

Raubolt, R. (2006). *Power Games: Influence, Persuasion, and Indoctrination in Psychotherapy Training.* New York: Other Press.

Reid, J.A. (2011). An exploratory model of girl's vulnerability to commercial sexual exploitation in prostitution. *Child Maltreatment* 16(2): 146–157.

Ribando Seelke, C. (2015). *Trafficking in Persons in Latin America and the Caribbean.* Washington, DC: Congressional Research Service.

Shaw, D. (2014). *Traumatic Narcissism, Relational Systems of Subjugation.* New York: Routledge.

Shively, M., Kliorys, K., Wheeler, K., and Hunt, D. (2012). A national overview of prostitution and sex trafficking demand reduction efforts, final report. Retrieved from https://www.ncjrs.gov/pdffiles1/nij/grants/238796.pdf

Silver, K.E., Karakurt, G., and Boysen, S.T. (2015). Predicting prosocial behavior toward sex-trafficked persons: the roles of empathy, belief in a just world, and attitudes toward prostitution. *Journal of Aggression, Maltreatment and Trauma* 24(8): 932–954.

Teo, T. (2015). Critical psychology: a geography of intellectual engagement and resistance. *American Psychologist* 70(3): 243–254.

Trafficking Victims Protection Act. (2000). 22 U.S.C. § 7101 (b)(2).

Tummala-Narra, P., Kallivayalil, D., Singer, R., and Andreini, R. (2012). Relational experiences of complex trauma survivors in treatment: preliminary findings from a naturalistic study. *Psychological Trauma: Theory, Research, Practice, and Policy* 4(6): 640–648.

UN. (2014). Global Report on Trafficking in Persons 2014. Vienna: United Nations Office on Drugs and Crime.

US Department of State. (2016). Trafficking in Persons Report 2016. Washington, DC: US Government Printing Office.

Verhaeghe, Paul. (1998). Trauma and hysteria within Freud and Lacan. *The Letter (Dublin)* 14: 87–106.

Yeatman, A. (2015). A two-person conception of freedom: the significance of Jessica Benjamin's idea of intersubjectivity. *Journal of Classical Sociology* 15(1): 3–23.

6 Psychological Treatment

Application of Feminist Theory

AnnJanette Alejano-Steele and Katherine Miller

Drawing from feminist counseling theory roots in the women's movement of the 1960s, current approaches take into consideration intersectional identities within the sociocultural context that surrounds survivor psychological functioning.

Human trafficking negatively impacts survivors, their families, and the community (Farley et al., 2003; Miller et al., 2007; Pierce, 2009; Roe-Sepowitz, 2012; Silbert and Pines, 1981, 1982b; Williamson and Prior, 2009), and this chapter takes into consideration feminist approaches to psychological treatment. Feminism focuses on the role of social, political, and cultural contexts of individuals' issues as they relate to gender and power. Feminist therapists attend to a range of tenets as they apply to post–trauma psychological functioning and complex trauma recovery. As a compliment to the previous chapters, feminist frameworks are powerful enhancements to clinical approaches, given the abusive power dynamics between survivor and perpetrator and the larger societal power structures that dictate how survivors are provided services. Broadly, the feminist movement asserts the belief in the equal worth of all human beings; recognition that each individual's personal experiences and situations are reflective of and an influence on society's institutionalized attitudes and values; and a commitment to political and social change that equalizes power among people (Rave and Larsen, 1995). The basic tenets central to this chapter include the following.

Tenet 1. Feminist practitioners attend to hierarchies of power and dominance among and between people in all practice settings. They also make explicit the values and biases they bring into their clinical practices (Brabeck, 2000; Egharevba, 2001; Enns, 1997; Wyche and Rice, 1997).

Tenet 2. Feminist practitioners promote and support survivor-led anti-trafficking initiatives. Feminists critique dominant narratives that frame how survivors are perceived.

Tenet 3. Feminist practitioners consider survivors' social, historical, cultural, and institutional contexts that surround them and anti-trafficking community efforts. Social ecology frameworks help feminist researchers to centralize survivor experience within a series of systems including family, community and institutions. Social and political contexts that frame an individual's experience must be acknowledged.

Tenet 4. Feminist researchers and practitioners attend to the complexities of intersectional identities, whereby gender identity, race, class, sexualities, nationalities, size (among others) compound vulnerability to human trafficking (APA, 2014). Intersectional identities of survivors can create barriers to access, availability, and treatment, creating hierarchies of who is worthy of support (Laboratory to Combat Human Trafficking, 2016). With these intentions, the range of lived experiences and identities of survivors of human trafficking can be honored through therapeutic practice.

Feminist Theory Underpinnings

Feminist work has changed social, political, and cultural beliefs about the role of women globally, attentive to: a) power of knowledge and epistemology; b) boundaries, marginalization, silences, and intersections; c) relationships and their power differentials; and d) individual sociopolitical location (Ackerly and Attanasi, 2009; Ackerly and True, 2010). Notable feminist theorists Karen Horney (1932), Melanie Klein (1921–1945), Juliet Mitchell (1971); Germaine Greer (1971); Dorothy Dinnerstein (1977); Nancy Chodorow (1978); Carol Gilligan (1982); and Lillian Rubin (1984) merged psychological and feminist theory that laid the foundation for subsequent research, professional practice, educational programs, community activism, and policy implementation (Worell and Johnson, 1997, p. 1). The conduct of feminist research draws upon theoretical, methodological, and empirical insights from a diverse body of feminist theories. Feminist-informed research is self-reflective, critical, political, and versed in multiple theoretical frameworks in order to enable the researcher to "see" people and processes lost in gaps, silences, margins, and peripheries (Ackerly and True, 2010). Recent priorities, articulated by the National Women's Studies Association (2014–2017) (see NWSA, 2017)—the formal interdisciplinary professional association of feminist scholars—have featured dialogues on recent topics including: intersectional identities; complexities of transgender identity; transnational borders; community precarity; and decoloniality. Focus upon political power (evidenced by recent Women's marches and resistance to gender violence and the actions catalyzed by the silence breakers of the #metoo movement), all share the quest for access, availability, and empowerment of all. Recent feminist critiques on the national anti-trafficking movement have included critiques of language and the framing of survivors (Laboratory to Combat Human Trafficking, 2017); binaries of identity and the social contract to protect children (O'Connell Davidson, 2005); critiques on policy, prostitution and sex work (Kempadoo and Doezema, 1995; Outshoorn, 2005); and, moral outrage and bifurcated feminist positions on sex work (Weitzer, 2007), among others.

Feminist Therapy Foundations and Foremothers

Building upon the range of feminist theories and analytical tools, the path for feminist therapy was paved by an array of clinicians, including Laura S. Brown (1994); Paula Caplan (1995); Carol Zerbe Enns (1997); Olivia Espín (1993); Beverly Greene (1994); Mary Harvey (1995); Judith Herman (1992); Hope Landrine (1989, 1995); Maria P.P. Root (1997) and Lenore E. A. Walker (1989, 1994); and Judith Worell (2000). (See Evans et al. (2005) and Webster and Dunn (2005) for reviews.) Like their predecessors, these clinicians addressed socially constructed biases against women and focused upon the impact of feminist theory on practice. Feminist therapy focuses upon centrally keeping present gender issues in order to actively engage in understanding how societal issues affect their behavior (Nathan, 2012). Brown (1994) summarizes feminist therapy as

> the practice of therapy informed by feminist political philosophy and analysis, grounded in multicultural feminist scholarship on the psychology of women and gender, which leads both therapist and client toward strategies and solutions advancing feminist resistance, transformation, and social change in daily personal life, and in relationships with the social, emotional, and political environment.
>
> (1994, p. 22)

One primary goal of offering feminist therapy includes an empowerment focus. This enables clients to focus on strengths instead of deficits; to recognize, claim and embrace personal power; and value and affirm diversity. Feminist therapists are also accountable for the management of the power differential within the therapist/client relationship.

Feminist counseling has evolved, attentive to the range of identities, beginning with race/ethnicity by incorporating multicultural counseling theories (Enns and Williams, 2013), expanding its scope beyond sex and gender to "explore the complex biopsychosocial intersections of multiple identities, multiple privileges, and multiple oppressions as they emerge during multiple time periods, multiple developmental phases, and multiple life tasks" (Enns and Williams, 2013, p. 4).

Currently, feminist therapeutic literature lacks in evidence-based practices for treating trafficking survivors therapeutically. Broadly, empirical support for feminist therapy approaches are limited due to research challenges; among them convenience samples, instrument validity, anecdotal evidence, and lack of long term outcomes (APA, 2014). For example, of those available, several publications narrowly focus upon women and girls trafficked in Southeast Asia. While this area of focus is valuable, this gap in research on effective therapeutic practices perpetuates myths that human trafficking is something that happens only in developing and Global South countries.

Because there are no "typical" profiles of human trafficking survivors (APA, 2014), there are no one-size-fits-all treatment plans to assist survivors. As long-term evidence is gathered, feminist therapy treatment models for practitioners will continue to evolve. The most closely related body of evidence on feminist therapy has been conducted with survivors of domestic violence and sexual assault, and although many interventions may be effective with survivors of trauma, they may not be effective for trafficking survivors. It bears repeating that any recommendations come with the caveat that feminist therapy approaches and interventions must be tailored to each individual client.

Webster and Dunn (2005) provide an overview of feminist efforts and historical challenges faced while bringing public and professional attention to gender violence through feminist theory and therapeutic methods. Bound by a commitment to shared feminist values, these clinicians recognize the power differentials between privileged and oppressed populations, both cross-culturally and internationally, and the need to acknowledge the social and political contexts in which gender violence occurs. Feminist therapists depathologize the individual responses to violence and hold accountable those who perpetrate the violence or refuse to provide safety for all of a society's citizens (Webster and Dunn, 2005).

In the area of gender violence, feminist theorists have directly challenged the culture's dominant explanatory frameworks regarding violence against women, countering widespread beliefs about violent acts and the survivors who broke their silences. First and foremost, priorities should be laid on platforming survivor voice and participation in anti-trafficking initiatives. The feminist work of Ginny NiCarthy's (1984) experience with rape survivors laid the groundwork to better understand the need to prioritize survivor voice, whereby the only real experts on the subject are the individuals with lived experience.

NiCarthy's (1984) perspective invites researchers and practitioners to reflect upon the benefits gained in adapting practices as they learn directly from human trafficking survivors in this burgeoning field. Services for human trafficking survivors will likely fail if they do not match the identified needs of survivors, but rather reflect what service providers *assume* survivors want or need. It is reasonable to presume, then, that survivor voices need to guide the design of these initiatives (APA, 2014; Caliber, 2007; Clawson et al., 2009; Iman et al., 2009; Pierce, 2009; Raphael and Ashley, 2008; Raymond and Hughes, 2001). Feminist practitioners advocate for survivors by creating spaces that are survivor inclusive. In the words of survivor leader Minh Dang,

> I urge all of you to continue to partner with survivors—to ask survivors not just about their stories, but also about their policy recommendations, their ideas for improved intervention, as well as their hopes and concerns for the movement.
>
> (Cited in Murphy, 2014)

In the next section, the work of Judith Herman, Mary Harvey, and Maria P.P. Root are featured to illustrate specific feminist therapy contributions to best advocate and guide treatment interventions for human trafficking survivors.

Judith Herman

Psychiatrist Judith Herman bridged her commitments to interdisciplinary research and social change. With the 1992 publication of *Trauma and Recovery: The Aftermath of Violence from Domestic Abuse to Political Terror*, she laid the foundations for understanding human trafficking today by addressing violence and human suffering. She developed the argument for a new Diagnostic and Statistical Manual of Mental Disorders (DSM) diagnosis of "Complex Post-Traumatic Stress Disorder," resulting from the effects of early and/or repeated acts of terror, captivity, and disconnection (as in the case of human trafficking), and how they differ significantly from single-event trauma that may be experienced alongside other survivors (Herman, 1992). Her work invites exploration of multidisciplinary perspectives on the meaning of advocacy and justice for human trafficking survivors.

The effects of complex trauma are wide reaching and persistent, affecting a multitude of areas in a person's life, including: physical and emotional health; the ability to form secure attachments and build trusting relationships; challenges with emotional identification and regulation; dissociation; cognitive problems (unclear thought patterns, reasoning, and inability to problem solve); behavior problems such as impulse control, extreme outbursts, risk taking, unpredictability, and aggressiveness (or conversely, being overly complicit and compliant with authority, rigidness, and appearing overcontrolled); and lack of future planning, hope, and healthy self-concept (NCSTN, 2016).

While there is much evidence to support the use of cognitive behavioral therapy and dialectical behavior therapy when working with trauma, multi-model approaches have developed in recent decades to address complex trauma. This framework has become a cornerstone in trauma treatment due to Herman's (1992) *Trauma and Recovery* work that drew from literature on survivors of combat, torture, and Holocaust survivors. Herman's approach focuses primarily on individual safety, ability to identify and regulate emotions, development of trusting relationships, and the consequences of interpersonal trauma (Courtois, 2013). Herman's 1992 work outlines a process of three recovery phases: safety, remembrance and mourning, and reconnection.

Herman's (1992) first critical phase—safety—acknowledges that no meaningful work can be done to diminish symptoms of trauma if the client does not feel safe. This phase can often be the longest, as safety may take days, weeks, months, or even years to establish depending on the severity of trauma. Building a strong, secure therapeutic alliance is critical to client safety and education helps clients to understand their treatment, identify and name their reactions, and recognize their symptoms (Courtois, 2013).

Education encourages empowerment to regain control and power (Herman, 1992).

Herman's (1992) second phase—remembrance and mourning—involves sharing the trauma narrative in order to process memories and emotions related to traumatic events (Courtois, 2013). The act of storytelling empowers clients, providing choice in confronting the past and engaging in meaning making while the counselor holds the role of witness or ally. Survivors may mourn the loss of their former self, their childhood, their relationships, or their innocence (Herman, 1992). This phase requires collaborative planning between the client and counselor, with cautions that this phase may not be empowering for all survivors of human trafficking.

Reconnection, Herman's (1992) final phase, is a time of growth centered on moving forward from the past to creating a future. The trauma narrative provides opportunity to determine a new identity, build relationships, and form new life meanings (Courtois, 2013). Further, constructing meaning around fear responses and rebuilding responses to be trusted help reestablish client control and power (Herman, 1992). Additionally, the client may wish to seek a "survivor mission" as a resolution to their trauma through the form of social action (Herman, 1992), providing an opportunity to develop a voice for public awareness and public outrage against violence.

Art therapy. One example of incorporating tools of empowerment in the ways that Herman notes is art therapy. Art is a motivating tool of empowerment in grassroots social justice movements, whether through music, poetry, murals, photography, documentaries, art galleries, dance, or drama. Art has demonstrated the power to move people, and illustrates perspectives and provides a mode of outlet and expression, thereby simultaneously promoting healing and social change. Art can be a vehicle to regain power and control, to reauthor a trauma narrative, and to transition an individual from surviving to liberation after traumatic experiences.

Art therapy has been proven to help with issues such as conflict resolution, improvement of interpersonal skills, decreasing negative emotions and stress, managing problematic behaviors, and gaining personal insight (AATA, 2016). Clients can nonverbally express themselves (AATA, 2016; Rosen Saltzman et al., 2013), when finding the words may pose challenges or re-traumatization. Additionally, art can engage clients physically, allowing space for healing from somatic symptoms of trauma. It allows clients to take stances that are proactive, promoting empowerment, resiliency, and the desire for change (Backos and Pagon, 1999). Herman's stages of recovery are illustrated in the ways in which art can: 1) establish safety within the group and sit with their anger; 2) begin a process of mourning their former selves; and 3) reconnect through the decision to participate in the movement calling for public awareness of gender violence (Backos and Pagon, 1999). Art serves to heal and empower.

Art as a therapeutic modality for creative expression and social change after trauma has also been successful in international settings, such as post-trauma recovery in Palestinian refugee camps and post-disaster areas like Sri

Lanka. In Palestinian refugee camps, Sawhney (2009) founded a creative engagement program entitled Voices Beyond Walls, where youth were provided avenues for creative expression and advocacy through digital storytelling and new media production. Art provides an opportunity to document trauma symbolically without becoming overwhelmed (Stronach-Buschel, 1990, c.f. Chilcote, 2007). Art allows practitioners to tailor therapeutic interventions while creating space for people to tell their stories in their own voices.

Mary Harvey

Like all community members, human trafficking survivors have lived experiences that have shaped their knowledge, attitudes, beliefs. However, their experiences (both positive and negative) are gained relationally with family, friends, fellow classmates, work colleagues. These relationships develop in community—whether that be their neighborhood, workplace, and community institutions (e.g., local businesses, governmental and non-governmental agencies, religious organizations, etc.). Widening the scope beyond local community, county-, state-, and national-level decisions also impact everyone's lives. Further, national cultural norms dictate whether behaviors and social relationships are acceptable—examples include individualism, patriotism, racism, sexism, and classism, among others (Stokols, 1992). It is in this type of analysis that feminist therapist Mary Harvey laid the groundwork for feminist therapies to address political forces that shape survivors' lives.

Her feminist work has shaped the way treatment promotes the recovery and resilience of human trafficking worldwide, noting that gender violence is not an individual problem, but a community problem burdened by all of its members. Harvey applied an ecological framework to describe the causes and clinical implications of trauma (Koss and Harvey, 1991; Harvey, 1996; Harvey and Harney, 1995), emphasizing the critical role of community in treating and preventing victimization by describing the multiple interrelationships between the individual and the community. Her ecological framework of victimization placed the relationships among the person characteristics (i.e., internal traits, abilities); event characteristics (i.e., the nature, severity, frequency and duration of victimization), and environment characteristics (i.e., degree of safety and protection provided post-trauma, attitudes toward the victim and available resources) form the individual's unique ecology and serve as the foundation from which recovery will occur (Harvey, 1996).

For human trafficking survivors, person and event characteristics are likely to be stable, while the environment characteristics may range in the degree to which they promote or hinder recovery. Survivors from communities that support a valued role for survivors and view gender violence as a form of patriarchy and oppression will likely fare better than individuals who are from communities which uphold patriarchal (and other and multiple privileged) views. Survivors who belong to multiple communities (i.e., cultural, racial, professional) as victims of violence must negotiate their recovery amid potentially disparate messages heard from multiple communities. Harvey further described how the provision or absence of supports to heal within the community (e.g., availability of human trafficking-appropriate crisis referrals) will shape the recovery process and play a vital role in supporting survivor well-being following trauma (Harvey, 1985; Koss and Harvey, 1991). For a detailed examination of these community-level factors as they are applied to Colorado and anti-trafficking responses, see Chapter 11.

Harvey's contributions reframed ways in which ecological factors (i.e., racism, poverty, misogyny, patriarchy, and political disinclination towards diversity and pluralism) serve as mechanisms to promote violence. Harvey's treatment model further platforms the ecological framework, to help clinicians provide the appropriate level of intervention to assist victims who are at different stages of recovery, and takes personal ecology into account. Since victimization is the result of a loss of power and control, interventions must guide the victim in restoring these internal and external facilities (Koss and Harvey, 1991; Harvey, 1996). For human trafficking survivors, Harvey's principles guide clinicians to focus on:

> the range of potential reactions to violence and multidimensional trauma (physical, psychological, relational, cognitive, behavioral and spiritual) and give power and control of the internal and external environment back to the victim by establishing physical and emotional safety, providing information, allowing for ventilation and validation of experience, mobilizing internal and external resources and preparing and planning for the future.
>
> (Webster and Dunn, 2005, p. xx)

Harvey's indicators of recovery after trafficking include: 1) authority over the remembering process; 2) integration of memory and affect; 3) affect tolerance; 4) symptom mastery; 5) self-esteem and self-cohesion; 6) safe attachment; and 7) establishing new meaning to experience prior, during, and after the period of being trafficked (Harvey and Harney, 1995). Finally, Harvey and her colleagues' work helps to account for the variation in goals of each stage for human trafficking survivors. The amount of time clients typically spend at each stage and the cyclical and non-linear nature of progression through the stages (Lebowitz et al., 1993; Yassen and Harvey, 1998) should be taken into account for the range of experiences of human trafficking survivors.

Maria Primitiva Paz Root

Therapists and other practitioners from the United States can also benefit from the plethora of global initiatives and perspectives on violence incurred throughout human trafficking operations. Maria Primitiva Paz Root's feminist orientation on global gender violence implored practitioners to ask critical questions concerning definitions of trauma and what groups of people have been included or excluded from historically accepted therapeutic frameworks. Her work further focused upon the long-term sequelae of victimization, reconceptualizing definitions of trauma and calling for further research on violence against women of color, particularly the structural factors (i.e. language barriers, economic disenfranchisement, conceptual, cultural and research) that surround them (Root, 1991). Women of color have historically had devalued status in society (multiplied by other intersectional identities like sexual orientation, class and nationality) and disinclination to report trauma out of fear of being mistreated, stereotyped, or for fear that disclosing will have little or no effect. Survivors' intersectional identities further play a significant role in access to services (assuming the services have skilled staff who understand human trafficking). An example might be an individual who is transgender female to male, low income American-Indian-Latino from Mexico who also has a disability. With a lived experience of being trafficked for labor that included sexual violence might prove to pose difficulties in receiving the array of services they need.

Root's focus on the aftermath of victimization helped to refine therapeutic inquiry to include victimization history and support clinician resilience as they discuss trauma with clients (Root and Fallon, 1989; Root, 1989; Root, 1991). Root's multidimensional definition of trauma can be applied to work with human trafficking survivors by critically considering: 1) historical and sociopolitical contexts in how human trafficking is framed and response is resourced; 2) the biopsychosocial spiritual impact of trauma; 3) how trauma is conceptualized by survivors (including threat, poverty, discrimination); and 4) how trauma impacts dimensions of safety.

By expanding comprehensive definitions of trauma, Root's feminist work calls for categorizing trauma based on the proximity to the perpetrator (Root, 1992; Root, 1997), both as direct recipient and observer. The malicious, often isolated intentions of trauma should also be taken into account to address attribution of blame, support received, and healing process (Root, 1992). For example, in human trafficking situations, victims of malicious trauma may suffer in isolation, receive little support and may be viewed as uniquely vulnerable

> If the victim experiences the trauma in deliberate isolation, the perpetrator's coercion will likely lead the victim to blame (themselves) for the crime. The connection with at least one other person, on the other hand, will provide social support and diminish feelings of self-blame and vulnerability.
>
> (Root, 1992, p. 134, cf. Webster and Dunn, 2005)

Feminist Initiatives

This section provides examples of putting feminist principles into practice beyond therapeutic settings. Feminist tenets can be identified in several policy arenas and services for survivors, most importantly beginning with policy recommendations posed by survivors.

National Advisory Council on Human Trafficking Recommendations

The United States Advisory Council on Human Trafficking Council is comprised of 11 diverse survivors of labor and sex trafficking. Guided by the US Department of State, the Council is a formal platform for trafficking survivors to advise and make recommendations on federal anti-trafficking policies to the President's Interagency Task Force to Monitor and Combat Trafficking in Persons (PITF). Amongst the areas that the United States Advisory Council on Human Trafficking has reviewed regarding rule of law, public awareness, labor laws, and grant making, the recommendations relative to Victim Services reflect the tenets and feminist sensitivities reviewed in this chapter. They are as follows.

- DOJ, HHS, DOS, USAID, and DOL provide comprehensive services for all survivors of human trafficking.
- Establishment of housing preferences for survivors of human trafficking at the federal and local levels.
- DOJ and HHS anti-trafficking grantees use standardized screening questions developed with survivors' professional input.
- The council believes that there is a need to shift the language currently used in survivor services and would like to work with agencies to ensure a more holistic and survivor-informed approach that is trauma-informed and sensitive to cultural and religious beliefs.
- Survivors would also like to work with regional HHS offices to develop a holistic approach to victim identification. Additionally, we would like to observe and advise anti-trafficking trainings for the foster care system, which could include trainings on survivor-specific services, trauma caused by human trafficking, and the effects of trauma on adolescent development.

American Psychological Association Task Force on the Trafficking of Women and Girls Recommendations

Similar feminist principles appear in the general recommendations for psychologists, put forth by the American Psychological Association Task Force on the Trafficking of Women and Girls, stewarded by the Women's Programs Office (WPO). The work of the Women's Programs Office aims to:

> improve the status, health and well-being of women psychologists and consumers of psychological services by promoting those aspects of psychology that involve solutions to the fundamental problems of human justice and equitable and fair treatment of all segments of society. The

Office encourages the utilization and dissemination of psychological knowledge to advance equal opportunity and to foster empowerment of those who do not share equitably in society's resources. Another goal is to increase scientific understanding and training in regard to those aspects that pertain to, but are not limited to, culture, class, race/ethnicity, gender, sexual orientation, age and discrimination; and to support improving educational training opportunities for all persons.

(APA, 2017)

The Task Force's recommendations also reflect a regard for feminist principles:

- Examine assumptions and biases toward at-risk groups as they consider engaging in work on human trafficking issues.
- Be culturally sensitive in all endeavors related to human trafficking (research, education and training, advocacy and public policy, public awareness, and practice).
- Remain cognizant that internationally and domestically trafficked persons are a diverse and multicultural group.
- Recognize that no "one-size-fits-all" approach exists to comprehensively address the victim/survivor experience.
- Support the creation of cultural shifts among law enforcement and service providers in anti-trafficking efforts to create a greater understanding of and respect for all trafficked populations.
- Examine the impact of paternalistic attitudes and the "rescue" approach on survivors' outcomes and well-being.
- Advocate for survivor-centered, survivor-informed, and survivor-led efforts guiding policymaking, protocol development, research design, methodology, and clinical approaches.
- Support recommendations of the APA Task Force on the Sexualization of Girls (APA, 2010) regarding social norms, attitudes, and culture of tolerance for sexual exploitation.
- In addition to policy recommendations, feminist principles are woven into programs serving survivors of human trafficking.

Feminist Service Provision: Colorado Network to End Human Trafficking Hotline

The delivery of services to trafficking victims necessitates case-by-case attention requiring coordinated efforts from several organizations. These services often include a combination of needs encompassing: immigration resources; legal and criminal defense; counseling for trauma and other mental abuses; resources for health (including physical trauma and sexually transmitted diseases); and protection from violence.

One example of a local area network providing resources from a feminist perspective is the Colorado Network to End Human Trafficking (CoNEHT), a statewide resource and referral network accessible by a statewide hotline. Hotline advocates often fill the role of first responders to survivors who are able to call. The impact of trauma can strongly influence how survivors interact with hotline advocates, where trust and rapport must be established quickly to assess immediate needs (Clawson et al., 2008). The development of trust, especially vocally, can be challenging, as survivors are likely to experience complex trauma (NCTSN, 2016). Engagement may be further complicated by the fact that their protective survival skills may be well-honed (APA, 2014). Many survivors may be suspicious of agencies that are meant to keep them safe, especially when the system has let them down or caused harm (Richardson, 2014; Trauma Center, 2014). Some survivors may dismiss the idea that anyone could make a difference in their situation or keep them safe (Trauma Center, 2014). Due to these complexities, services must operate collaboratively, where empowerment is the central goal of service to the survivor (Clawson et al., 2008).

Further, the CoNEHT hotline ensures access to available resources, without the necessity of engaging law enforcement response. Hotline advocates operate from a feminist framework, attending to power and privilege dynamics, recognizing that many communities see law enforcement response as one of last resort. If the caller's prior experiences with law enforcement were violent, exploitive, or dismissive, they would be less apt to call for assistance if a crime report is required. Many callers are undocumented migrants, people of color and are unhoused; the risks for many are not worth the assistance, therefore they say silent.

Feminist Research: Shelter services in Israel

Where women's studies scholars and practitioners integrate their work as knowledge producers, APA (2014) has identified research as one of the primary foci for psychologists in the quest to understand the nature of human trafficking and the fight to end it. An example of feminist research on gendered service provision is a study focusing on shelter service operations in Israel. In a study by Hacker et al. (2015), comparisons were made between gendered state-funded shelters for human trafficking survivors, revealing clear distinctions between services offered for men and women. Women were favored to receive emotional support and therapy, while men received greater support for labor force reintegration. Identification of these and other discrepancies enabled researchers to advise law-makers and funders about the detriment of gendered approaches to rehabilitation.

Feminist Research: Colorado Project to Comprehensively Combat Human Trafficking

Another example of feminist research involves community-based research methods, designed to create sustainable social change to support survivors. A three-year longitudinal project, named the Colorado Project to Comprehensively Combat Human Trafficking utilized feminist pedagogies and research design. Conducted by the Laboratory to Combat Human Trafficking, its interdisciplinary project team (with the guidance of a national advisory board composed of researchers and practitioners) collected promising practices for Prevention, Protection, Prosecution and Partnerships to assess strengths and gaps in community responses to human trafficking. Much of the work was conducted by way of creating shared learning spaces, and earning trust to build bridges across parallel movements (e.g., gender-based violence advocates; advocacy for the unhoused; immigrant and labor rights groups, amongst others) to address human trafficking. Further, feminist frameworks enabled researchers to identify how systems of power and oppression fuel the trafficking of persons across Colorado communities, and how community precarity supports or prohibits survivors from receiving services. Current efforts with the Colorado Project include the monitoring of a data-driven Colorado Action Plan, replication in other states, and future research incorporating survivor-driven research. For a full review of how community-based research enhances service provision at the community level, see Chapter 11.

Feminist Framework Resources

In alignment with the key tenet of continuing education and sustainability for social change efforts around human trafficking this chapter concludes with suggested resources to support infusing feminist approaches into practice.

National Women's Studies Association

Established in 1977, the National Women's Studies Association (www. nwsa.org) has as one of its primary objectives promoting and supporting the production and dissemination of knowledge about women and gender through teaching, learning, research and service in academic and other settings. Their commitments are to: illuminate the ways in which women's studies are vital to education; to demonstrate the contributions of feminist scholarship that is comparative, global, intersectional and interdisciplinary to understandings of the arts, humanities, social sciences and sciences; and to promote synergistic relationships between scholarship, teaching and civic engagement in understandings of culture and society. NWSA recognizes that women's studies is broader than what happens in the classroom and acknowledges women's centers staff as feminist educators. Campus-based women's centers have a long history of working together with women's studies to transform the curriculum, the campus environment, and society at large.

Through their scholarship and pedagogy our members actively pursue knowledge to promote a just world in which all persons can develop to their fullest potential—one free from ideologies, systems of privilege or structures that oppress or exploit some for the advantage of others. The Association has more than 2,000 individual and 350 institutional members working in varied specialties across the United States and around the world.

American Psychological Association Women's Programs Office (WPO) works to improve the status, health and well-being of women psychologists and consumers of psychological services by: Promoting those aspects of psychology that involve solutions to the fundamental problems of human justice and equitable and fair treatment of all segments of society; Encouraging the utilization and dissemination of psychological knowledge to advance equal opportunity and to foster empowerment of those who do not share equitably in society's resources. WPO's **Committee on Women in Psychology** furthers the major purpose of the APA—"to advance psychology as a science and a profession and as a means of promoting health, education and human welfare"—by ensuring that women in all their diversity achieve equality within the psychological community and in the larger society, nationally and globally in order that all human resources be fully actualized. Its mission shall be to function as a catalyst by means of interacting with and making recommendations to the various parts of the APA's governing structure, to the APA's membership, and particularly to the Society for the Psychology of Women, Association for Women in Psychology and other relevant organizations, including groups whose missions address the status of women.

Race Forward

Founded in 1981, Race Forward (www.raceforward.org) brings systemic analysis and an innovative approach to complex race issues to help people take effective action toward racial equity. Founded in 2002, CSI catalyzes community, government, and other institutions to dismantle structural racial inequity and create equitable outcomes for all. Race Forward is home to the Government Alliance on Race and Equity (GARE), a national network of government working to achieve racial equity and advance opportunities for all. Race Forward publishes the daily news site Colorlines and presents Facing Race, the country's largest multiracial conference on racial justice. Race Forward's mission is to build awareness, solutions, and leadership for racial justice by generating transformative ideas, information, and experiences. We define racial justice as the systematic fair treatment of people of all races, resulting in equitable opportunities and outcomes for all and we work to advance racial justice through media, research, and leadership development.

Creating Change

The National LGBTQ Task Force sponsors and organizes Creating Change (www.creatingchange.org). Creating Change 2018 is the 30th anniversary of the conference. The Creating Change Conference is the foremost political, leadership, and skills-building conference for the LGBTQ social justice movement. Since 1988, Creating Change has created opportunities for many thousands of committed people to develop and hone their skills, celebrate victories, build community, and to be inspired by visionaries of our LGBTQ movement and allied movements for justice and equality.

Laboratory to Combat Human Trafficking

The Laboratory to Combat Human Trafficking (LCHT; www.combathumantrafficking.org) is a 501(c)3 nonprofit organization based in Denver, Colorado. LCHT exists to inform social change that eliminates human exploitation. Since 2005, we have trained over 25,000 professionals and community members; conducted community-based research to drive action and inform policy change; operated the statewide 24/7 human trafficking hotline; and developed over 125 future human rights leaders. Note this feminist/ social justice organization for feminist community-based research and work prioritizing survivor leadership.

References

AATA. (2016). American Art Therapy Association. Retrieved from https://arttherapy.org

Ackerly, B., and Attanasi, K. (2009). Global feminisms: theory and ethics for studying gendered injustice. *New Political Science*, 31(4), 543–555.

Ackerly, B., and True, J. (2010). *Doing Feminist Research in Political and Social Science*. London: Palgrave Macmillan.

APA. (2010). Report of the APA Task Force on the Sexualization of Girls. Retrieved from https://www.apa.org/pi/women/programs/girls/report-full.pdf

APA. (2014). Task Force Report on the Human Trafficking of Women and Girls. American Psychological Association Task Force on Human Trafficking. Division 35 Psychology of Women.

APA. (2017). Report of the Task Force on Trafficking of Women and Girls: Executive Summary. Retrieved from www.apa.org/pi/women/programs/trafficking/executive-summary.pdf

Backos, A. K., and Pagon, B. E. (1999). Finding a voice: art therapy with female adolescent sexual abuse survivors. *Art Therapy*, 16(3), 126–132.

Brabeck, M. M. (2000). *Practicing Feminist Ethics in Psychology*. Washington, DC: American Psychological Association. doi:10.1037/10343-000

Brown, L. S. (1994). *Subversive Dialogues: Theory in Feminist Therapy*. New York: Basic Books.

Brown, L. S. (2008). *Cultural Competence in Trauma Therapy: Beyond the Flashback*. Washington, DC: American Psychological Association.

Chilcote, R. L. (2007). Art therapy with child tsunami survivors in Sri Lanka. *Art Therapy*, 24(4), 156–162.

Caliber (2007). Evaluation of Comprehensive Services for Victims of Human Trafficking: Key Findings and Lessons Learned. Retrieved from https://www.ncjrs.gov/pdffiles1/nij/grants/218777.pdf

Caplan, P. (1995). Weak ego boundaries: One developing feminist's story. *Women & Therapy*, 17(1–2), 113.

Clawson, H. J., Salomon, A., and Goldblatt Grace, L. (2008). Treating the hidden wounds: Trauma treatment and mental health recovery for victims of human trafficking. US Department of Health and Human Services, Office of the Assistant Secretary for Planning and Evaluation.

Clawson, H. J., Dutch, N. M., Salomon, A., and Goldblatt Grace, L. (2009). Study of HHS programs serving human trafficking victims. US Department of Health and Human Services. Retrieved from https://aspe.hhs.gov/report/study-hhs-programs-serving-human-trafficking-victims

Courtois, C.A. (2013). Feminist counseling with traumatized individuals. In C.Z. Enns and E.N. Williams (eds.), *The Oxford Handbook of Feminist Multicultural Counseling Psychology*. London: Oxford University Press.

Egharevba, I. (2001). Researching an-'other' minority ethnic community: reflections of a black female researcher on the intersections of race, gender and other power positions on the research process. *International Journal of Social Research Methodology*, 4(3), 225–241.

Enns, C. Z. (1997). *Feminist Theories and Feminist Psychotherapies: Origins, Themes, and Variations*. Lanham, MD: Harrington Park Press/The Haworth Press.

Enns, C. Z., and Williams, E. N. (eds.). (2013). *The Oxford Handbook of Feminist Multicultural Counseling Psychology*. Oxford and New York: Oxford University Press.

Espín, O.M. (1993). Feminist therapy: Not for or by white women only. *The Counseling Psychologist*, 21(1), 103–108.

Evans, K. M., Kincade, E. A., Marbley, A. F., and Seem, S. R. (2005). Feminism and feminist therapy: Lessons from the past and hopes for the future. *Journal of Counseling and Development*, 83, 269–277.

Farley, M., Cotton, A., Lynne, J., Zumbeck, S., Spiwak, F., Reyes, M. E., Alvarez, D., and Sezgin, U. (2003). Prostitution and trafficking in nine countries: an update on violence and posttraumatic stress disorder. *Journal of Trauma Practice*, 2(3/4), 33–74.

Foot, K. (2016). *Collaborating against Human Trafficking: Cross-Sector Challenges and Practices*. London: Rowman & Littlefield.

Greene, B. (1994). Teaching ethics in psychotherapy. *Women & Therapy*, 15(1), 17–27. Co-published in N. Gartrell (ed.), *Bringing Ethics Alive: Feminist Ethics in Psychotherapy Practice*, New York: Haworth Press.

Hacker, D., Levine-Fraiman, Y. and Halili, I. (2015). Ungendering and Regendering Shelters for Survivors of Human Trafficking. Social Inclusion. Retrieved from http://www.cogitatiopress.com/ojs/index.php/socialinclusion/article/viewFile/173/pdf_14

Harvey, M. R. (1985). *Exemplary Rape Crisis Programs: A Cross-Site Analysis and Case Studies*. Rockville, MD: National Institute of Mental Health.

Harvey, M. R. (1996). An ecological view of psychological trauma and trauma recovery. *Journal of Traumatic Stress*, 9(1), 3–23.

Harvey, M. R. and Harney, P. (1995). Individual psychotherapy. In C. Classen and I. D. Yalom (eds.), *Treating Women Molested in Childhood* (pp. 63–93). San Francisco, CA: Jossey-Bass/Pfeiffer.

Herman, J. L. (1992). *Trauma and Recovery: The Aftermath of Violence from Domestic Abuse to Political Terror*. New York, NY: Basic Books.

Iman, J., Fullwood, C., Paz, N., Daphne, W., and Hassan, S. (2009). *Girls Do What They Have to Do to Survive: Illuminating Methods Used by Girls in the Sex Trade and Street Economy to Fight Back and Heal: A Participatory Research Study of Resilience and Resistance*. Chicago, IL: Young Women's Empowerment Project.

Kempadoo, K., and Doezema, J. (eds.). (1998). *Global Sex Workers: Rights, Resistance, and Redefinition*. London: Psychology Press.

Koss, M. P. and Harvey, M. R. (1991). *The Rape Victim: Clinical and Community Interventions*. Thousand Oaks, CA: Sage Publications.

Lebowitz, L., Harvey, M. R. and Herman, J. L. (1993). A stage-by-dimension model of recovery from sexual trauma. *Journal of Interpersonal Violence*, 8(3), 378–391.

Laboratory to Combat Human Trafficking (2012). *Prostitution-Related Arrests in the City and County of Denver: Who Pays?*Denver, CO: Laboratory to Combat Human Trafficking.

Laboratory to Combat Human Trafficking (2013). *Colorado Project National Survey Report*. Denver, CO: Laboratory to Combat Human Trafficking.

Laboratory to Combat Human Trafficking (2016). Weblog. Retrieved from https://combathumantrafficking.org/2016/12/applying-research-end-human-trafficking

Laboratory to Combat Human Trafficking (2017). Weblog. Retrieved from https://combathumantrafficking.org/2017/12/not-my-story-to-tell-how-to-rethink-the-ways-we-support-survivors

Landrine, H. (1989). The politics of personality disorder. *Psychology of Women Quarterly*, 13(3), 325–339.

Landrine, H. (1995). *Bringing Cultural Diversity to Feminist Psychology: Theory, Research, and Practice*, Washington, DC: American Psychological Association.

Miller, E., Decker, M. R., Silverman, J. G., and Raj, A. (2007). Migration, sexual exploitation, and women's health: a case report from a community health center. *Violence Against Women*, 13(5), 486–497.

Murphy, Laura T. (ed.). (2014). *Survivors of Slavery: Modern-Day Slave Narratives*. New York: Columbia University Press, p. xvii.

Nathan, P. E. (2012). *The Oxford Handbook of Feminist Counseling Psychology*. Oxford: Oxford University Press.

NCTSN (2016). Complex trauma. National Child Traumatic Stress Network. Retrieved January 29, 2016, from www.nctsn.org/trauma-types/complex-trauma

NiCarthy, G., Merriam, K., and Coffman, S. (1984). *Talking It Out: A Guide to Groups for Abused Women*. Seattle, WA: Seal Press.

NWSA (2017). National Women's Studies Association, https://www.nwsa.org/about

O'Connell Davidson, J. (2005). Beyond contract? Dualist legacies, late-modern anxieties and the sanctity of the child. In J. O'Connell Davidson, *Children in the Global Sex Trade*, Cambridge: Polity Press.

O'Connell Davidson, J. (2006). Will the real sex slave please stand up? *Feminist Review*, 83(1), 4–22.

Outshoorn, J. (2005). The political debates on prostitution and trafficking of women. *Social Politics: International Studies in Gender, State and Society*, 12(1), 141–155.

Pierce, A. (2009). *Shattered Hearts: The Commercial Sexual Exploitation of American Indian Women and Girls in Minnesota*. Minneapolis: Minnesota Indian Women's

Resource Center. Retrieved from http://www.miwrc.org/shattered_hearts_full_report-web_version.pdf

Raphael, J., and Ashley, J. (2008). *Domestic Sex Trafficking of Chicago Women and Girls.* Washington, DC: DePaul University.

Raymond, J., and Hughes, D. (2001) *Sex Trafficking of Women in the United States.* Washington, DC: National Institute of Justice/Coalition Against Trafficking in Women.

Rave, E. J., and Larsen, C. C. (1995). *Ethical Decision Making in Therapy: Feminist Perspectives.* New York: Guilford Press.

Richardson, M. (2014). The complex trauma of sex trafficking. Retrieved January 29, 2016, from www.seethetriumph.org/blog/the-complex-trauma-of-sex-trafficking.

Roe-Sepowitz, D. E. (2012). Juvenile entry into prostitution: the role of emotional abuse. *Violence Against Women,* 18(5), 562–579.

Root, M. P. P. (1989). Treatment failures: the role of sexual victimization in women's addictive behavior. *American Journal of Orthopsychiatry,* 59(4), 542–549.

Root, M. P. (1991). Persistent, disordered eating as a gender-specific, post-traumatic stress response to sexual assault. *Psychotherapy: Theory, Research, Practice, Training,* 28(1), 96–102.

Root, M. P. P. (1992). Reconstructing the impact of trauma on personality. In L. S. Brown and M. Ballou (eds.), *Personality and Psychopathology: Feminist Reappraisals* (pp. 229–265). New York: Guilford Press.

Root, M. P. P. (1997). *Filipino Americans: Transformation and Identity.* Thousand Oaks, CA: Sage Publications.

Root, M. P. P. and Fallon, P. (1989). Treating the victimized bulimic: the functions of binge–purge behavior. *Journal of Interpersonal Violence,* 4(1), 90–100.

Rosen Saltzman, M., Matic, M., and Marsden, E. (2013). Adlerian art therapy with sexual abuse and assault survivors. *Journal of Individual Psychology,* 69(3), 223–244.

Sawhney, N. (2009). Voices Beyond Walls: The Role of Digital Storytelling for Empowering Marginalized Youth in Refugee Camps. Retrieved from http://homepage.divms.uiowa.edu/~hourcade/idc-workshop/sawhney.pdf

Silbert, M. H., and Pines, A. M. (1981). Sexual child abuse as an antecedent to prostitution. *Child Abuse and Neglect,* 5(4), 407–411.

Stokols, D. (1992). Establishing healthy environments: toward a social ecology of health promotion. *American Psychologist,* 47(1), 6–22.

Stronach-Buschel, B.(1990). Trauma, children, and art. *The American Journal of Art Therapy,* 29, 48–52.

Trauma Center. (2014). Utilizing trauma-informed approaches to trafficking-related work. Retrieved January 29, 2015, from www.traumacenter.org/resources

Trafficking Victims Protection Act (2000). § 7101, 22 U.S.C. (b)(2).

Walker, L. E. A. (1989) Psychology and violence against women. *American Psychologist,* 44, 695–702.

Walker, L. E. A. (1994). *Abused Women and Survivor Therapy: A Practical Guide for the Psychotherapist.* Washington, DC: American Psychological Association.

Webster, D. C., and Dunn, E. C. (2005). Feminist perspectives on trauma. *Women & Therapy,* 28(3–4), 111–142.

Weitzer, R. (2007). The social construction of sex trafficking: ideology and institutionalization of a moral crusade. *Politics & Society,* 35(3), 447–475.

Whiteley, J. M. (1999). Conceptual Social Ecology. University of California at Irvine. Retrieved from http://socialecology.uci.edu/csc/cse.html

Williamson, C., and Prior, M. (2009). Domestic minor sex trafficking: a network of underground players in the Midwest. *Journal of Child & Adolescent Trauma*, 2, 1–16.

Worell, J. (2000). Feminism in psychology: revolution or evolution? *The Annals of the American Academy of Political and Social Science*, 571(1), 183–196. doi:10.1177/000271620057100113

Worell, J. E., and Johnson, N. G. (1997). *Shaping the Future of Feminist Psychology: Education, Research, and Practice*. Washington, DC: American Psychological Association.

Wyche, K. F., and Rice, J. K. (1997). Feminist therapy: from dialogue to tenets. In J. Worell and N. G. Johnson (eds.), *Shaping the Future of Feminist Psychology: Education, Research and Practice*. Washington, DC: American Psychological Association.

Yassen, J., and Harvey, M. R. (1998). Crisis assessment and interventions with victims of violence. In P. M. Kleespies (ed.), *Emergencies in Mental Health Practice: Evaluation and Management* (pp. 117–144). New York: Guilford Press.

7 Creative Approaches for Working with Trafficking Survivors with Disabilities

Susan O'Rourke and Kevin Spencer

Introduction

According to the *Trafficking in Persons Report* (Department of State, 2016), individuals with disabilities are particularly vulnerable to human trafficking. Although accurate calculations of disability rates in particular countries or regions are difficult to measure, these individuals represent between 12% and 20% of the population. Most alarming is the limited resources devoted to understanding the intersection of disability and vulnerability to human trafficking. The combination of societal and cultural norms associated with disability and consequently the limited options of employment exacerbates vulnerability for this population. "Systemic social, cultural, and economic policies or practices may marginalize or discriminate against individuals and groups because they are poor, are intellectually or physically disabled, or because of their gender or ethnicity" (Department of State, 2016).

Individuals with disabilities are at greater risk of being exploited by human traffickers because they are vulnerable. Some of the factors include: 1) limited access to employment, may make individuals with disabilities more apt to take on risks associated with unusual employment; 2) a lifetime of dependency on others may result in an acceptance of relinquishing control to another; 3) repeated negative experiences with relationships and caregivers may create a condition of "learned helplessness" (LoLordo and Overmier, 2011), in which the victim believes that it is futile to avoid the distressing situation; 4) limited ability to comprehend when someone may be taking advantage, individuals with intellectual disabilities may not recognize these attempts; and 5) fewer personal relationships or friends may lead them to crave any relationship and tolerate abusive tactics presented by the trafficker.

Cultural beliefs affect the significant number of individuals with disabilities who are subjected to human trafficking. In some countries, mothers who give birth to a child with a disability are viewed as being cursed and therefore more susceptible to selling their child to uncertain circumstances. Children with disabilities are particularly vulnerable to being trafficked even by their families and subjected to working as beggars especially when the disability is visible.

The percentage of victims of human trafficking with disabilities is also magnified by the fact that many survivors become disabled as a result of the conditions in captivity and/or as a result of the experiences resulting in mental health crisis. These factors present a challenge for agencies that provide support services to victims of human trafficking as they will encounter a significant number of individuals with disabilities but often lack experience in working with this population.

Further exacerbation of the victimization of survivors occurs after the trauma through ineffective processing by law enforcement and limitations in our judicial courts (Farrell et al., 2008). It is important to keep in mind that individuals with disabilities may not have equal access to criminal justice systems. This discrimination within the justice system is affected by many factors and may be due to circumstances from limited access to interpreters for the deaf to devaluation of testimony provided by individuals with disabilities.

Exposing Ableism

According to WHO (2017), "People with disabilities are among the most marginalized groups in the world. People with disabilities have poorer health outcomes, lower education achievements, less economic participation and higher rates of poverty than people without disabilities." According to the American Community Survey (ACS), 12.6 % of persons in the US has a disability (Kraus, 2017). Disability rates vary from state to state and from country to country. The employment gap for persons with disabilities stands a 41.1 % and the disparity in wages consistently remains over $10,000 annually (Kraus, 2017). The poverty percentage gap, or the difference between the percentages of individuals living in poverty with and without disabilities, has been between 7.4 and 8.3 percentage points for the past seven years. Eighty-eight percent (88%) of these are termed "invisible," meaning that they cannot be determined by casual observation. These statistics reflect and increased level of vulnerability for persons with disabilities and their resulting risk for trafficking.

Merriam Webster defines ableism as, "the discrimination or prejudice against individuals with disabilities." Historically, individuals with disabilities have been discriminated against and this marginalization by society in the form of ableism continues to be a factor in how these individuals see the world and their place in it. This marginalization of individuals with disabilities creates additional concerns around their perception of the world and their opportunities for growth and personal development.

Consideration of the impact of a lifetime of confronting ableism and its effects on interactions with individuals with disabilities is essential when working with this population. Direct care workers must keep in mind that individuals with disabilities have been subjected to marginalization throughout their lives and made to feel "less than." This marginalization has not been given equal attention as other prejudicial conditions such as racism, misogyny or homophobia have received in recent decades. As recently as 2014 the British Broadcast Corporation (BBC) introduced the concept of ableism to their readers. Similar to any discriminated minority, individuals with disabilities may exhibit their response to ableism through behaviors that indicate anger, anxiety, and depression. It is essential to create a safe space where individuals feel valued, supported, and empowered.

Accommodations and Disability Status

In 1975 the US Congress passed legislation (P.L. 94–142) that resulted in educational reform for persons with disabilities. Prior to this legislation, school systems were not required to provide a free and appropriate education for children with disabilities. What has come to be known as the Individuals with Disabilities Education Act (IDEA), identifies 13 categories of disabilities. For the purposes of this chapter, the categories of disabilities will be combined in an effort to simplify adaptations and accommodations which are typically employed given the ability status rather than focus on a disability category. These include: 1) sensory impairment (VI/blind, HI/deaf, etc.); 2) physical disability (PD); 3) intellectual disability (ID); and 4) mental health disorder. It is important to understand that disabilities may be present at birth or appear later in life as in the case of a disability resulting from conditions during captivity.

Another consideration when providing accommodations to persons with disabilities is the difference between what is equal and what might be equitable. Society may provide equal compensation, however, as illustrated in Figure 7.1, this may not allow for equitable access. It is important to consider the perspective of the individual with a disability in determining how best to accommodate conditions.

Access

One of the first considerations for creating an environment in which the person with a disability feels welcome is access. Individuals with physical disabilities (PD) must have access to meeting spaces and many of these are not friendly for persons using a wheelchair or walker. Providers must examine entryways, hallways, bathroom facilities and space. Considerations around transportation should also be examined for potential barriers. Individuals with limited cognitive abilities (ID) may require assistance in following signs and directions. Individuals with visual impairments (VI) may require signs that include braille.

Providing access is not limited to physical barriers. Communication barriers must also be given consideration. Some individuals may have limitations in receptive language. Interpreters for the deaf and hearing impaired

Figure 7.1 Equal support may not be equitable to all

(HI) may be necessary. If these are not available, adaptive equipment to allow for easily written and shared communication should be provided.

Individuals with intellectual disabilities benefit from simplified language and repetition of information. Cognitive processing speed is often affected and consequently verbal information may be more easily understood when the information is simplified, repeated, rephrased and background noises are limited. Strategies may include constructing a list of things to do, relying on a calendar for appointments or setting reminders through text messages. Instructions provided auditorily disappear after spoken and may be forgotten. Pairing these with written directions can improve outcomes. Often individuals with intellectual disabilities may be able to express themselves through drawings rather than constructing complex sentences. This process will be described more thoroughly later in this chapter.

Challenges in communication are a common characteristic in individuals with autism spectrum disorder (ASD). Speech patterns are often affected resulting in unusual tone and delivery. Non-verbal communications may not be interpreted correctly. The individual with ASD tends to take things literally and may come across as blunt in their communications. They may display an unconventional use of language which includes echolalia (words and phrases are mimicked) or neologisms (made-up words). The ability to articulate speech may be present while the meaning of language escapes them. This can be confusing to others who are unfamiliar with their methods of communication. Some individuals with ASD are non-verbal and may communicate via augmentative communication devices such as pictures on a communication board or using electronic devices such as the

Figure 7.2 Barriers to accessibility

Dynavox© or simple applications on an iPad. It is important to become familiar with the individual's communication capabilities and methods and work within those parameters.

Practitioners must also consider any limitations in expressive language that include verbal and written communication. An individual's physical disability may impact their ability to speak or their fine motor skills required for written communication. Alternate communication methods including augmentative communication devices are helpful in these cases. Competency in sign language allows for free-flowing communication with individuals who are deaf. It is critical to fully understand the individual's methods of expressing themselves and if this is not apparent, professionals should begin the conversation by establishing an understanding of their preferred method for communication.

General Strategies for Improved Outcomes

Many individuals with disabilities have well-honed skills in employing adaptations to meet the demands of their environment. It is essential to respect these strategies and allow the individual to display their independence. Additional time may be needed to allow for this independence however, providing this time increases feelings of accomplishment and self-efficacy (Wehmeyer and Palmer, 2003).

Successful approaches are those that build upon the individual's strengths rather than focusing on their disability (Niemiec et al., 2017). Emphasizing character strengths such as perseverance, self-regulation, honesty, humor, and spirituality, to name a few, can be foundational to building the individual's basic belief system that most likely has been damaged through their experience. Recognition of the individual's strengths provides opportunities to develop the safe relationship that are associated with improved outcomes.

Specific strategies increase the likelihood of improved outcomes when working with individuals with disabilities. Some of these target the development of time management skills, assistance in setting goals, and general organization of information. A daily planner can add structure that promotes self-determination and includes identified action steps. Spending time reviewing plans can reduce procrastination and encourage follow through with plans. Modeling skills prior to expecting independent utilization of planning tools has been shown to be effective (O'Brien and Wood, 2011).

Individuals with disabilities may require an adjustment in how information is presented to them. For instance, consider providing audio recordings in replace of reading text; reduce or simplify the amount of information given both auditorily or in written form; enlarge text or increase the white space on written materials; record a session for reference at a later time; provide visual representation or visual organizers; and encourage verbal or written repetition of expectations or future intentions. It is also helpful to verify in any means appropriate that the individual understands your conversations.

Individuals with disabilities may also require alternative methods of expression for communication. This accommodation is even more critical when one recognizes the holistic impact of trauma that will, inevitably, compound the communication challenges of those with disabilities. Adjustments for expressive communication can provide opportunities for accurate sharing of evidence, recounting events and conveying feelings.

The emergence of neuroscience, developmental psychopathology, and interpersonal neurobiology has generated significant amounts of research data that reveal the effects of psychological trauma and physical abuse on the development of mind, brain, and body (Van der Kolk, 2014). It fundamentally changes the victim's way of thinking, reorganizes the way their mind and brain manage perceptions, and disrupts the systematic functioning of their nervous system. People who have experienced trauma tend to superimpose their traumatic experience(s) on every event in their daily lives making it difficult to make sense of their world. Every new experience is poisoned by the past allowing it to play out in the battlefield of their bodies without a conscious connection between the past and the present. This can be especially difficult to grasp for anyone whose mental capacities are already diminished or whose physical limitations necessitate accommodations. When the individual has a dual diagnosis, PTSD or traumatic symptomology may be further exacerbated.

Consideration of the compounding effects of trauma on disabilities is essential for practitioners. Alternative methods for communication and understanding that are outside of what is typically expected is advised. For decades, practitioners have recognized the benefits of expressive art therapy approaches that engage the whole person, allowing for alternative ways of receptive and expressive communication that avoid the limitations of language. The Arts provide a unique window for revealing underlying emotions. The American Art Therapy Association provides a definition for art therapy in which it, "employs the creative process of art making to improve and enhance the physical, mental, and emotional well-being of individuals of all ages with the aim of resolving conflicts and problems." The creative process that requires personal engagement through expression for sharing ideas and emotions can provide an opportunity for improved therapeutic outcomes. The remainder of this chapter explores a variety of techniques to employ with any client, but can be especially effective in working with individuals with disabilities.

How Does Trauma Change Us?

In order to fully explore the effectiveness of the expressive arts therapy approach for all individuals, including those with developmental or intellectual disabilities, a basic understanding of the language centers of the brain is needed. The availability of neuroimaging helps us understand that past trauma activates the right hemisphere of the brain which is involved in the expression and comprehension of nonverbal communication and deactivates the left hemisphere which negotiates verbal communication, organizes problem-solving tasks, and processes information (Davidson and Tomarken, 1989; Van der Kolk 2000, 2014). This lack of activation of the left brain has a crippling effect on the individual's ability to organize their experience into logical sequences, express their emotions, and accurately verbalize what they are experiencing. Van der Kolk writes (2000), "The person may feel, see, or hear the sensory elements of the traumatic experience, but he or she may be physiologically prevented from being able to translate this experience into communicable language" (p. 15). This is compounded when the traumatized individual also has a disability.

The Broca's area—located in the left frontal lobe of the cerebral cortex—assists in accurately communicating ideas to others *through speech* (Flinker, 2015) and when it does not function properly (or is deactivated), one cannot put thoughts and feelings into words (Van der Kolk, 2014). The victim's past experience is fractured into emotions, images, thoughts, smells, sounds, and awareness that are relived in the present. Flinker (2015) asserts that Broca's area is critical for "integrating and coordinating information across brain regions" (p. 2873). Providing ways for victims to organize their traumatic experiences into a logical and consistent narrative with a beginning, a middle, and an end is a difficult task, made even more challenging when the victim has a developmental or intellectual disability. This new understanding has accelerated the exploration of alternative therapeutic techniques (Van der Kolk, 2000). Understanding that language is stifled and constrained, the expressive arts therapies can provide an alternative means of communicating when clients find themselves in a safe and secure environment.

Purpose and Process of Expressive Arts Therapy

Expressive arts therapy recognizes the uniqueness of each person's therapeutic process and integrates therapeutic tools and techniques from a variety of art forms. These creative approaches are grounded in several models including developmental theory (i.e. the inability of a child to verbalize thoughts), trauma theory, biopsychosocial models, and neuropsychological evidence of the storage of memory in non-verbal parts of the brain (Westrhenen and Fritz, 2014). These techniques provide multiple pathways by which an individual may find meaning, clarity, and healing. Incorporating the creative process through arts techniques under the guidance of a professional counselor can be used for self-expression and personal growth while augmenting traditional talk therapy. These techniques may be especially appropriate when the client is no longer able to participate in talk therapy.

According to neuroscientist Rex Jung, creativity and intelligence are *not* closely correlated in the brain and may provide an explanation as to why some individuals who struggle with typical intellectual tasks, in fact, think creatively. This may provide an opportunity for expression that is unexpected given their cognitive abilities (Jung, 2014).

Enhancing communication in all forms is a critical component of the healing process. According to Smyth and Nobel (2015), the expression of one's feelings, thoughts, or ideas through artistic articulation may be beneficial in solving conflicts, managing behaviors, improving self-esteem, developing self-awareness and insight, managing stress, and developing interpersonal skills. The expressive arts therapy techniques focus on the *process of creating* rather than the artistic outcome or product. An important consideration is that clients are not required to possess any artistic skill. The only requirement is their willingness to engage their imagination, feelings, and awareness in order to process and support their healing. Another significant factor is that each expressive arts technique has its own unique qualities suggesting that different approaches might be considered for different clients with different abilities and under a variety of situations and conditions. The readiness and level of comfort of the client are important elements that should always be considered.

Attributes of Expressive Arts Therapy

Expressive arts interventions can help bridge communication barriers for people with disabilities by bringing distinct attributes to counseling not typically found in strictly verbal techniques: self-expression, imagination, active participation, and mind–body connections. The therapeutic approach is described as integrative when different expressive arts techniques are intentionally used in combination with traditional medical practices to promote improved client outcomes.

Self-Expression

All effective therapies encourage clients to engage in self-exploration and expression; however, expressive therapies foster in-depth self-exploration through one or more techniques as an integral part of the therapeutic process. Research suggests that the use of the arts in psychotherapy may expedite the process of self-exploration encouraging a deeper self-understanding that may result in a sense of well-being and a resolution of conflict (Gladding, 1992). Under the guidance of a therapist, these techniques act as a catalyst for the discovery of personal meaning and a greater sense of understanding.

As stated earlier, stressful memories are stored in the right hemisphere of the brain, typically in imagistic form, outside of conscious awareness. For individuals who have suffered traumatic experiences, these memories encoded in the right hemisphere may not be fully integrated with the left hemisphere. Because thoughts and feelings are not solely stored in the brain as verbal language, the use of expressive therapies can provide an important means of helping people discover and communicate memories, feelings, and thoughts.

Imagination

Imagination is the wonderful ability to conjure images and ideas in our mind without any immediate input to our other senses. It is an essential component of creativity, problem solving, and self-expression. As previously stated, the expressive arts therapy techniques focus on the *process of creating* rather than the *artistic outcome*. Clients may not generate a final work of art—drawing, poem, song, or story—but the process of creating engages their imaginative thinking utilizing their senses and giving rise to self-expression and discovery that may lead to resolution and reparation.

Active Participation

All therapies require clients to participate in the process; however, expressive therapies are defined by psychology as *action therapies* (Weiner, 1999). These interventions go beyond simply asking clients to participate. They require clients to become fully involved, to invest themselves in the art discipline thereby redirecting their awareness to visual, tactile, and auditory channels. This process compels them to explore issues and communicate their thoughts and feelings throughout the process. Malchiodi (2005) writes, "The experience of doing, making, and creating actually energize individuals, redirect attention and focus, and alleviates emotional stress, allowing clients to fully concentrate on issues, goals, and behaviors" (p. 10).

Mind–Body Connections

When interventions take into consideration the ability of the client's thought processes to influence bodily functions and symptoms, these are defined as mind–body interventions (Malchiodi, 2005). Expressive arts therapies capitalize on the sensory aspects of engaging in the process of making art but they also empower individuals to recognize their natural competencies and skills, both of which can effect change in the life of the client. The process of making art may also be an enjoyable distraction during exposure therapy which can provide access to difficult memories without prompting negative reactions (Becker, 2015). Trauma recovery is a process that takes time and happens in intentional stages.

Framework of Trauma Recovery

Dr. Pierre Janet formulated a phased framework of trauma recovery that was later developed by Dr. Judith Herman (1992, 1997) in the works, *Trauma and Recovery*. It is appropriate to examine the effectiveness of expressive arts therapies within this three-phrase theoretical framework as it is currently recognized as best practice (ISSD, 2006). It is important to remember that each of the phases can overlap and they may be nonlinear. Each phase involves providing information and support to clients and the use of creativity, imagination, and techniques that will help with emotional regulation. These three phrases are: 1) safety and stabilization; 2) remembrance and mourning; and 3) reconnection and integration.

Phase One: Safety and Stabilization

People affected by trauma tend to feel unsafe in their bodies and in their relationships with others. For individuals with Autism Spectrum Disorder (ASD) and those who are tactile defensive as a result of a Sensory Processing Disorder, these conditions may be further aggravated. People may also struggle with regulating difficult emotions in everyday life which they might not associate directly with the trauma. This can be even more challenging if the individual has an intellectual disability or emotional behavior disorder (EBD).

This phase concentrates on helping individuals gain a sense of mastery over their bodies, emotions, and environment; however, it is important to remember that those with disabilities may have already struggled with these areas prior to any trauma. Finding innovative ways to facilitate a better understanding about the dynamics of abuse, e.g. shame, loss of power, and loss of control, will be critical when working with individuals with disabilities. Recently, both therapists and researchers have been exploring nonverbal ways to foster emotional regulation and improve understanding of these dynamics (Rothschild, 2000; Van der Kolk, 2014). This provides viable opportunities for therapists to incorporate one or more of the expressive arts therapies into the treatment process.

Phase Two: Remembrance and Mourning

Attending to safety allows the person affected by trauma to move through the second phase—putting words and emotions to the trauma and making meaning of it. This phase involves the important task of exploring and mourning the losses associated with the trauma, processing and integrating the story of the trauma, and providing space to grieve and express their emotions. These emotions may be jumbled and unrealistic based on an inaccurate appreciation or notion of who they are and a true understanding of their skills and abilities. Because verbal language is often impaired in individuals with disabilities, the therapist is tasked with finding alternative ways for clients to move through phrase two, opening the door to the utilization of the expressive arts.

Phase Three: Reconnection and integration

This final phase focuses on redefining oneself in the context of meaningful relationships, moving beyond the trauma as the defining and organizing principle in one's life. The trauma becomes one of many stories that define them rather than the only story that defines them. The individual recognizes the impact of the victimization and is ready to take positive, definitive steps towards empowerment and the ability to resolve conflicts within themselves. However, when the victim has ASD, intellectual limitations, developmental disabilities, or a mental health diagnosis, they may have difficulties understanding their trauma and embracing a way forward. They may have a distorted perception of their abilities and self-concept presenting a greater challenge for conflict resolution.

The Expressive Art Therapies and Trauma Recovery

The capacity of the arts to circumvent the speechlessness that comes with trauma and provide an alternative method of exploring these phases of recovery may explain why they have been an integral part of treatment in cultures around the world (Van der Kolk, 2014). In the following pages, we will examine more fully four creative arts therapy practices: music, dance, drama, and visual art.

Music Therapy

According to the American Music Therapy Association (n.d.), "Music therapy is the clinical and evidence-based use of music to accomplish individualized goals within a therapeutic relationship by a credentialed professional who has completed an approved music therapy program."

Music Therapy and Phase One

Studies published by the American Music Therapy Association demonstrate that the direct use of music is highly effective in helping clients develop coping strategies. Patients may consider talk therapy as intrusive and difficult but music engages them in a context they consider safe and enjoyable (Carr et al., 2012). Orth (2005) suggests that music offers an approach for victims of trauma to relate to their healthy identity, encourages understanding and the expression of feelings of anxiety and helplessness. It creates and provides a safe environment that fosters stability and relaxation (Orth, 2005). Music is a form of sensory stimulation and can arouse responses because of the familiarity, predictability, and feelings of security that are often associated with it. Music is a common denominator of all levels of developmental functioning and could be a preferred method for children and adolescents to express and process their traumatic experiences. According to Schlabach (2014), music therapy can provide an opportunity for empowerment by focusing on an individual's strengths while dealing with the underlying trauma. And this approach can be instrumental in fostering positive attachment and building trust.

Music is an effective way to stimulate and focus a person's attention and some genres of music might provide a calming effect when the client's anxiety obstructs their cognitive focus (Davis et al., 2008). These attributes assist in achieving the objectives of phase one—safety and stabilization.

Music Therapy and Phase Two

The therapist can guide the client through phase two—remembrance and mourning—using music to assist in expressing and experiencing emotions. Clients can use their imagination and creativity to produce something musical, giving them a platform to express emotions and a means by which they can control emotional surges or outbursts (Davis et al., 2008). As music is being created, it can be changed from moment to moment in alignment with, or to alter, the mood of the person who is listening or participating. Music therapy provides a course of action for nonverbal communication as well as stimulating/motivating a person's speech (Davis et al., 2008). Davis et al. (2008) report that music has successfully encouraged spontaneous speech with children with developmental disabilities and promotes nonverbal communication through bliss symbols or sign language.

Music Therapy and Phase Three

Music therapy can be specifically designed to develop and cultivate the reciprocal social capacities that are essential to trauma recovery and healthy development (Hussey et al., 2008). This ability to motivate interaction with others addresses phase three—reconnection and integration. Individuals with developmental and intellectual disabilities have fewer opportunities for social interaction.

Music therapy can provide options to interact with peers through a shared experience and provide a means and outlet for appropriate self-expression (Hussey et al., 2008). PTSD has a severe impact on mood which can present as extreme anger, irritability and depression. In several studies (Frewen and Lanius, 2006; Van der Kolk, 2006), patients reported music therapy as a beneficial way of expressing and regulating emotions. The therapeutic importance of social support is consistent with current developments in psychosocial support of traumatized communities (Davidson, 2010). Providing individuals with disabilities the opportunity for positive social interactions in a safe and stable environment that incorporates the universal qualities of music can assist in reconnection and integration of self and others.

Dance/Movement Therapy

According to the American Dance Therapy Association (n.d.), "dance/movement therapy is the psychotherapeutic use of movement to further the emotional, cognitive, physical and social integration of the individual."

Dance/movement therapy (DMT) is an alternative way to express emotions when clients are unable to express them verbally. Individuals with disabilities who also have communication deficits can use movement to relate thoughts and feelings and the expressive elements of DMT are appropriate as a method of assessment and intervention. Dancing can bring changes to emotions and attitudes and build confidence, self-esteem, communication and social skills.

Recall that language and communication are often impacted by trauma (Broca's area) and integration of memories, sights, and sounds in the right brain is essential for recovery. Pierce (2014) proposed a theorized application of DMT to support the development of a holistic and effective treatment model in which DMT aids in the facilitation of right brain integration.

Dance/Movement Therapy and Phase One

Neuroscience has confirmed Maslow's basic principle that humans must experience a basic sense of safety for higher-order learning and integration to occur (Cozolino, 2002). For many clients who have experienced trauma, they are often more orientated to survival than the integration and resolution of their traumatic experience (Cozolino, 2002).

Maiese (2016) notes that Mills and Kaniluk observed that "spontaneous physical movement was perceived not only as an avenue to access [a client's] inner world, but also as a vehicle for the physical expression and release of sometimes intensely painful emotions" (p. 255). Movement is a universal language communicated through our bodies by which people gain the basic, implicit, non-verbal capacities for emotional expression, self-regulation, and bonding. This can support the client in developing a sense of acceptance or nonverbal attunement (Siegel, 2012) resulting in the essential (but often unconscious) foundation of a secure attachment relationship (Tortora, 2011).

DTM has proven effective with a variety of disability diagnoses because it has the potential to open an entry point for building these connections (Devereaux, 2014). As human beings, each of us has the biological need to feel understood. People with disabilities are no exception. However, therapists must be aware that this imperative is often reflected in different and difficult ways when the individual has a disability. A client with an ASD diagnosis may have language deficits that restrict their social interactions and prevent social reciprocity. Their sensory systems may be over stimulated causing agitation, anxiousness, and aggression. Movement may provide an outlet that can calm them allowing them to focus and dissipate some of the sensory overload and realize a feeling of security (Devereaux, 2014). For this reason, Colombetti (2014) suggests that imitation and synchronization of movement be used at the beginning of a session to foster a relationship, invite acceptance, and encourage self-awareness.

In her pioneering study on DMT and trauma, Baum (1991) reported her subjects (female victims of trauma) felt more present in their physical bodies when engaged in dance/movement allowing them to achieve a greater awareness of physical and psychological integration. When the therapist mirrored their movements, it increased their sense of validation resulting in a positive level of security and stability. DMT can also play a significant role in assisting clients in the learning of an additional set of movement interventions to aid in self-regulation of arousal and emotion (Pierce, 2014). For example, pressing one's feet into the floor while imagining roots growing into the earth can help a client feel grounded. Freely moving hands and arms in this planted position can give them a sense of freedom while maintaining stability and security (Van der Hart, 2012).

Dance/Movement Therapy and Phase Two

Johnson et al. (2009) propose that DMT interventions can be viewed as a type of exposure therapy that supports trauma processing because it brings awareness to sensations, thoughts, and images resulting in a coherent narrative that reinforces meaning making and the integration of self. It offers an entry point to mindfulness through nonjudgmental observation of feeling, awareness, consciousness, and movement. In this processing phase, traumatic memories may be more manageable through symbolic imagery, sound and gesture (Pierce, 2014). According to Berger (2012), DMT offers "structures to fulfill the needs and wishes not available through life experience" (p. 7) and allows the client to "recreate themselves" (p. 7) using symbolism through expression. These symbols and metaphors enlist the right brain at a nonverbal level "stimulating connections between the integrative pathways that have been demonstrated as foundational in organizing the sense of the corporeal and emotional self" (p. 258). Maiese (2016) suggests that movement can help a client make meaning of trauma by moving beyond their cognitive defenses and becoming more aware of their inner emotions. This results in a reconnection of brain, body, and emotion.

Dance/Movement Therapy and Phase Three

DMT involves the process of social interaction between the therapist and patient and, when conducted in a group, among multiple patients. This dynamic of group movement offers clients an opportunity to apply their newly acquired skills in the context of a social environment. Marian Chace (1993) wrote, "Dance, man's basic form of communication, is a way for a mental patient to … become more aware of himself as an entity functioning with others in relative safety" (p. 217). When movement is offered as a group activity, it provides an approach for people to relate to one another as a larger community and to express themselves within that community (Pierce, 2014). These group sessions help to establish rapport and empathy while building trust. Colombetti wrote, "moving in synchrony with others or coordinating movements in response to what others do can foster a feeling of togetherness and contribute to social cohesion" (2014, p. 197).

These sessions can be as meaningful and effective with children and adolescents with disabilities. Devereaux (2014) recounts a session with a young girl on the autism spectrum:

> I remember a day very vividly when we were moving together in a dance/ movement therapy group with other children and we were warming up our torso, twisting from side to side and joining through a unifying rhythm. Just the experience of moving in rhythm together meant we were joined together. This was joyful and enlivening. At one point, in our twisting dance we actually began twisting towards each other spontaneously, and then away. This dance became a metaphor in our relationship, the movement towards, and the movement away. I am often reminded that even if these children move away from me, the action of choosing to "reject" my social invitations is still a way of relating. Rejection is still a form of social communication. Therefore, when the twisting towards and away happened that day, I invited it, and used the dance process to expand it and turn it into a dance of communication. As we twisted towards each other, I put my hand up and non-verbally offered to connect with her hand. She took me up on this offer and touched her hand with mine. Our twisting dance became less about moving away and more about moving towards each other. This spontaneous greeting that occurred non-verbally then turned into a wave, then grew spontaneously into a high five, and culminated in a verbal expression, she said, "hi" (para. 4).

Drama Therapy

According to the National Drama Therapy Association (n.d.), "Drama therapy is the intentional use of drama and/or theater processes to achieve therapeutic goals."

There are two theories regarding the use of drama as a therapeutic intervention. The first method is psychodrama developed and introduced by Dr. J. L. Moreno from 1920 to 1940 (Moreno, 1983). In this technique, the therapist plays the role of a director and the client is the main character. The therapist leads the session, assisting the client in the exploration of feelings and behaviors. It is directed and structured but it requires the client to be able to verbalize personal conflicts and feelings. This can be problematic for individuals with disabilities who may have a primary deficit with language.

The second method is drama therapy. This approach focuses on processes and interactions rather than issues and conflicts. It utilizes several techniques from theatre (role play, stories, improvisation, etc.) and integrates them with theories and methods of therapy. Drama therapy accesses the imagination and the act of imagining is the first act of creating—creating relationships as well as an environment where trust and connections are possible. Drama therapy is more playful, less self-disclosing, and better able to assist clients in developing a sense of safety and freedom (Emunah, 1997). Through drama techniques, individuals can take on a different identity in a safe environment.

David Read Johnson is a licensed clinical psychologist and Associate Clinical Professor in the Department of Psychiatry, Yale University School of Medicine. He is also a pioneer in the field of drama therapy. He proposed a three-stage process for using drama therapy with trauma victims that aligns with Herman's three phases of recovery (1992, 1997) discussed earlier in this chapter. Johnson's (1987) phases include: 1) a critical period of securing safety for the client; 2) a period of restructuring; and 3) a conclusion that culminates in societal reintegration.

Drama Therapy and Phase One

Those who have survived trauma are frightened to experience their emotions on a deep level, afraid that it could lead to a loss of control. For someone with a disability, this can be even more terrifying because they are unable to communicate both their fears and their feelings. Drama therapy techniques can be effective in helping clients move beyond this paralysis by allowing them to assume a role and play someone other than themselves. This can bring about a sense of stability and security to help move them into phase two of recovery.

Children often do not use words to communicate their emotions and thoughts. They use the language of play and make believe—*the language of theatre*. Because drama is about assuming different roles, it encourages clients to pretend to be someone other than themselves. Children and adolescents are accustomed to dramatic play. It avails them with an opportunity to process information and aides them in their communication with others. This concept is foundational to theatre and gives the individual the freedom to express emotions through symbolism. When feelings are overwhelming, drama activities can provide moments where persons can distance themselves from what they are feeling.

Regarding trauma and children, Pifalo (2006) states, "Children often have fewer mental capacities to construct a coherent, verbal narrative regarding their abusive experiences" (p. 181). Individuals with intellectual disabilities may have access to even fewer mental and cognitive capacities. This approach may have significant advantages given their child-like and often limited ability to process information and communicate their thoughts and emotions. This process can bring about the safety and stabilization needed to move them into phase two of recovery.

Drama Therapy and Phase Two

In this phase, treatment should focus on the impact of the traumatic experiences on the individual, how they affect their self-concept and self-image, and their influence on choices and behaviors (Silberg, 2004). Johnson's phase two (restructuring) and Herman's phase two (remembrance and mourning) require a way for clients to express complicated and confusing emotions and experiment with new ways of being. Drama offers individuals a different way to access a full range of emotions and to explore alternative ways of engaging with life (Van der Kolk, 2014). Theatre activities can help them make sense of the changes and challenges they are experiencing by providing a structured environment where they can take risks and openly explore difficult feelings. Through this process, they can build trusting relationships, develop verbal and nonverbal communication skills, explore choice, self-responsibility and self-affirmation. Drama therapy is active and experiential and can provide the context for participants to tell their stories, set goals and solve problems, express feelings, or achieve catharsis.

Traumatized individuals are disorganized and chaotic: inhibited, out of sync, inarticulate, uncoordinated, and purposeless. They are easily triggered and often depend on action rather than words to release their feelings (Van der Kolk, 2014, 2000; Maiese, 2016). Theatre is about structure, story, and spirit. Trauma is about trying to forget, hiding how scared, enraged, or helpless the person feels. Theatre is about finding ways of telling the truth and revealing emotion to an audience. Theatre and drama require pushing through blockages so the client can discover their own truth, explore and examine their own internal experience. This process of discovery and examination can empower them to bring together their body and voice in performance (Van der Kolk, 2014) and help them translate their trauma into metaphors, stories, and themes (Craig, 2005).

Drama Therapy and Phase Three

Theatre activities give trauma survivors a chance to connect with one another by deeply experiencing their common humanity. At the Trauma Center of Justice Resource Center in Brookline, MA, the drama program uses mirroring exercises to help clients get in tune with one another. The process is to go slowly and engage them little by little, using simple prompts at first and gradually becoming more complex. Clients move body parts and make facial expressions that are mimicked or mirrored by others in the group. Mirroring helps them focus less on what other people think of them and helps them attune viscerally, not cognitively, to someone else's experience (Tortora, 2011; Van der Kolk 2014).

Another effective group therapy program is New York City's Possibility Project (2018) for at-risk, traumatized inner-city youth. When adolescents become a part of the program, they move through three phases of processing and creating. The first phase emphasizes group building including the development of basic agreements among group members that include responsibility, accountability, respect, and developing the rules. In this phase, they focus on collaboration. The second phase involves listening to one another, sharing their life stories, discovering their shared experiences, and breaking through the isolation they feel because of their trauma. This level of communication is deeply personal and is the beginning of writing their script and creating their own production. Rehearsals begin in the third phase as participants take on the roles they've created. Performance takes priority. In this phase, they are witnesses to the consequences of their imaginative and artistic decisions. Paul Griffin is the founder and president of the Possibility Project. He sums it up like this:

If you want to give them a sense of control, you have to give them power over their destiny rather than intervene on their behalf. You cannot help, fix, or save the young people you are working with. What you can do is work side by side with them, help them to understand their vision, and realize it with them. By doing that, you give them back control. We're healing trauma without anyone ever mentioning the word (Van der Kolk, 2014).

Art Therapy

According to the American Art Therapy Association (2016), art therapy is defined as,

> A mental health profession in which clients, facilitated by the art therapist, use art media, the creative process, and the resulting artwork to explore their feelings, reconcile emotional conflicts, foster self-awareness, manage behavior and addictions, develop social skills, improve reality orientation, reduce anxiety, and increase self-esteem.

Art therapists are trained to assess and treat individuals using the creative process of two- and three-dimensional media to meet the preferences and needs of the client. Neuroscience supports the benefits of action-oriented interventions (Van der Kolk, 2006) and making art has been shown to enable people to become conscious of and verbally process dissociated traumatic memories (Buk, 2009). The literature documents the successes of art therapy techniques to empower trauma survivors to symbolically express and process emotions they find difficult or impossible to put into words (Buk, 2009; Collie et al., 2006; Crenshaw, 2006; Klorer, 2005; Talwar, 2007; Tripp, 2007; Becker 2015).

Researchers maintain that the value of art therapy as a form of trauma intervention is predicated on two principles. The first is that it provides purposeful psychotherapeutic experiences that take advantage of the body's senses (the visual, tactile and kinesthetic characteristics of art making) in ways that talk therapy does not (Malchiodi, 2003; Steele and Malchiodi, 2012). This allows memories to be retrieved, restructured, and repaired (Malchiodi, 2016). Second, there is evidence that art therapy may associate implicit memories with explicit memories, i.e. connect feeling with thinking (Malchiodi, 2003; Steele and Raider, 2001). Researchers contend that an important phase in trauma integration is the reconnection of these two forms of memory (Malchiodi, 2016; Van der Kolk, 2014; Rothschild, 2000).

Art Therapy and Phase One

One way for clients to gain a sense of environmental mastery is to create an atmosphere where they can create art of their own choosing while freely sharing thoughts and random words with no regard for how coherent or appropriate these thoughts may be (Johnson, 1987; Buk, 2009). This freedom builds trust and safety for clients and reinforces a positive, judgement-free relationship between client and therapist.

The creation of art provides individuals with an opportunity to draw on their own experiences and connect their artistic creations to their personal lives. Making art gives them an opportunity to explore their own perceptions, thoughts, and feelings in a non-threatening, supportive space. This exploration happens at their own pace in an environment that encourages risk taking, problem solving and creative thinking.

Persons with disabilities often need alternate ways to communicate their thoughts, feelings, knowledge, and ideas. Children, including those with disabilities, use art and the process of creating art to communicate information about themselves and their world and to express emotion in appropriate ways (Mason et al., 2008). The arts can help them build resilience, contributing to the development of emotional regulation, peer relationships, and positive well-being (Lester and Russell, 2008). In the safe and self-contained environment of the therapist's office, the therapist and the client become witnesses to the trauma through the making of art.

Art Therapy and Phase Two

Research has shown that art therapy can help shift memories from non-verbal expression to declarative memory (Becker, 2015) while encouraging a cogent trauma narrative (Van der Kolk, 2000, 2006, 2014). This is a critical aspect of processing traumatic experiences. Following the terror attacks of 9/11, research with children who experienced the nightmare found that when they were engaged in drawing *and* talking about the event compared to only talking, the results yielded two to three times more narrative (Malchiodi, 2011).

Once the client has been able to externalize their memories and feelings, there is evidence that they find it easier to talk about them using metaphor and stories (Johnson, 1987; Becker, 2015). The artwork created by the client becomes an extension of their inner world and the therapist communicates the value and importance of the art by the way it is physically managed and stored.

Art Therapy and Phase Three

Malchiodi (2016) reports that clients often refer to art therapy as a positive form of expressing emotional content when they are unable to find words. Art making recruits regions in both hemispheres of the brain that aid in the integration of traumatic images and memories (Malchiodi, 2011; Koch and Harvey, 2006; Van der Kolk, 2006), shifting a client's locus of control from external to internal. Evidence suggests art making also facilitates this shift for individuals with developmental disabilities (Robey et al., 2018).

The person's will to be understood and connect with others can be channeled into making art allowing "the different language of the mind [to] be spoken and a concrete place [to] be found for the traumatic memories to exist without dominating everyday life" (Buk, 2009, p. 73).

Results of Expressive Arts Therapy

Empirical evidence of expressive arts therapy substantiates the effectiveness of these interventions to improve social anxiety, impulse control/self-regulation, aggressive behaviors, social isolation, communication, and depression (Henley, 1999; Stuckey and Nobel, 2010). A qualitative case study found that individuals with a mental health diagnosis who participated in creative experiences demonstrated improvements in three psychological processes: motivation, concentration, and connection with others (Secker et al., 2007). The National Rehabilitation Information Center (2013) reports typical results of increased awareness, the release of repressed emotions, general relief from depressive feelings, an increase in energy levels, and resolving internal conflict. Fraser et al. (2014) performed an extensive review of the literature from 2011 to 2014 on artistic interventions in a clinical setting and reported the majority of studies indicated an improvement in psychological well-being, a reduction in anxiety levels, and appreciable satisfaction in life. Becker (2015) reports the integration of expressive arts therapy interventions with other therapy techniques, e.g. exposure, grounding, and narrative therapy, also demonstrated positive results.

Individuals with disabilities are *individuals* first. Each is unique in their talents, their experiences and their dreams for the future. Just as hair color or handedness doesn't define a person, neither does their disability. As commonly expressed, disability is not an inability. A combination of respect for the individual while employing creative techniques for expression will lead to understanding.

References

American Art Therapy Association. (2016). What is art therapy? Retrieved from https://sta tic1.squarespace.com/static/56155efbe4b04a78cb3c160a/t/57b60e9029687f4116957 311/1471549072950/What+is+Art+Therapy.pdf

American Dance Therapy Association. (n.d.). What is dance/movement therapy? American dance therapy association website. Retrieved fromhttps://adta.org/faqs

American Music Therapy Association. (n.d.). What is music therapy?Retrieved fromhttps://www.musictherapy.org

Baum, E. (1991). Movement therapy with multiple personality disorder patients. *Dissociation: Progress in the Dissociative Disorders*, 4(3), 99–104.

Becker, C. J. (2015). Integrating art into group treatment for adults with Post-Traumatic Stress Disorder from childhood sexual abuse: a pilot study. *Art Therapy: Journal of the American Art Therapy Association*, 32(4), 190–196.

Berger, M. R. (2012). Marian Chace Foundation annual lecture: the improvisation of order. *American Journal of Dance Therapy*, 34(1), 6–19, doi:10.1007/s10465-012-9128-8.

Bowman, S. L. and Plourde, L. A. (2012). Andragogy for teen and young adult learners with intellectual disabilities: learning, independence, and best practices. *Education*, 132(4), 789–798.

Buk, A. (2009). The mirror neuron system and embodied simulation: clinical implications for art therapists working with trauma survivors. *The Arts in Psychotherapy*, 36, 61–74.

Carr, C., d'Ardenne, P., Sloboda, A., Scott, C., Wang, D., and Prebe, S. (2012). Group music therapy for patients with persistent post-traumatic stress disorder—an exploratory randomized controlled trial with mixed methods evaluation. *Psychology and Psychotherapy: Theory, Research and Practice*, 85, 179–202.

Chace, M. (1993). The power of movement with others. In S. L. Sandel, S. Chaiklin, and A. Lohn (eds.), *Foundations of Dance/Movement Therapy. The Life and Work of Marian Chace* (pp. 234–246). Columbia, MD: The Marian Chace Memorial Fund of the American Dance Therapy Association.

Collie, K., Backos, A., Malchiodi, C., and Spiegel, D. (2006). Art therapy for combat-related PTSD: recommendations for research and practice. *Art Therapy*, 23(4), 157–164.

Colombetti, G. (2014). *The Feeling Body: Affective Science Meets the Enactive Mind*. Cambridge, MA: MIT Press. doi:10.7551/mitpress/9780262019958.001.0001

Cozolino, L. (2002). *The Neuroscience of Psychotherapy*. New York: Norton.

Craig, H. (2005). Rebuilding security: group therapy with children affected by September 11. *International Journal of Group Psychotherapy*, 55(3), 391–414.

Crenshaw, D. (2006). Neuroscience and trauma treatment: Complications for creative arts therapists. In L. Carey (ed.), *Expressive and Creative Arts Methods for Trauma Survivors* (pp. 21–38). London: Jessica Kingsley.

David, W., Gfeller, K., and Thaut, M. (2008). *An Introduction to Music Therapy: Theory and Practice*. Silver Spring, MD: American Music Therapy Association.

Davidson, S. (2010). Psychosocial support within a global movement. *The Psychologist*, 23, 304–307.

DavidsonJ., and TomarkenA. (1989). Laterality and emotion: an electrophsyiological approach. In F. Boiler, and J. Grafman (eds.), *Handbook of Neuropsychology* (pp. 419–441). Amsterdam, The Netherlands: Elsevier.

Davis, W. B., Gfeller, K. E., and Thaut, M. H. (2008). *An Introduction to Music Therapy: Theory and Practice* (3rd edn.). Silver Spring, MD: American Music Therapy Association, Inc.

Department of State (2016). Trafficking in Persons Report.

Devereaux, C. (2014). Dance/movement therapy: building relationships through movement. *Psychology Today*, April 2.

Emunah, R. (1994). *Acting for Real: Drama Therapy, Process, Techniques, and Performance*. New York: Brunner-Routledge.

Emunah, R. (1997). Drama therapy and psychodrama: An integrated model. *International Journal of Action Methods*, 50(3), 108–134.

Farrell, A., McDevitt, J. and FahyS. (2008). *Understanding and Improving Law Enforcement Responses to Human Trafficking*. Final Report, June. Research Gate.

Flinker, A. (2015). Redefining the role of Broca's area in speech. *Proceedings of the National Academy of Sciences*, 112(9) (March 3), 2871–2875. doi:10.1073/pnas.1414491112

Fraser, A., Bungay, H., and Munn-Giddings, C. (2014). The value of the use of participatory arts activities in residential care settings to enhance the well-being and quality of life of older people: A rapid review of the literature. *Arts & Health* 6(3), 266–278. doi:10.1080/17533015.2014.923008

Frewen, P., and Lanius, R., (2006). Toward a psychobiology of posttraumatic self-dysregulation: re-experiencing hyperarousal, disassociation, and emotional numbing. *Annals of the New York Academy of Sciences*, 1071, 110–124, doi:10.1196/annals.1364.010

Gladding, S. (1992). *Counseling as an Art: The Creative Arts in Counseling*. Alexandria, VA: American Counseling Association.

Henley, D. (1999). Facilitating socialization within a therapeutic camp setting for children with attention deficits utilizing the expressive therapies. *American Journal of Art Therapy*, 38(2), 40.

Herman, J. L. (1992). *Trauma and Recovery*. New York: Basic Books.

Herman, J. L. (1997). *Trauma and Recovery: The Aftermath of Violence from Domestic Abuse to Political Terror*. New York: Basic Books.

Hussey, D., Reed, A., Layman, D., and Pasiali, V. (2008). Music therapy and complex trauma: a protocol for developing social reciprocity. *Residential Treatment for Children & Youth*, 24(1–2),111–129.

ISSD. (2006). Guidelines for treating dissociative identity disorder in adults. *Journal of Trauma & Dissociation*, 6(4), 69–149. doi:10.1300/J229v06n04_05

Johnson, D. R. (1987). The role of the creative arts therapies in the diagnosis and treatment of psychological trauma. *The Arts in Psychotherapy*, 14, 7–13.

Johnson, D. R., Lahad, M., and Gray, A. (2009). Creative therapies for adults. In E. B. Foa, T. M. Keane, M. J. Friedman, and J. A. Cohen (eds.), *Effective Treatments for PTSD: Practice Guidelines from the International Society for Traumatic Stress Studies* (pp. 479–490). New York: Guilford Press.

Jung, R. (n.d.) Speaking of Psychology: The Neuroscience of Creativity. Podcast with Audrey Hamilton. American Psychological Association. Retrieved from http://www.apa.org/research/action/speaking-of-psychology/neuroscience-creativity.aspx

Jung, R. (2014). Evolution, creativity, intelligence, and madness: "Here Be Dragons." *Frontiers in Psychology*, July 23. doi:10.3389/fpsyg.2014.00784

Klorer, P. G. (2005). Expressive therapy with severely maltreated children: neuro-science contributions. *Art Therapy*, 22(4), 213–220.

Koch, S. and Harvey, S. (2012). Body memory, metaphor, and movement. *Advances in Consciousness Research*, 84(2012), 369–385.

Kraus, L. (2017). *2016 Disability Statistics Annual Report*. Durham, NH: University of New Hampshire.

Lester, S. and Russell, W. (2008). *Play for a Change: Play, Policy, and Practice: A Review of Contemporary Perspectives*. Play England. National Children's Bureau.

LoLordo, V. M., and Overmier, J. B. (2011). Trauma, learned helplessness, its neu-roscience, and implications for posttraumatic stress disorder. In T. R. Schachtman and S. Reilly (eds.), *Associative Learning and Conditioning Theory: Human and Non-Human Applications* (pp. 121–167). New York: Oxford University Press.

Maiese, M. (2016). *Embodied Selves: Divided Minds*. New York: Oxford University Press.

Malchiodi, C. (2003). *Handbook of Art Therapy*. New York: The Guilford Press.

Malchiodi, C. A. (ed.). (2005). *Expressive Therapies*. New York: The Guilford Press.

Malchiodi, C. (2016). Expressive arts therapy and self-regulation: Your expressive arts therapist understands sensory-based attunement. *Psychology Today*. Retrieved from https://www.psychologytoday.com/us/blog/arts-and-health/201603/exp ressive-arts-therapy-and-self-regulation

Mason, C., Steedly, K., and Thormann, M. (2008). Impact of arts integration on voice, choice, and access. *Teacher Education and Special Education*, 31(1), 36–46.

Moreno, J. L. (1983). *The Theatre of Spontaneity*. Ambler, PA: Beacon House, Inc.

National Rehabilitation Information Center (2013). Arts as therapy. Retrieved from https://www.naric.com/?q=en/publications/volume-10-issue-1-arts-therapy

Niemiec, R. M., Shogren, K. A., and Wehmeyer, M. L. (2017). Character strengths and intellectual and developmental disability: a strengths-based approach from positive psychology. *Education and Training in Autism and Developmental Disabilities*, 52(1), 13–25.

O'Brien, C. and Wood, C. L. (2011). Video modeling of cooperative discussion group behaviors with students with learning disabilities in a secondary content-area classroom. *Journal of Special Education Technology*, 26(4), 25–40.

Orth, J. (2005). Music therapy with traumatized refugees in a clinical setting. Voices: A World Forum for Music Therapy. Retrieved from http://www.voices.no/ma inissues/mi40005000182.html

Ouch blog. (2014). First there was racism and sexism, now there is ableism. BBC Ouchlets: A series on small but significant insights into disability. June 16. Retrieved from http://www.bbc.com/news/blogs-ouch-27840472

Pifalo, T. (2006). Art therapy with sexually abused children and adolescents: exten-ded research study. *Art Therapy: Journal of the American Art Therapy Association*, 23(4), 181–185.

Pierce, L. (2014). The integrative power of dance/movement therapy: Implications for the treatment of dissociation and developmental trauma. *The Arts in Psy-chotherapy*, 41(2014), 7–15.

Possibility Project (2018). Retrieved from http://the-possibility-project.org

Robey, K., Reed, M., Steiner, P., and Wilkenfeld, B. (2018). Fine arts participation, self-determination, and locus of control among persons with developmental dis-abilities. *Arts & Health*, 10(1), 45–56.doi:10.1080/17533015.2016.1247900

Rothschild, B. (2000). *The Body Remembers: The Psychophysiology of Trauma and Trauma Treatment*. New York: W. W. Norton & Company.

Schlabach, J. (2014). Central Ohio Music Therapy. Retrieved from https://centra
lohiomusictherapy.com/music-therapy-and-trauma

Secker, J., Spandler, H., Hacking, S., Kent, L., and Shenton, J. (2007). Empowerment and
arts participation for people with mental health needs. *Journal of Public Mental Health*, 6,
14–23. Retrieved from https://www.researchgate.net/publication/254191435_Emp
owerment_and_arts_participation_for_people_with_mental_health_needs

Siegel, D. (2012). *The Developing Mind: How Relationships and the Brain Interact to
Shape Who We Are* (2nd edn.). New York: Guilford Press.

Silberg, J. (2004). Guidelines for the evaluation and treatment of dissociative symptoms in children and adolescents. International Society for the Study of Dissociation. *Journal of Trauma & Dissociation*, 5(3), 119–150. doi:10.1300/J229v05n03_09

Smyth, J., and Nobel, J. (2015). Creative, artistic, and expressive therapies for PTSD.
Arts & Healing. Retrieved from http://www.marketingnavigators.com/FAH2/
wp-content/uploads/2015/12/PTSD-White_Paper_Smyth_Nobel.pdf

Steele, W., and Malchiodi, C. A. (2012). *Trauma-Informed Practices with Children and
Adolescents*. New York: Taylor & Francis.

Steele, W., and Raider, M. (2001). *Structured Sensory Intervention for Children, Adolescents and Parents: Strategies to Eliminate Trauma*. Lewiston, NY: Edwin Mellen Press.

Stuckey, H. L., and Nobel, J. (2010). The connection between art, healing, and
public health: A review of current literature. *American Journal of Public Health*, 100(2),
254–263. doi:10.2105/AJPH.2008.156497

Talwar, S. (2007). Accessing traumatic memory through art making: an art therapy
trauma protocol (ATTP). *The Arts in Psychotherapy*, 34(1), 22–35.

Tortora, S. (2011). The Need to Be Seen: From Winnicott to the Mirror Neuron
System Dance/Movement Therapy Comes of Age. *American Journal of Dance
Therapy*, 33, 4–17. doi:10.1007/s10465-011-9107-5

Tripp, T. (2007). A short term therapy approach to processing trauma: art therapy
and bilateral stimulation. *Art Therapy*, 24(4), 178–183.

Van der Hart, O. (2012). The use of imagery in phase 1 treatment of clients with
complex dissociative disorders. *European Journal of Psychotraumatology*, 3.
doi:10.3402/ejpt.v3i0.8458

Van der Kolk, B. (2000). Posttraumatic stress disorder and the nature of trauma.
Dialogues in Clinical Neuroscience, 2(1) (March), 7–22. Retrieved from https://
www.ncbi.nlm.nih.gov/pmc/articles/PMC3181584

Van der Kolk, B. (2006). Clinical implications of neuroscience research in PTSD.
Annals of the New York Academy of Sciences, 1071, 227–293. doi:10.1196/
annals.1364.022

Van der Kolk, B. (2014). *The Body Keeps the Score: Brain, Mind, and Body in the
Healing of Trauma*. New York: Penguin Books.

Wehmeyer, M., and Palmer, S.B. (2003). Adult outcomes for students with cognitive disabilities three-years after high school: the impact of self-determination.
Education and Training in Developmental Disabilities, 38(2), 131–144.

Westrhenen, N., and Fritz, E. (2014). Creative arts therapy as a treatment for child
trauma: an overview. *The Arts in Psychotherapy*, 41(2014), 527–534.

Wiener, D. (1999). Beyond talk therapy: Using movement and expressive techniques in clinical practice. doi:10.1037/10326-000.

WHO. (2017). 10 facts on disability. World Health Organization. Retrieved from
http://www.who.int/features/factfiles/disability/en

8 Understanding Sex Trafficking through the Lens of Coercion

A Closer Look at Exploitation, Threats, and Betrayal

Susan Brotherton and Jamie Manirakiza

Introduction

Often and mistakenly viewed as a mere social ill, sex trafficking is actually a pervasive phenomenon with significant sociocultural and psychological implications. Hidden within plain sight in our communities are victims enduring trauma-inducing emotional and physical abuse at the hands of a sex trafficker. This chapter will focus on the coercive elements of sex trafficking including early childhood victimization, tactics used by pimps to control and exploit victims, and the often unintended coercive nature of mandated treatment that victims endure. We will define parallel-process in terms of the manner in which the system and survivor enter into an all too familiar dance of power dynamics: trust and betrayal, compliance for reward, and punishment for breaking the contract. Methods employed by traffickers to manipulate and coerce their victims into compliance is a complex process often marked by developing a trusting relationship with the victim, a relationship which is then exploited in a variety of ways. Social services, law enforcement, residential treatment, outpatient treatment programs, secure facilities, and housing programs all use strategies to ensure compliance. We assert that many of these strategies ignite victim–trafficker behaviors, rekindle trauma bonds, and impede the process of healthy recovery.

Coercion Defined

Coercion, in human trafficking, has a specific legal definition. The Trafficking Victims Protection Act (TVPA) of 2000 and Reauthorizations of 2003, 2005, 2008, and 2013 state that:

> sex trafficking is the recruitment, harboring, transportation, provision, obtaining, patronizing, or soliciting of a person for the purposes of a commercial sex act, in which the commercial sex act is induced by force, fraud, or coercion, or in which the person induced to perform such an act has not attained 18 years of age.
>
> (22 USC § 7102)

While there are three specific means by which trafficking is carried out (i.e. force, fraud and coercion), in this chapter the focus is on the nuances and complexities of coercion. The TVPA definition of *coercion*, more specifically, is found in 22 U.S.C. 7102 (3) as:

> (a) threats of serious harm to or physical restraint against any person; (b) any scheme, plan, or pattern intended to cause a person to believe that failure to perform an act would result in serious harm to or physical restraint against any person; or (c) the abuse or threatened abuse of the legal process.

This definition is often misunderstood, in part because elements of coercion are not always observable. Threats, which are often invisible to the investigator or therapist, are an incredibly powerful psychological tool used to control an individual and to push them to do something against their will. Threats to the victim or their family members, even if never carried out, are often enough to compel a victim to behave in ways that are compliant to the trafficker. For example, tactics used to cause a victim to believe that serious harm will occur if they do not earn enough money for their trafficker are not observable by the bystander or by a law enforcement officer patrolling the streets at night. However, verbal threats of physical harm are often enough to force compliance of the victim, so much so that she or he will continue to engage in sex acts against their will, to ensure enough money is made to avert physical harm by the trafficker.

Traffickers are skilled at identifying and exploiting vulnerabilities. In a process referred to as grooming, traffickers may prey on a victim's need for love, attention, even survival: fulfilling every need until the victim trusts them implicitly. Traffickers gain power and control as they isolate victims from friends and family. Victims become reliant on the trafficker, and often love the trafficker, which leaves them especially vulnerable. Slowly and methodically, traffickers express their control and coerce victims through violence or threats of violence: cultivating fear. Victims are lured by a false sense of security. These relationships are remarkably complex yet in many ways resemble similar betrayals and exploitation many victims experienced earlier in their lives.

Coercion Through Exploitation, Threats and Betrayal in Prior Childhood Trauma

A review of the literature reveals commonly identified risk factors and vulnerabilities that coexist for those who have reported being victims of sex trafficking. Our experience as service providers has led us to similar findings. It should be noted, however, that not all victims of sex trafficking have a history of prior sexual or physical abuse, nor will all victims have the vulnerabilities we are about to explore. Vulnerabilities highlighted in this section are not noted to blame the victim, but to bring attention to our belief that human trafficking is a public health issue and to make recommendations for identification, intervention, and treatment. They are not causal factors, but common associations.

Sexual, Physical, and Emotional Abuse

In our experience as clinicians working with sex trafficking survivors, most of the victims with whom we work were raised in extreme poverty. In addition, violence in the community and in the home is commonly reported; as well as parents or family members struggling with addictions to drugs and/or alcohol. While parents are working to make ends meet or are incapacitated due to their drug/alcohol use, children raised under these circumstances are vulnerable when left to fend for themselves. Children may be bullied at school for not having clean or fashionable clothes. Children may be forced out of their homes due to sexual orientation, gender expression, or a variety of other reasons. All these factors increase vulnerability to a trafficker who may buy the child or adolescent fancy clothes, provide a place to live, or offer love and companionship where there has been loneliness and isolation. For example, data from the National Incidence Studies of Missing, Abducted, Runaway and Throwaway Children (NISMART), "suggest a large percentage of these children left home because of physical, sexual, and psychological abuse. Many of these children often have low self-esteem and are extremely vulnerable."[1]

Clear and consistent research is difficult with commercially sexually exploited individuals. Victims rarely identify as victims of human trafficking. One study in a review of the literature found that while most research shows an "association between prior child sexual abuse histories and sexual exploitation as well as prostitution, the prevalence rates of trauma reported in these studies ranges widely from 33% to 84%."[2] This range in data may suggest problematic data gathering, variability in operational definitions or confounding variables not known to the researchers. However, it also shows a consistent presence of prior sexual abuse in a large number of victims of sex trafficking. Other forms of early childhood trauma have been identified as well. A study of 278 women in commercial sexual exploitation found that of this sample, "51% had experienced physical abuse and 65% had experienced emotional abuse, in addition to 53% who had experienced sexual abuse."[3] Interestingly, another study found that "childhood emotional abuse is also significantly associated with commercial sexual exploitation and may contribute to a younger age of entry into prostitution." [4] Regardless of the numbers reported through formal research, many of the victims we serve have disclosed histories of childhood sexual abuse. The trauma associated with early childhood sexual abuse can lead a young person to have a sense of worthlessness, feel betrayed by family members, and to leave the family home to escape abuse. Traffickers seek to prey upon low self-esteem; if a boy or girl seems lost and lacking in confidence, a trafficker knows he can use that to his advantage.

Family Challenges

Family dynamics and other vulnerabilities within the family unit can also be linked to many individuals who have reported being trafficked. For example, children who are in child protective services, chronic runaways, and in the foster care system are at a much higher risk than the general population to be targeted by a trafficker. This is because the trafficker can easily prey upon the need for family, safety, security and acceptance that these youth are missing. Consider the example of a youth who has been sexually abused by her mother's partner since she was five years old. At age seven, the child tries to report the abuse to her mother. However, when this, child tells her mom about the abuse, the mother's response is that of shame and secrecy. She tells her daughter that she should not speak of this, as her boyfriend provides for the family and if she talks they will lose their home. The child is solely dependent on her mother for her basic needs, love, and safety. While mother's response has a number of implications in terms of attachment, we want to highlight the foundation for coercive exploitation, threats, and betrayal from a loved one on whom the child depends. The child is betrayed by her protector, forced to endure the abuse and then threatened with jeopardizing the safety of her entire family if she acts in a way to protect herself from harm. We suggest that not only the resulting trauma from the abuse but also the coercive process employed by the mother increases the vulnerability of the child to traffickers or others seeking to exploit her, whether through the process of traumatic re-enactment or simply being a victim of circumstance.

> A study exploring 174 women who were exploited when they were children found associations between factors in the home such as familial IPV and drug use, as well as, lack of supervision, food and medical care, and love. Failures of these particular social institutions, such as the family, serve as contributing factors toward the pathway into prostitution.[5]

The study went on to state that, "pimps, traffickers, or exploiters are often family members or family friends themselves".[6] In fact, the study found that 16% of individuals trafficked were recruited by a family member.[7] We too have observed similar findings in our work with victims. As stated above, we seek to highlight common themes in early childhood: betrayal, coercive abuse, threats or perceived threats to maintain abuse, and early life-defining relationships. We know that interpersonal relationships and boundary violations early in childhood have a lasting impact on re-victimization and risk factors.

The impact of early childhood exposure to adverse experiences and trauma has been widely supported by the Adverse Childhood Experiences (ACEs), with their research finding clear links between early childhood traumas and later physical and mental health issues in the future. Interesting to note that as one ACE score increases so does one's vulnerability to victimization by violence. Renowned trauma researcher and author, Sandy Bloom, states, "Children and adults who are exposed to interpersonal violence are not likely to experience only a single incident. Interpersonal violence is likely to be repetitive, haunting the lives of victims."[8] Victims of early childhood exploitation begin to find means to cope with the trauma and even the interpersonal betrayal. Traffickers replicate the process of betrayal and exploitation that the child has experienced in their immediate family. Initially drawn to the trafficker, who offers love and all that has been missing in their young lives, the child is easily coerced as the dynamic is familiar; they have lived through this before. Vulnerabilities the child carries with him or her from early childhood include feelings such as a:

> negative sense of identity, trust, and place in the world. But human beings are adaptive, so children will adapt to adversity by changing their definitions of "normal"—and human beings resist changing anything that has come to feel "normal" one of the many important consequences of this adaptation is an increased likelihood that the child will reenact the trauma and in doing-so will be re-victimized or may turn to victimizing others.[9]

At some point, the "prostitution of these vulnerable children becomes a continuation of the victim's sexual exploitation and abuse, not just the beginning."[10]

Coercion Through Exploitation, Threats and Betrayal in the Pimp Relationship

Traffickers use deliberate tactics to lure victims into situations of complex control. The beginning phase of this process of grooming often mirrors that of a romantic boyfriend relationship. The trafficker steps in to provide what the victim is lacking in family structure, offering the illusion of safety, sense of belonging, and emotional and financial security. The trafficker has most likely spent time targeting victims who experience the vulnerabilities noted above, and capitalizes on those vulnerabilities to create a new narrative for the exploitation he is about to inflict. The trafficker takes time to get to know his victim, learning about his or her family life and abuse or betrayal. He then takes times to validate those experiences as wrong telling the victim things like "you should never have had to live like that that or feel that way," "I will protect you," "You are with me now," "We will be a new family." Sometimes the trafficker will even encourage the victim to refer to him as "daddy" fulfilling a void in the victim's need for a safe and protective father figure. If the victim lacks financial means, he demonstrates his financial security by taking her out to eat, buying her clothes, getting her hair and nails done, and showing her that he can take care of her financially. If she has lived in poverty he will show her that she can be financially secure with him. If he notices that her self-esteem and trust of others is broken or nonexistent, he will focus his time on making her feel known, loved, and beautiful. The grooming phase may last anywhere from one week to a few months, but at some point, there is a shift and the trafficker starts to isolate the victim from others and starts to exert control that will allow him to entrap her in a life of commercial sexual exploitation, yet another form of betrayal. However, this time the betrayal takes a new coercive form. The trafficker or pimp tells his victim a series of lies as to why she must sell her body to make money for him, lies that are enmeshed in his methods of conditioning. As is explained in the notoriously sadistic book "Pimpology," Pimpin' Ken explains the basic rules of the game for how to be a pimp by creating dependence, exploiting weakness, playing mind games, and manipulation. Pimpin' Ken states:

> it's important that a ho doesn't feel like she's ho'ing for nothing. She has to constantly have an incentive, a carrot dangled in front of her face. A pimp has to keep her distracted with the things she thinks she wants, and he has to constantly fill her head with more and more things for her to want.[11]

The betrayal in this case is masked by the notion that she has to do this for the mutual dream of her trafficker and herself. Prostitution is just the cost of getting ahead, together. The victim is being betrayed by the trafficker and exploited for his gain; however, the abuse is interwoven within a complex system psychological manipulation tactics or what is known as coercive conditioning.

So deliberate and manipulative, the coercive process a trafficker uses to gain physical, emotional, financial, and psychological control over a victim has been paralleled to the tactics used to torture political prisoners. In 1973, Amnesty International published their *Report on Torture* detailing and explaining systematic coercive tactics used by the military to torture political prisoners. These tactics are referred to as "Biderman's Chart of Coercion" (see Fig. 8.1).[12]

Biderman's Chart of Coercion includes tactics such as: isolation; demonstrating omnipotence; degradation; enforcing trivial demands; and occasional indulgences. Strikingly, what is important to point out is that within Biderman's Chart of Coercion "few of the methods necessitate brute force, but instead rely heavily on tactics of mental abuse—abuse that may leave few outward indicators to the casual, untrained observer."[13] Further substantiating the premise of this chapter which is that coercive tactics must be intricately understood as a foundation by any practitioner working with

General Method	Effects (Purposes)	Variants
1. Isolation	Deprives victim of all social support of his ability to resist. Develops an intense concern with self. Makes victim dependent upon interrogator.	Complete solitary confinement. Complete isolation. Semi-isolation. Group isolation.
2. Monopolization of Perception	Fixes attention upon immediate predicament. Fosters introspection. Eliminates stimuli competing with those controlled by captor. Frustrates all action not consistent with compliance.	Physical isolation. Darkness or bright light. Barren environment. Restricted movement. Monotonous food.
3. Induced Debilitation and Exhaustion	Weakens mental and physical ability to resist	Semi-starvation. Exposure. Exploitation of wounds. Induced illness. Sleep deprivation. Prolonged constraint. Prolonged interrogation. Forced writing. Over-exertion.
4. Threats	Cultivates anxiety and despair	Threats of death. Threats of non [return?]. Threats of endless interrogation and isolation. Threats against family. Vague threats. Mysterious changes of treatment.
5. Occasional indulgences	Provides positive motivation for compliance. Hinders adjustment to deprivation.	[Occasional?] favors. Fluctuations of interrogator's attitudes. Promises. Rewards for partial compliance. Tantalizing.
6. Demonstrating "Omnipotence" and "Omnipotence"	Suggests futility of resistance.	Confrontation. Pretending cooperation taken for granted. Demonstrating complete control ever victim's fate.
7. Degradation	Makes cost of resistance more damaging to self-esteem than capitulation. Reduces prisoner to 'animal level' concerns.	Personal hygiene prevented. Filthy infested surrounds. Demeaning punishments. Insults and taunts. Denial of privacy.
8. Enforcing Trivial Demands	Develops habits of compliance.	Forced writing. Enforcement of minute rules.

Figure 8.1 Biderman's Chart of Coercion (from Amnesty International, 1975)

those who have been victimized by this crime. Let's try to briefly understand this concept with a case example.

Esther met her trafficker at age 14. He was a nice-looking guy who used
to hang outside her school with some other friends. He would always smile
at her, and tell her she looked beautiful. He asked for her name and found
her on social media. He began talking to her online each night. They fell
in love through these late night conversations, Esther said. She lived in a
small apartment with her drug-addicted mother and two younger brothers
from a different father. Mom allowed the boy's father to sell drugs out of
their home and strangers were in and out all day and night. Esther had
been sexually assaulted on more than one occasion by these strangers in her
home. Her mother ignored her complaints, telling her she was worthless
anyway. Eventually Esther left her abusive home to move into his apartment. At first everything was wonderful. She was in love and trusted him
implicitly. She allowed him to take nude pictures of her, believing that he
would keep them just for himself. Then one night he brought her to a
party. There were a lot of adult men there and he told her to dance for
them. When she refused he pulled up the pictures he had taken on his
phone and threatened to post them on social media where all her friends
and family could see them if she didn't strip and dance for the men, she
complied. Later that night he asked her to perform sex acts with the men,
she adamantly refused saying she loved only him and didn't understand. He
then showed her a gun he had concealed and, again, sadly she complied.

The trafficker in this scenario did not have to use physical force on
Esther. Everything was invisible to the naked eye, and yet so powerfully
life-threatening and forcefully coercive.

Coercive Relationship: Victimized to Perpetrate; The Bottom Bitch

Pimps act in deliberate ways to coerce victims to perform sex acts, acts of
violence, and often minor crimes through coercive tactics. Pimps commonly refer collectively to their victims as their "stable". Often in a
"stable", there is one woman, usually the one who has been there the
longest, who is referred to as the "bottom bitch". If you consider the
trafficker's operation as a pyramid with him at the top, the "bottom"
represents the foundation or actual bottom. The bottom handles the
money, recruits others to the stable, and keeps the others in line. The
"bottom bitch" phenomenon is one that is characterized by even more
complex and constant coercion and betrayal. Often times this individual
victim is someone who has a deep loyalty to the trafficker. She is someone who has most likely experienced and witnessed horrific abuse leaving
her grateful to the trafficker for being allowed to live. She has also been
forced to commit acts of violence against others in the stable, should they
refuse to do what is asked of them, come home without earning their

quota or simply as a demonstration of loyalty to the trafficker. Pimpin' Ken states about his bottom girl that:

> she helped me elevate my pimpin'. I would talk to her about my plans for myself and for her. I would write down my plan on paper and I would make her read my plan every day. I talked to her until I was blue in the face. It was my duty to instill in her the drive to get money and let her know that once she commits to this game, it's a part of her. She had to eat, sleep, and shit my pimpin', until she believed in everything I was telling her. If I told her something was going to happen, in her mind it was already done.[14]

Again the nature of the pimp/bottom coercion is difficult to see. Understanding the actions of the bottom and the violence she inflicts on others is challenging to reconcile. We have seen occasions where these women have been treated by law enforcement like their traffickers as perpetrators. A bottom has not only experienced everything else that other victims of sex trafficking have endured but she has, often times, experienced more abuse and manipulation by the trafficker to participate in criminal acts and abuse of others that she would not have done otherwise. She may seem to have more privileges than the others in the stable, but is equally considered property of the pimp. This relationship is indicative of complex trauma-bonding that is sequentially reinforced one act of violence after another as she proves her loyalty. Bottoms are not readily identifiable to law enforcement during investigations. She may be arrested in a police sting operation in possession of drugs and a cell phone that contains content for arranging all of the "dates" for the other girls. Once in the court system, she may appear to have a blunted affect with seemingly no remorse when confronted with other victims' statements or accusations. The pimp has her walking a legally fine line with him, so as to keep himself at a distance from his operations and prosecution. This bottom girl is victim of trafficking. She has suffered the same coercive abuse and threats of abuse if she refused to comply with the orders given by the trafficker as the other girls in the stable, if not more. She knows firsthand what happens when a girl does follow with the rules of the game.

Trauma Implications from the Pimp Coercive Relationship

Earlier in this chapter we discussed Biderman's Chart of Coercion. The chart outlines coercive tactics that may be employed to effectively crush an individual's will until they comply with the exploiter's demands. Traffickers use similar methods and while the impact may be invisible on the outside, sustained manipulation and torture greatly impact our bodies and our brains. These tactics actually inflict damage to the body's fight-or-flight response system and create an internal state of dysregulation of hyper- and/or hypo-arousal. This flood of stress hormones impacts our emotions, our ability to process information and our ability to accurately perceive the world around us. When victims leave the life, they may leave the trafficker behind but the impact of trauma remains. All of those who seek to support victims, across all disciplines, need to fully grasp the impact of complex trauma in order to create effective healing spaces. We know that any perceived or actual threat to the body sends off a host of hormones in one's body to signal the fight, or flight response. These very basic reactions serve to save us from extreme situations such as driving down the highway and steering to avoiding a near death accident when another car swerves into your lane. However, in the life of the trafficking victim, this stress response is being triggered too frequently often times creating "dysregulation in the body's nervous system."[15] Over time the effects of "survival oriented" biological responses may begin to "compromise three key self-regulation systems in the brain, 1) The reward/motivation systems, 2) the distress tolerance systems, and 3) the executive systems for emotions and information processing."[16] Following periods of victimization, individuals may have challenges with delayed gratification or future planning, excessive and blunted emotional reactions and rigid, impulsive and disorganized thinking and coping styles.[17]

Traumatic dysregulation impacts one's ability to self-regulate and self-soothe, but also one's ability to develop healthy interpersonal relationships. We have noted that many victims have suffered betrayal at the hands of those on who they were the most dependent. When one's focus is survival, trust is fleeting. Victims we have known have not been able to name a single trusted individual in their inner circle. Dr. Bessel Van der Kolk states, "Most traumas occur in the context of interpersonal relationships, which involve boundary violations, loss of autonomous action, and loss of self-regulation."[18] Victims of sex trafficking may be more likely to have experienced repeated boundary violations starting in early childhood, which creates a sense of helplessness deep within the body to protect itself from external threats. ACEs' data supports the notion that victims of trauma are likely to re-victimized. As creatures of habit, we often return to the familiar, even when it is not in our best interest.

A victim's history of manipulation, coercion, and trauma is likely to repeat until the pattern is disrupted. In our work with victims we have observed that those who desire to support the victim, often unintentionally do so in ways that are manipulative and coercive. Power is exerted to push compliance, privileges granted or withheld based upon behavior. We assert that healing is only possible when these dynamics of power are removed and replaced by self-determination and choice. In essence, let us not act like the will-imposing pimp.

Case Scenario

Let's return to Esther's story. Months have gone by since Esther found herself being trafficked by her boyfriend. She is arrested by the police in a sting operation at the hotel where she is being prostituted. During the bust, a small amount of heroin is found with her belongings. She is charged with possession. Her case is presented before a judge who is familiar with her history and who desires to help her. However, through Esther's lens, everyone is out to destroy her life; the police want her to talk so they can arrest her boyfriend who is actually her pimp, and the judge is trying to control her so that she complies with the police. The judge mandates Esther to an inpatient substance abuse program for thirty days due to her substance abuse history and current usage. Following completion of that program the judge recommends a referral to group home, where she can finish high school, receive therapy and get back her life. The judge has Esther's probation officer arrange transport to the inpatient program directly from court. Two weeks into the program the court is notified that Esther has left. Esther returned to the streets but keeps her court appointment to see the judge. She says that while in the program she felt trapped, staff wouldn't "leave her alone," the food was making her sick, she was vomiting almost nightly and states, "those people wanted to poison me." She couldn't sleep, as she felt unsafe. She went on to report that the daily support group discussions made her feel more ashamed and unheard. In group people made jokes about prostitutes. Esther felt ashamed and like she didn't belong there. She didn't identify with others in group because the only reason she ever used drugs was because her trafficker, also her boyfriend, forced her to, and then made her sell her body for sexual acts while high. She said the cause of her substance abuse wasn't the same as people who had chosen to pick up and use. She never wanted to use drugs. Esther explains in a more detached voice that if she didn't leave she was going to explode and hurt someone in the facility, so she left.

Esther's story highlights the paradox of traditional programming. Without an understanding of the dynamics of trafficking and trauma traditional programs are ill-prepared to meet the needs of these individuals and can actually cause greater harm. It is interesting to note that while Esther's needs simply didn't fit the program, it is Esther who endures the consequences. She is identified as non-compliant, not treatment-ready, and often in cases like Esther's, more restrictive consequences are given. Victims, like Esther, become the square peg in the round hole of traditional treatment. Ford and Blaustein (2013) could not explain this tension any better in discussing treatment programs for traumatized juvenile justice settings.

The experience of traumatic victimization, in many ways, violates the "social contract" that lies at the heart of societal laws and structures: the contract that suggests that good deeds and behavior are rewarded, that perpetrating harm should and will be punished, and that maintaining order is mutually beneficial. For youth who have experienced repeated violence and violation in their homes and communities, often in the absence of societal response (e.g., note the relatively low rates of prosecution of child abuse cases as compared with other felonies; Cross et al. 2003), this is a direct, immediate life experience that violates this implicit social contract. It is little wonder, then, that multiple psychologically traumatized youth may apply different standards in decision-making and in action (Fagan and Piquero

2007). For these youth, the rubric of survival ("When will get my needs met?") is likely to trump legality ("Is this behavior appropriate within the laws of our society?").[19]

Esther has demonstrated amazing survival skills. She chose to leave the facility before she acted out violently, and she did return to court to explain why she left. Here is where the process of power is again initiated. The judge, believing substance abuse treatment is the best thing for Esther, uses her power to send her to another facility miles away from the city. Esther is reminded that she is indeed powerless. How will she learn to manage choices in her life if not given the freedom to do so?

Trauma Experience Becomes Encoded in a Somatic World

Trauma theory teaches us that trauma is experienced by parts of our brain that are not verbal, not accessible by rational thought, and non-linear in content when expressed. The implications for those providing treatment and criminal justice are endless when one begins to understand how the body encodes traumatic experiences and stores those experiences throughout the body. One trauma survivor of prolonged sexual abused stated "the way to fix her mind was to listen to her body."[20] Expert in neurobiology of trauma, Dr. David Lisak states "not only can we react without the intervention of our cortex" referring to our amygdala based fight-or-flight response to fear, but "we can also store a great deal of information without it."[21] This has great implications for understanding how to communicate with survivors of sex trafficking. "It has been crucial to our survival that we be capable of encoding in memory particular stimuli, the recognition of which might determine life or death, and to do so without cortical involvement."[22] If we take the example of the car on the highway mentioned earlier, it is only when our bodies react to a stimulus, bypassing complex higher functioning systems that we continue to survive. For by the time the thought to steer out of the way of the oncoming car reached the cortex, we would be dead.

The key to working with victims of such complex trauma is understanding that "a human being who has been traumatized, will have far less flexibility in the activation of their fear system. For the traumatized human, the low road to fear predominates."[23] In this instance, the low road to fear is referring to the subcortical regions of the brain which do not possess higher level decision-making processes so often desired by society to maintain order and structure. The individual with a complex trauma history for example, has "very little capacity to squelch sensations, control emotional arousal or change fixed action patterns."[24] So often survivors of trafficking find themselves in a system where they are triggered by issues of power and control. The court room where a judge holds the power to decide one's fate. The residential program where every hour of the residents' days are rigidly structured: regimented food meals, regimented therapy, regimented medication. In all cases, compliance is expected to gain the reward of release. These are all hallmarks of power being exerted over the individual despite good intentions. Some of these examples may play a part in the survivor being triggered throughout the course of a day, causing an overtly aggressive irrational response to a situation that does not otherwise match the level of expressed emotion. "The fact that reminders of the past automatically activate certain neurobiological responses explains why trauma survivors are vulnerable to react with irrational—subcortically initiated responses that are irrelevant, and even harmful, in the present."[25] The victim, who has survived an experience of trafficking, is likely to react this way in program both because of triggers he or she may face, but also because of the parallel process of the coercive nature of the trafficker, the police, the court and even service providers. Each, in their own way, while not intending harm, uses coercive tactics encouraging the victims' participation. Victims learn what they have to do to get through this process rather than owning their care and their future. While we are not researchers, current trauma theory clearly explains the victim experience and supports the need for trauma-informed care. What we believe to be unique to trafficking is the repetitive experiences of coercion, betrayal, the exploitation victims experience in their early development, in their victimization, and sadly by those who seek to work with them to find freedom from traffickers.

Practice Recommendations

Traditional interventions fail to meet the needs of those who have survived the violence, abuse, and coercion of a trafficker. Beginning in 2010, we were introduced to law enforcement, court-ordered treatment, demanding child welfare policies, and limited treatment options prepared with our knowledge of trauma theory and a passion to support victims of this crime. The Salvation Army New Day to Stop Trafficking program of Greater Philadelphia, Pennsylvania was established in 2010 with the creation of a drop-in center, later to be called the New Day Drop-In Center. Our model incorporates principles of harm reduction, motivational interviewing, the Sanctuary Model® for trauma-informed care, as well as our shared social work values of service and self-determination addressing mind, body, and spiritual needs. The core value of the Drop-In Center is meeting the individual where they are, emotionally, physically, psychologically, and spiritually. Services are focused on building relationships and having a consistent presence in the community, while offering a trauma-informed safe space. Safety is paramount to the work of anti-trafficking. Sanctuary training taught us that without being socially, physically, psychologically, and morally safe,[26] victims cannot begin to explore future options. The focus of the drop-in center is to provide services in a nonjudgmental, safe, and respectful environment that welcomes women no matter in what state they enter, whether sober or under the influence of a controlled substance, tired, angry, happy, or simply in need of a space to be out of the weather and off the street. The Drop-In Center has been widely successful in reaching women directly forced into commercial sexual exploitation along an open air street track notorious for the sex trade, and building relationships that inspire hope and a foundation for change. Change, however, is based upon the individual's readiness for change, never on program expectations or time frames. Staff is trained in de-escalation, Sanctuary values, motivational interviewing and the tenets of harm reduction. For women who choose to seek services and leave the life, TSA-NDSTP offers a residential program for survivors of sex or labor trafficking. We like to refer to New Day Home as the place you choose, not the place you end up. Residential support, in this setting, is guided by the principles and values discussed above and are outlined below as practice recommendations.

Survivor-Led Services

Our social work values guide us to give voice to those we serve. Sanctuary training guides us to establish a democratic environment where everyone has a voice. In this manner our program is guided by those we serve. Survivors of trafficking must be engaged, in any way possible, in developing or running victim services. We value survivors as the experts in this field, although participation is never forced, opportunities for input and participation are offered. Survivors can and should be offered jobs, leadership roles, and/or serve in other capacities within a program, committee, or coalition. At any level, survivors can be influential and can participate in making decisions within a program. It is up to the agency to create this space for shared governance of policies and procedures.

Autonomy, Choice, and Self-Determination

As we have described throughout this chapter, the coercive nature of the trafficking experience is the abuse of power and control which strips a victim of their identity and ability to have a voice or choice. The trafficker literally breaks the victim in order to exert control with the intent to exploit. It is essential for the survivor to rediscover and regain a sense of self and a voice. Change is an arduous process. As Sandy Bloom has advised, change is not easy, creating new norms are challenging, "In reality, no one changes habits easily or quickly—that is what makes habits habitual—they resist change."[27] Recovery from trafficking-induced trauma, like any form of recovery, more often than not, includes relapse, or in this case, a return to the life. As terrifying as this return may be to us as clinicians, we are guided by the principle of self-determination. Respect for choice is respect regardless of the choice. Faced with the dire consequences of a return to the life, it can be tempting to want to mandate treatment. However, in our experience, genuine respect for choice, and an open door for return coveys a true sense of autonomy and respect for a victim. In order to foster genuine authentic healing processes, the victim needs to realize that he or she has the right to his or her own body and has free will and freedom to make choices about recovery. In this way we start to disrupt the process of coercion deeply instilled by the trafficker. Only when choice is respected with dignity can one gain personal power and begin to heal. Recovery is not a linear process. A ballerina learning to perfect the pirouette must stumble and fall to learn how to position her body correctly to complete the turn. Recovery is also a process of learning. Relapse is not a failure; it is just a step along the way.

Explore Alternative Forms of Therapy

Traditional models of insight-oriented talk therapy may not be immediately effective for a survivor who does not identify as a victim. As we discussed earlier, the experience of trauma is preverbal, and trying to put the story together can be re-traumatizing. Immediate needs of survivors relate to the management of symptoms such as the hyperarousal, disassociation, depression, and emotional dysregulation that victims experience. Van der Kolk points out that:

> in order to deal with the past, it is helpful for traumatized people to learn to activate their capacity for introspection and develop a deep curiosity about their internal experience. This is necessary in order to identify their physical sensations and to translate their emotions and sensations into communicable language—understandable, most of all, to themselves. Traumatized individuals need to learn that it is safe to have feelings and sensations.[28]

When we consider the violence endured by victims of trafficking, the internal protective function of fight-or-flight response often did not protect them from the abuse they endured as a child or as a victim of trafficking, resulting in a sense of learned helplessness and loss of control. It is challenging enough for an individual who has not experienced these elements of coercive abuse to face their feelings and emotions, but it can be evermore challenging when those feelings come with a flood of hormones signaling a threat to one's safety. "For therapy to be effective it might be useful to focus on the patient's physical experience and increase their self-awareness, rather than focusing exclusively on the *meaning* that people make of their experience—their narrative of the past."[29] Utilizing alternative forms of therapy such as expressive art groups, movement groups, equine therapy, and recreational activities have all proven to be more engaging for individuals in TSA-NDSTP and are supported by research regarding complex trauma and individuals living with PTSD and related disorders. TSA-NDSTP has drawn from various theoretical frameworks for understanding trauma and merged these theories with firsthand knowledge of the coercive process of sex trafficking victimization. Effective service provision incorporates trauma theory, and an understanding and knowledge base of victimization and human trafficking. Van der Kolk has asserted that "introspective, body-oriented therapies can directly confront a core clinical issue in PTSD: traumatized individuals are prone to experience the present with physical sensations and emotions associated with the past" he goes on to note that, "it seems that, in order to come to terms with the past it may be essential to learn to regulate one's physiological arousal."[30] There is no proven technique for this, but there are promising practices such as mindfulness, trauma focused yoga, equine therapy, and other body-oriented therapies. We have found that by deliberately creating a healing community, in our case using the Sanctuary Model, forming and maintaining transformative relationships, mirroring healthy boundaries, establishing new norms for daily routines, and offering opportunity to seek meaning and explore one's spirituality, we can influence change and recovery in a non-coercive loving way.

Relationship, Boundaries, and Spirituality

The Salvation Army is a part of the international Christian church and values faith and spirituality in all programming. It is interesting to note that anti-human trafficking work has been a mandate of the TSA since its inception 150 years ago. What has been so transformational in the work being done by the New Day to Stop Trafficking programs is that it has sought to fully integrate both the values social work and spirituality and faith in a non-coercive manner. We know that many anti-trafficking efforts led by faith-based organizations tend to mandate religious services or bible study. Yet, a primary tenet in the values of the TSA is to meet basic needs regardless of faith, gender, or orientation. Inherent in the Army's motto of "Soup, Soap, & Salvation" is the understanding that people are not free to embrace spirituality, or faith, until their basic needs are met. Our practice in New Day is consistent with the values of the Salvation Army and our stance that service delivery should not be coercive in nature. Just like we do not mandate therapy, we do not mandate religious compliance, lest we replicate the process of the trafficker. We believe that authentic transformation comes from within the individual, not from anything we can do to mandate that transformation which includes one's psychological and spiritual state of mind and heart. We acknowledge the role of spirituality and faith in recovery. Finding meaning, forgiving and seeking connection through community are all essential for healing.

Conclusion

We have explored at length, in this chapter, the need to understand the role complex trauma, from repeated betrayal, abuse, and coercion, plays in the victimization at the hand of a trafficker. Healing occurs when relationships are formed which allow for safety, freedom, and choice. Sadly, those who enter victims' lives, even with the best intentions, offer help, but with the expectation of compliance. Law enforcement may lessen charges for information. Courts may demand treatment before reunification with family. Service providers arbitrarily set goals to meet program needs, ignoring the needs of the victim. In many ways these mandates, coercive in nature, force victims to comply rather that offering avenues for healing. Victims do not learn how to be independent, but how to work the system much like how they learned to service a trick to avoid punishment. This process simply replicates the process of the trafficker. True healing comes from the establishment of safety: safety to make choices without threat of consequence; safety in saying no; safety in knowing that your support system will not abandon you because you make a mistake. As social workers, we accept the work of Maslow and his hierarchy of needs as canon. Until basic needs are met, higher level needs are unattainable. Victims of trafficking have the same basic needs and require the freedom to get these needs met without threat of consequence. If we believe in such basic human rights, then we must create and foster systems that strive to do this work from a victim-centered and non-coercive stance.

Notes

1 Jordan, J., Patel, B., and Rapp, L. (2013). Domestic minor sex trafficking: A social work perspective on misidentification, victims, buyers, traffickers, treatment, and reform of current practice. *Journal of Human Behavior and the Social Environment*, 23(3), 356–369.

2 Gerassi, L. (2015). From exploitation to industry: definitions, risks, and consequences of domestic sexual exploitation and sex work among women and girls. *Journal of Human Behavior and the Social Environment*, 25(6), 591–605.

3 Gerassi, L. (2015). From exploitation to industry: definitions, risks, and consequences of domestic sexual exploitation and sex work among women and girls. *Journal of Human Behavior and the Social Environment*, 25(6), 591–605.

4 Gerassi, L. (2015). From exploitation to industry: definitions, risks, and consequences of domestic sexual exploitation and sex work among women and girls. *Journal of Human Behavior and the Social Environment*, 25(6), 591–605.

5 Gerassi, L. (2015). From exploitation to industry: definitions, risks, and consequences of domestic sexual exploitation and sex work among women and girls. *Journal of Human Behavior and the Social Environment*, 25(6), 591–605.

6 Gerassi, L. (2015). From exploitation to industry: definitions, risks, and consequences of domestic sexual exploitation and sex work among women and girls. *Journal of Human Behavior and the Social Environment*, 25(6), 591–605.

7 Gerassi, L. (2015). from exploitation to industry: definitions, risks, and consequences of domestic sexual exploitation and sex work among women and girls. *Journal of Human Behavior and the Social Environment*, 25(6), 591–605.

8 Bloom, S. (2010). Mental health aspects of IPV/DV: survivors, professionals, and systems. In Giardino, A. P., and Giardino, E. R. (eds.), *Interpartner Violence, Domestic Violence and Spousal Abuse: A Resource for Professionals Working with Children and Families*. St. Louis, MO: GW Medical Publishing.

9 Bloom, S. (2010), Mental health aspects of IPV/DV: survivors, professionals, and systems. In Giardino, A. P., and Giardino, E. R. (eds.), *Interpartner Violence, Domestic Violence And Spousal Abuse: A Resource for Professionals Working with Children and Families*. St. Louis, MO: GW Medical Publishing.

10 Jordan, J., Patel, B., and Rapp, L. (2013) Domestic minor sex trafficking: a social work perspective on misidentification, victims, buyers, traffickers, treatment, and

reform of current practice. *Journal of Human Behavior and the Social Environment*, 23(3), 356–369.

11 Ivy, K., and Hunter, K. (2008). *The 48 Laws of the Game: Pimpology*. New York: Gallery Books.

12 Dalla, R., Baker, L., DeFrai, J., and Williamson, C. (2011)., *Global Perspectives on Prostitution and Sex Trafficking: Europe, Latin America, North America, and Global*. New York: Lexington Books.

13 Dalla, R., Baker, L., DeFrai, J., and Williamson, C. (2011). *Global Perspectives on Prostitution and Sex Trafficking: Europe, Latin America, North America, and Global*. New York: Lexington Books.

14 Ivy, K., and Hunter, K. (2008). *The 48 Laws of the Game: Pimpology*. New York: Gallery Books.

15 Ford, J., and Blaustein, M. (2013). Systemic self-regulation: a framework for trauma-informed services in residential juvenile justice programs. *Journal of Family Violence*. DOI: 10.1007/s10896-013-9538-5

16 Ford, J., and Blaustein, M. (2013). Systemic self-regulation: a framework for trauma-informed services in residential juvenile justice programs. *Journal of Family Violence*. DOI: 10.1007/s10896-013-9538-5

17 Ford, J., and Blaustein, M. (2013). Systemic self-regulation: a framework for trauma-informed services in residential juvenile justice programs. *Journal of Family Violence*. DOI: 10.1007/s10896-013-9538-5

18 Van der Kolk, B.A. (2006). Clinical implications of neuroscience research in PTSD. *New York Academy of Sciences Journal*, 1071(1), 277–293.

19 Ford, J., and Blaustein, M. (2013). Systemic self-regulation: a framework for trauma-informed services in residential juvenile justice programs. *Journal of Family Violence*. DOI: 10.1007/s10896-013-9538-5

20 Green, Matthew (2017). A radical new therapy could treat the "untreatable" victims of trauma. *Newsweek* (US edition), 23 March. Available at: https://www.newsweek.com/2017/03/31/trauma-ptsd-therapy-comprehensive-resource-model-treats-untreatable-572367.html, para. 7.

21 Lisak, D. (2002). Neurobiology of trauma. Unpublished article, University of Massachusetts, Boston.

22 Lisak, D. (2002). Neurobiology of trauma. Unpublished article, University of Massachusetts, Boston.

23 Lisak, D. (2002). Neurobiology of trauma. Unpublished article, University of Massachusetts, Boston.

24 Van der Kolk, B.A. (2006). Clinical implications of neuroscience research in PTSD. *New York Academy of Sciences Journal*, 1071(1), 277–293.

25 Van der Kolk, B.A. (2006). Clinical implications of neuroscience research in PTSD. *New York Academy of Sciences Journal*, 1071(1), 277–293.

26 Bloom, S. (2010). Mental health aspects of IPV/DV: survivors, professionals, and systems. In Giardino, A. P., and Giardino, E. R. (eds.), *Interpartner Violence, Domestic Violence and Spousal Abuse: A Resource for Professionals Working with Children and Families*. St. Louis, MO: GW Medical Publishing.

27 Bloom, S. (2010). Mental health aspects of IPV/DV: survivors, professionals, and systems. In Giardino, A. P., and Giardino, E. R. (eds.), *Interpartner Violence, Domestic Violence and Spousal Abuse: A Resource for Professionals Working with Children and Families*. St. Louis, MO: GW Medical Publishing.

28 Van der Kolk, B.A. (2006). Clinical implications of neuroscience research in PTSD. *New York Academy of Sciences Journal*, 1071(1), 277–293.

29 Van der Kolk, B.A. (2006). Clinical implications of neuroscience research in PTSD. *New York Academy of Sciences Journal*, 1071(1), 277–293.

30 Van der Kolk, B.A. (2006). Clinical implications of neuroscience research in PTSD. *New York Academy of Sciences Journal*, 1071(1), 277–293.

9 Relapse

Clinical Considerations

Brian D. Bruijn and Lucy L. Bruijn

Upon exiting a life of domestic sex trafficking, adult survivors face numerous barriers that work against their restoration effort. Complex trauma, disordered attachments, dehumanization, and childhood abuse are all reported survivor experiences (Hom and Woods, 2013; Muftić and Finn, 2013). This is the level of abuse that survivors bring to aftercare. Therefore, when survivors do not perceive service providers' boundaries as healthy or beneficial, it is because there is often a long-standing history of getting close to people and getting hurt. For survivors, the service providers' well-intended policies and procedures implemented to protect survivors feel more like another means of control. This is an example of one of many things that can trigger a relapse in adult survivors of sex trafficking. This chapter will briefly examine the differences between trafficking and prostitution, explore relapse, provide an overview of some of the reasons why survivors run away from aftercare, and discuss possible ways to mitigate the potential for a relapse.

Definitions

Aftercare—The program or coalition of programs a survivor of sex trafficking utilizes in the restorative process.

Prostitute—One who engages in numerous, emotionally detached transient sexual acts for money.

Relapse—The process of reentering a life of sex trafficking, after having exited.

Survivor—The person who has exited a life of sex trafficking.

The Life—A term used to denote the time in which someone was actively in prostitution.

Typical Society—A term used to refer to society-at-large or the people who have been living life apart from a life of prostitution or sex trafficking.

Victim of Sex Trafficking—A person who is forced to engage in commercial sex as a result of being exploited by the use of force, fraud, or coercion.

Context

In 2005, members of the United Nations came together to establish a unified definition of human trafficking.

> Trafficking in persons shall mean the recruitment, transportation, transfer, harboring or receipt of persons, by means of the threat or force or other forms of coercion, of abduction, of fraud, of deception, of the abuse of power, or of a position of vulnerability or of the giving or receiving of payments or benefits to achieve the consent of a person having control over another person, for the purpose of exploitation. Exploitation shall include, at a minimum, the exploitation of the prostitution of others or other forms of sexual exploitation, forced labor or services, slavery or practices similar to slavery, servitude or the removal of organs.
>
> (Europol, 2005, p. 10)

Over the past decade there has been a distinct increase in attention drawn to the existence of human trafficking, and specifically sex trafficking. Sex trafficking occurs when force or coercion, fraud, and/or deception are used as a means to induce the performance of a commercial sex act. While coercion is often construed as the threat of physical, emotional, or sexual violence, it is not always that straightforward for victims of sex trafficking. For some individuals, the need for safety, childcare, or having no reasonable means of supporting oneself can instantiate a sense of desperation, and that desperation functions as a means of coercion (Hernandez, 2001). While both sex trafficking victims and those who choose prostitution as a profession engage in sex acts in exchange for money, it is the sex trafficking victim that does so outside of her or his personal choice.

There was a time when typical society viewed prostitution as a career choice that was made by an individual. As mentioned above, some may have freely chosen prostitution as a profession; for others, the label of prostitute is not as clear or accurate. Better victim identification methods are revealing that an increasing number of those labeled as prostitutes actually meet the legal criteria as victims of adult sex trafficking. However, as improved as the identification methods may be, these methods often only serve to identify victims and not necessarily provide an avenue of escape. Nor does identification address the environmental, political, social, and structural barriers that foster an environment in which sex trafficking flourishes. Identification of a victim does not always equate to an opportunity for a person to exit the life and become a survivor. The individual identified as a victim of sex trafficking, if provided with a viable means of escape, may not see herself or himself as a victim, or think she or he needs help.

When a victim of sex trafficking does take advantage of an opportunity (often provided by an aftercare agency that specializes in working with trafficking victims) to exit the life, there are no assurances that she or he will not go back. The instability and trauma that survivors experienced prior to and during captivity influences their experiences with aftercare, and thus their experiences with the helping professionals with whom they are working. The coping mechanisms and skills used for survival on the streets (typically skills in manipulation or negotiation) consistently manifest in the aftercare setting. If an organization does not utilize a strengths-based model of service provision, these coping mechanisms, while adaptive in one environment (typically on the streets), can serve to destabilize restoration efforts. Many organizations that are dedicated to the restoration of survivors of sex trafficking also have rules, policies, and procedures that guide (and sometimes dictate) how situations (i.e., crises, unexpected behaviors, deliberate infractions) should be handled. This juxtaposition of the life (unstable and typically known) with aftercare (typically stable and unknown) occurs in an environment where survivors don't know what to think or how to act. The security of knowing what to expect, even if abusive and unstable, is a powerful draw when faced with the uncertainty of what it might be like to live with boundaries, rules, and people who say that they want to love and care for the survivor. The notion of stability can be overwhelming, and it can feel like they are trading one controlling entity for another.

While age has some influence on how likely someone is to come out of and stay out of the life, complex trauma short circuits rational decisions. Not only are survivors and aftercare providers working against maladaptive adjustment, they also have to address the repeated trauma that could have started as early as childhood. All of these factors come together to influence the likelihood of a survivor staying out of the life. For the remainder of the chapter, relapse will be discussed in the context of events or circumstances that could trigger a relapse. Each potentially triggering event will be followed by recommended courses of action that can be used to mitigate the potential for relapse. Lastly, there will be a brief discussion of relapse in the context of clinical implications for support workers.

Relapse

Relapse occurs when a survivor of sex trafficking, after having exited a life of forced commercial sex with the intention of not going back to the perpetrator, returns at some point to the life. It should be noted that this scenario is different from that of those who engage in prostitution as their profession. There are cases in which a victim has escaped from her or his trafficker and still engaged in prostitution of her or his own choosing. When working with sex trafficking victims and prostitutes, operating from a nonjudgmental, strengths-based stance is vital to provide the scaffolding necessary to empower people to make choices that are best for their needs. Exiting a life of sex trafficking is a difficult process, and, consequently, relapse happens on a regular basis. The reasons for relapse are as individual as the client, and there are some consistent themes.

- Trauma bond / Stockholm Syndrome
- Drug addiction
- Protecting loved ones
- Aftercare boundaries and rules are felt to be too much to deal with
- Disorganized and unprepared agencies
- The participation in religious worship is a requirement to receive services
- Lack of social acceptance
- Money

While these are certainly not all of the reasons someone may relapse back into the life with her or his trafficker, they account for a good portion of why participants go back. This list consists of three categories: relapse influences that stem from abuse and consequences of having been in the life, working with aftercare, and interacting with typical society. These categories serve to illustrate the complexity of interactions that survivors have to work through as they move through care and into a new way of living.

Relapses that Result Because of Influences from the Life

Attachment Exploitation. When in the life, traffickers utilize numerous means to maintain control of victims. One form of control involves utilizing victims' maladaptive attachment patterns to establish an emotional bond. This typically happens when the victim is an adolescent, involves promises of love, the meeting of basic needs, and/or protection from a volatile home life. Entrance into sex trafficking by this avenue can have an initial modicum of stability before the trafficker begins coercing the victim into prostitution in order to start making money off of her or him.

After the attachment is made, traffickers utilize numerous resources to maintain control of victims. They will manipulate circumstances so as to convince the victim that being with the trafficker is her or his only means of survival. Traffickers will utilize the victims' emotional connection by coercing them with phrases like "if you love me, you will ... ", or the perpetrator may become physically aggressive. Traffickers will do whatever is necessary to maintain control.

Mitigating Maladaptive Attachment. Because of the unstable nature of attachments that have developed over the course of a survivor's life, it is important to address the need for secure and healthy attachments. Often a person who has been in the life did not have a positive figure with whom to develop a secure attachment (Parrish and Eagle, 2003). To address not only the trauma bonding but also the complex trauma, there are a range of modalities that can be implemented, including Contextual Therapy (Gold, 2009), Sensorimotor Psychotherapy (Fisher and Ogden, 2009), Cognitive Behavioral Therapy (Jackson et al., 2009), and Experiential and Emotion-Focused Therapy (Fosha et al., 2009). Another consideration for treatment is to implement a relational approach while integrating trauma and attachment theories (Briere et al., 2010; Ford et al., 2005; Pearlman and Courtois, 2005).

Chemical Dependence. Drugs are introduced as another means of control through manipulating the victims into chemical dependence or by exploiting preexisting addictions. By utilizing the victim's addiction to substances, traffickers bypass the victim's ability to make logical decisions. Thus, the traffickers implement another layer of control by establishing themselves as the victim's substance provider.

Mitigating Chemical Dependence. Because a survivor's chemical dependence is often tied to the complex trauma she or he has experienced, it is important to connect the survivor with a trauma-informed substance abuse treatment program (Harris and Fallot, 2001). Amaro et al. (2007) found that trauma-informed substance abuse treatment programs have better retention rates than standard programs. Covington (2008) recommended that treatment programs be designed for specific genders. The vast majority of persons who are addicted to substances and trafficked for sex are female identified, and they share some common-lived experiences including stigmatization, shame, abuse, and lack of financial resources (Covington, 2008).

Protecting Children. Experiencing victimization in the life does not preclude victims from having children or families of origin they care about. Traffickers not only produce children with victims, but they also use those children as another means of maintaining control of the victim. By making the victims the sole persons responsible for ensuring their children's safety, traffickers exploit the bond victims have for their children. In this case, if a victim does not meet the trafficker's demands, the victim's children may suffer.

To say that this situation is a tough circumstance is an understatement. The desire to protect those we love is strong, and if a person has had children in the life and they are in an aftercare setting, they may have entered the aftercare setting at the behest of leaving children behind. Rhodes et al. (2010) examined the concerns of mothers who have experienced violence in intimate relationships. They found that mothers expressed concern for violence against their children; freedom from violence was not as easy as leaving, and some were drawn back because a perpetrator was also a child's father. Working with child protective services also was a barrier to gaining access to support.

Mitigating the Draw of Protecting Children. In this instance, establishing a safe place for parent and child is needed. It is also important to provide parenting support in the form of childcare while the parent is engaged in services. Part of the reason for relapse in this instance is the worry that the survivor's children are not safe. Another complicating layer, in this case, is the need to establish interventions to protect the child or children. Assuming that an aftercare service provider can keep the child or children and parent together, services that affect child safety need to be evaluated strongly. Developing positive parenting classes, regular home-based visits to monitor child safety, Parent Child Interaction Therapy, trauma- informed therapy for the child (ren) and potentially utilization of the foster care system may be necessary while the survivor parent is working on wellness (MacMillan et al., 2009).

Relapses that Occur as a Result of the Aftercare Environment

Boundaries and Structure. In order to provide quality services, aftercare service providers should have established policies and procedures, rules and boundaries, and an overall organizational structure of operations to function and carry on their work. A solid understanding of the services the provider offers and how to consistently access these services is needed greatly when setting the survivors' expectations of service provision. These boundaries are (or should be) developed for the survivor's safety and service providers. However, for the survivor who has lived in an environment where the primary structure involved emotional and coercive control, engaging with service providers and the amount of rules that need to be followed can be overwhelming. For the survivor, the rules are seen as antagonistic and difficult to follow. Victimization while in the life is chaotic, inconsistent, and volatile. Aftercare tends to be structured, organized, and full of expectation. Survivors having come out of the life typically do not have experience with navigating the expectations of aftercare.

Mitigating Organizational Structural Triggers. Culturally sensitive trauma-informed care cannot only occur in the therapy room. The entire service organization should consistently train staff on how to respond appropriately survivors' traumatic reactions. The therapeutic bond that people in the organization develop with the survivor, combined with the consistent presentation of services provides a safety net of reconnection if a survivor were to relapse. The boundaries and expectations may be overwhelming because the survivor may never have experienced anything like this. Agencies that remain consistent, operate from a strengths-based approach, and remain non-judgmental model an example of a different way to live.

Disorganized and Unprepared Agencies. However consistent and organized aftercare agencies may be, the reality is that there is no widely accepted standard of care for working with adult survivors of sex trafficking. There are no governmental policies or regulations that service organizations are required to follow to maintain a baseline of appropriate care. In other words, presently there is no accepted standard of care for aftercare service organizations. Service organizations can state that they engage in restorative care and need only establish themselves as a non-profit agency (assuming they would like to operate tax free). Then, depending on the social capital they build, they can start promoting their organization to people in their community. There are well-intended organizations that have determined that sex trafficking is going to be their primary social justice issue to address, yet they have not researched fully what needs to be done during the organizations' planning phases. This is true particularly when it comes providing services to those who have experienced complex trauma. These aftercare service providers may promise a better life without the organizational structure in place or capacity to fulfill promises of a better life. These organizations' inability to fulfill promises made to survivors may be due to not having enough personnel to adequately care for the number of survivors in their care, inconsistency with service provision, or staff that has not received adequate training to address complex trauma. Aftercare providers in this category are often learning on the job and survivor care suffers as result.

Mitigating Disorganization and Lack of Preparation. To be able to offer the best services possible, it is important for organizations to conduct a needs analysis within their communities. It is important to develop relationships with those who are working presently in the anti-trafficking field and to research what needs are not being met. By building coalitions and working with other agencies, the local community is able to offer better service provision. Once the needs analysis is complete, it's important to consider consulting with experts in the area of need and to utilize outside expertise to develop a solid plan for service provision. Seeking relationships and sharing information with other groups that are doing the same type of work can help bolster the work of organizations and provide a sense of community. The nonprofit world is competitive (Thorton, 2006), and if service providers in local communities are not working together, survivors suffer (Bruijn, 2017).

Required Spiritual Participation for Services. Some aftercare programs are faith-based and operate with an evangelical stance that does not consider it an ethical dilemma to require religious worship in exchange for restorative services. The transactional nature of this interaction may induce trauma in survivors. Having a spiritual component to aftercare can be beneficial if a survivor has a faith to which she or he ascribes, and if a survivor sees that faith as a source of strength. Even when the survivor endorses a personal faith, it is incumbent on the provider not to push a particular dogmatic system, but rather to work with the faith that the survivor brings to the setting. When it comes to the inclusion of a spiritual component for aftercare, providers need to exercise caution and place the restorative needs of the survivor above the evangelical requirements of the organization.

Mitigating the Effects of Required Spiritual Participation for Services. If an aftercare provider is faith-based and offers spiritual services, then consider that those services should be offered on a voluntary basis with alternative programming available for those who do not choose to participate in religious activity. Additionally, the faith-based service provider will need to go to extra lengths to ensure that the survivor does not experience marginalization by the organization's staff or from other survivors participating in the religiously based services.

Relapses that Occur as the Result of Typical Society

Lack of Acceptance. There is a stigma that victims of sex-trafficking can suffer from, and that is never being able to be seen as anything other than prostitutes. Unless a survivor is able to go stealth or is able to live a life without anyone knowing about her or his past, the potential stigma of having once been a victim of sex-trafficking can feed into typical society interactions. Typical society's lack of understanding of how power and privilege shape daily interactions can lead to some paternalistic and condescending interactions with survivors. It is not uncommon for those with power and means to help fund aftercare services. However, those providing the funding seldom understand the contextual variables that continue to marginalize those who have been trafficked for sex.

While in the life, survivors had to daily contend with people telling them what to do, how to behave, and had very little, if any, power to do or react otherwise. In typical society, there is a different set of rules that tell survivors what to do and how to behave. Because of their often intersecting marginalized statuses (i.e., race, victim, gender), there is also very little power to do or act otherwise. The biggest difference is that survivors developed coping skills for surviving the life. The same cannot necessarily be said for living in typical society.

Mitigating Typical Society Ignorance. How does one shape the mindset of society? Interventions on this level require advocacy and community engagement. Advocacy involves engaging politicians to support changing laws that penalize victims and disproportionately let perpetrators go free. Community engagement can be achieved by awareness campaigns, hosting educational events, providing resources to religious and civic groups, and engaging with schools to provide age appropriate education programs. Raising awareness and helping to redefine a narrative that continues to marginalize individuals already victimized is necessary.

Money. Money is a motivator, and, even though in the life, victims often had access to quick money. Earning a living wage as a survivor can be challenging. To begin with, while in aftercare services, access to funds is limited. For instance, in the early stages of a residential program, a high priority is placed on stabilization and not on finances. Admittedly, residential programs will often provide for survivors' basic needs and/or help survivors gain access to social services that can assist with meeting these needs. The early momentum of aftercare is certainly in favor of stabilization. Even when survivors attain a certain level of stabilization, there is still no guarantee that they will be able to earn a living wage when they exit an aftercare setting. Structural barriers such as criminal records, marginalized identities, and an overall ignorance of the hidden rules of typical society serve as barriers that will need to be addressed. For survivors, there is often a distinct disadvantage when it comes to education. If a person entered the life while she or he was a minor, then it is likely she or he is not going to continue meeting social, emotional, and developmental milestones with those her or his age. This can include never completing a high school education.

From a developmental standpoint, those who are in their mid-20s to mid-30s are more likely to leave sex trafficking and stay out of the life if someone offers an avenue of escape (Bruijn, 2017). Adolescents have a tendency towards impulsivity and older victims (while more likely to come out than adolescents) tend to suffer from chemical dependence or have given up (Bruijn, 2017). Even if a survivor escaped from her or his trafficker at age 25 and graduated from a two-year program, she or he would still be 27 years old with no work history. The survivor may have earned a GED as the result of participating with an aftercare program, and yet would not have a resumé comparable to those of the same age range. Staffing agencies such as Randstad are trying to help breach the vocational gap by developing programs designed to help meet needs specific to the survivor experience. However, unless something is done to address the structural and social barriers that survivors experience, the survivor will almost always be at a disadvantage when competing for jobs.

Mitigating Money Barriers. The beginning of aftercare can be a difficult time. To begin addressing the financial challenges that survivors will face when they enter aftercare, it is important to reinforce that finances will be a significant component addressed during the course of aftercare. Some residential aftercare programs offer a mixed model of providing basic needs and a nominal stipend for residents until they have financial resources of their own. During the course of restoration, it is important to provide not only access to education in the form of a GED, vocational training, and/or community college, but also training on how to responsibly mange money. Fiscal literacy classes are valuable tools that can used to teach financial skills such as budgeting, saving, how to utilize banking services, and how to manage a personal bank account. While typical community can be ignorant about the challenges a survivor of sex trafficking faces, typical community can also be a good source for training in a trade skill, engaging with staffing agencies for training and access to employment, and providing exposure to healthier social networks (Bruijn, 2017). As mentioned above, Randstad (a Fortune 500 company) (https://www.randsta dusa.com/about/corporate-social-responsibility) is utilizing its expertise in job placement to provide job readiness training for survivors. Social enterprises are another means by which local communities can support survivors of sex trafficking. Organizations such as Freedom a la Cart (http://freedomalacart.org) and Thistle Farms (https://thistlefarms.org) are providing survivors of sex trafficking job skills in their communities.

Concluding Remarks

When treating adult survivors of sex trafficking, it takes a concerted effort on the part of community organizations to address and meet the biopsychosocial and sometimes spiritual needs of survivors. When survivors come into an aftercare setting, it is expected that they will be emotionally volatile. This volatility often can trigger a relapse.

For those who work with survivors, part of the restoration process involves developing a therapeutic alliance with the survivor. Therefore, when a survivor relapses, there is the potential for vicarious trauma. Kliner and Stroud (2012) found that helping professionals who work with sex

152 B. D. Bruijn and L. L. Bruijn

trafficking survivors are susceptible to vicarious trauma. Compassion fatigue and burnout are additional considerations to pay attention to as they represent symptoms that could potentially affect the quality of service survivors receive (Kliner and Stroud, 2012). Organizations who treat survivors should provide high levels of support and ample opportunities for staff to set appropriate boundaries and engage in self-care in order to mitigate the stress that vicarious trauma can cause (Kliner and Stroud, 2012; O'Halloran and Linton, 2000). Experiencing vicarious trauma is a real concern; a survivor relapsing can trigger it, and having way to mitigate its effects is not only helpful for the worker, but ultimately for the survivor as well.

References

Amaro, H., Chernoff, M., Brown, V., Arévalo, S., and Gatz, M. (2007). Does integrated trauma-informed substance abuse treatment increase treatment retention? *Journal of Community Psychology*, 35, 845–862.

Briere, J., Hodges, M., and Godbout, N. (2010). Traumatic stress, affect dysregulation, and dysfunctional avoidance: a structural equation model. *Journal of Traumatic Stress*, 23, 767–774.

Bruijn, B. D. (2017). Sex trafficking survivor-advocates' experience with aftercare. Unpublished doctoral dissertation. Memphis, TN: University of Memphis.

Covington, S. S. (2008). Women and addiction: a trauma-informed approach. *Journal of Psychoactive Drugs*, 40, 377–385.

Europol. (2005) *Legislation on Trafficking in Human Beings and Illegal Immigrant Smuggling*. The Hague: Europol.

Fisher, J., and Ogden, P. (2009). Sensorimotor psychotherapy. In C. A. Courtois and J. D. Ford (eds.), *Treating Complex Stress Disorders* (pp. 243–263). New York: Guilford Press.

Ford, J. D., Courtois, C. A., Steele, K., Hart, O. V. D., and Nijenhuis, E. R. (2005). Treatment of complex posttraumatic self-dysregulation. *Journal of Traumatic Stress*, 18(5), 437–447.

Fosha, D., Paivio, S. C., Gleiser, K., and Ford, J. D. (2009). Experiential and emotion-focused therapy. In C. A. Courtois and J. D. Ford (eds.), *Treating Complex Stress Disorders* (pp. 286–311). New York: Guilford Press.

Gold, D. (2009). Contextual therapy. In C. A. Courtois and J. D. Ford (eds.), *Treating Complex Stress Disorders* (pp. 227–242). New York: Guilford Press.

Harris, M., and Fallot, R. (2001). Envisioning a trauma-informed service system: a vital paradigm shift. *New Directions for Mental Health Services*, 89, 3–22. doi:10.1002/yd.23320018903

Hernandez, T. K. (2001) Sexual harassment and racial disparity: the mutual construction of gender and race. *University of Iowa Journal of Gender, Race and Justice*, 4, 183–224.

Hom, K. A., and Woods, S. J. (2013). Trauma and its aftermath for commercially sexually exploited women as told by front-line service providers. *Issues in Mental Health Nursing*, 34, 75–81. doi:10.3109/01612840.2012.723300

Jackson, C., Nissenson, K., and Cloitre, M., (2009). Cognitive-behavioral therapy. In C. A. Courtois and J. D. Ford (eds.), *Treating Complex Stress Disorders* (pp. 243–263). New York: Guilford Press.

Kliner, M., and Stroud, L. (2012). Psychological and health impact of working with victims of sex trafficking. *Journal of Occupational Health*, 54, 9–15. doi:10.1539/joh.11–0125-OA

MacMillan, H. L., Wathen, C. N., Barlow, J., Fergusson, D. M., Leventhal, J. M., and Taussig, H. N. (2009). Interventions to prevent child maltreatment and associated impairment. *The Lancet*, 373, 250–266.

Muftić, L. R., and Finn, M. A. (2013). Health outcomes among women trafficked for sex in the United States: a closer look. *Journal of Interpersonal Violence*, 28, 1859–1885. doi:10.1177/0886260512469102

O'Halloran, T. M., and Linton, J. M. (2000). Stress on the job: self-care resources for counselors. *Journal of Mental Health Counseling*, 22, 354–364.

Parish, M., and Eagle, M. N. (2003). Attachment to the therapist. *Psychoanalytic Psychology*, 20, 271. doi:10.1037/0736–9735.20.2.271

Pearlman, L. A., and Courtois, C. A. (2005). Clinical applications of the attachment framework: relational treatment of complex trauma. *Journal of Traumatic Stress*, 18, 449–459.

Rhodes, K. V., Cerulli, C., Dichter, M. E., Kothari, C. L., and Barg, F. K. (2010). "I didn't want to put them through that": the influence of children on victim decision-making in intimate partner violence cases. *Journal of Family Violence*, 25, 485–493.

Thorton, J. (2006). Nonprofit fund-raising in competitive donor markets. *Nonprofit and Voluntary Section Quarterly*, 35, 204–224. doi:10.1177/0899764005285951

10 Interdisciplinary Collaboration*
Working with Other Professions

Judy Hale Reed

Victims and survivors of human trafficking require complex care, and their needs vary from person to person and over time for the same person. In working with victims of human trafficking, clinicians coordinate care and work with non-clinicians, because victim and survivor treatment is necessarily collaborative. For this reason, this chapter will look at the perspectives of non-clinicians in working with clinicians to provides services to and support human trafficking victims.

Human trafficking victims and survivors require complex care, and their needs can vary both from person to person and over time for the same person. Different professions face different barriers in assisting victims and in working across professional boundaries. However, coordination can make victim-centered care effective and more practical.

In identifying and assisting trafficking victims, it is valuable to keep in mind that each profession has a "lens" of training, perspectives, goals, and barriers through which it works and through which each profession collaborates with other professions and agencies to varying degrees. For example, law enforcement officers and prosecutors are focused on gathering evidence, identifying actors, and preparing witnesses and their case for prosecution. Civil attorneys are focused on obtaining relief for their victims, such as immigration relief, a visa, family reunification, staying deportation, or monetary damages for victimization and exploitation. Victim advocates, including those in professions for which this book is primarily prepared, are focused on victims' healing, safety, and care. Other professionals, for instance dental and clinical medical care providers, may be focused on limited or narrow physical issues and clinical resolution of those needs.

However, by considering the different goals of partners, collaboration is achievable and brings better outcomes. Communication and cross training make this much easier, so that professionals have an opportunity to consider each other's goals and needs, especially prior to working with a victim or group of victims. Having common legal definitions, which can vary in different jurisdictions and different professions, is also helpful; this is also addressed elsewhere in this book. Opportunities to attend trainings on human

* This chapter has benefited from the author's conversation with Liz M. Chacko, Esq., Deputy Director, Friends of Farmworkers.

trafficking that include a variety of providers in your community is an excellent way to build professional understanding as well as informal connections.

Categories of Care and Services for Human Trafficking Victims

Identification

Unfortunately, victim identification remains the primary need for most victims of human trafficking. Although there are increasing identifications of sex trafficking victims, and media coverage of sex trafficking, labor trafficking in a variety of fields, including construction, services, agriculture, and domestic servitude, remains largely unidentified and unreported or under-reported in the press. Recent research indicates that police identification remains an area for increased training and effectiveness,[1] and so social service professionals are more likely to have the opportunity to identify trafficking victims. However, this can be highly dependent on the local office and leadership, and is changing as increasingly state laws require training and allocate funding, and training programs develop, implement, and improve trainings for law enforcement and other non-clinical professionals, including attorneys and law enforcement.

Identification: Indicators

- Living with employer, and/or in poor living conditions.
- Multiple people living in a cramped space.
- Inability to speak on one's own behalf.
- Answers appear to be scripted and rehearsed.
- Employer is holding identity documents.
- Unpaid or paid very little.
- Evidence of physical, mental, or emotional abuse.
- Working for long hours, often with little or no pay.
- Presence of another person, male or female, who seems controlling.
- Loyalty and positive feelings towards a suspected trafficker.
- Exhibition of fear, tension, shame, humiliation, nervousness; appearing submissive
- Lack of ability or unwillingness to identify him/herself as victim.
- Over-sexualized behavior and/or clothing from a younger person, and/ or under 18 and engaged in any form of sex trade (may be survival sex).

Identification: Screening Questions

- How is work going?
- What are you doing for work?

- How is your work situation?
- Are you being paid what was promised?
- Are you able to stay in touch with your family?
- (In a medical context) Are you here because of something from work?
- Can you leave your job if you want to?
- Are you able to come and go from home and work as you please? If not, have you or anyone else been hurt or threatened if you try to leave?
- Does anyone pressure you to do something illegal, or is someone profiting off of you?
- Do you owe anyone a debt that makes you uncomfortable?
- Have you ever been forced to do work you didn't want to do or didn't agree to do?
- Have you ever been forced to have sex to pay off a debt?
- Does anyone hold your identity documents (i.e. driver's license/ passport) for you? Why?
- Have physical abuse or threats from your employer made you fearful to leave your job?
- Has anyone lied to you about the type of work you would be doing?
- Were you ever threatened with deportation or jail if you tried to leave your situation?
- Where do you sleep and eat?
- Has your family been threatened?
- Do you live with your employer?

Barriers to Assisting Trafficking Victims

Human trafficking is hard to identify if you do not know what to look for; when you do identify a potential victim, it is hard to gain enough trust to get an individual to talk to you, and then again to talk to someone else about what is happening. For example, an attorney was once able to assist a hospitalized victim because, due to their medical condition, the victim could not leave the hospital. The only reason that this victim (and patient) was willing to talk to someone was because they could not leave hospital due to the extent of the victim's medical condition. Unfortunately, due to the fleeting nature of most medical situations, it is hard to identify a victim of trafficking in a medical context. To identify human trafficking, a person needs to open up space for conversation. Awareness among medical staff, training for hospital workers on identification, screening, and referral for services beyond medical services are all needed. Victims do not trust easily, and often do not identify as victims of severe crimes.

Medical Needs

Victims may face long-term medical needs due to exposure to toxic substances from farming or construction activities, as well as infections and physical trauma from sexual abuse. They may have dental and medical needs from long-term lack of access to hygiene and basic nutrition as well as from having suffered physical abuse. Some social services professionals in areas hit by the opioid epidemic are reporting sharp increases in sex trafficking of opioid addicted individuals, including in very rural areas in the US; therefore now more than ever, addiction treatment may also be indicated for trafficking victims.

Vocational, Educational, Employment, Spiritual, Financial, and Housing Needs

In addition to emergent medical and psychological needs, victims often need support for vocational or educational needs, employment, spiritual needs, financial support, and housing. Vocational, educational, employment, and financial support can generally be addressed by government and community agencies providing those services, and faith communities can provide a wide diversity of spiritual support. Housing, however, is complex and there are significantly inadequate services in the US. Survivors need safe, stable housing until they achieve stability, which may mean shelter that is not punitive and supports their healing while also keeping them safe from traffickers who would harm them or lure them to return to their trafficking situation through coercion, including threats and false promises of better treatment. A major conflict in the US currently is the tension regarding keeping victims safe from traffickers, especially with domestic sex trafficking victims, while also providing safe, empowering housing. There is a shortage in general of adequate shelters and safe housing, but there is a particular lack of safe housing that can balance the tension between providing an empowering space while also providing security from traffickers' influences.

Legal Services

Victims may need legal services for criminally prosecuting their traffickers, for defense of (or to clear their record of) crimes they were forced to commit as a part of their trafficking situation, to pursue civil damages after criminal cases are prosecuted, and/or for immigration relief if they are not citizens in the location where they are identified and receiving assistance. Victim restitution depends on state law, and most states have offices for crime victim services and social services for victim advocacy and counseling. In terms of immigration relief for foreign nationals in the US, there are two visa categories for foreign victims, the T visa for trafficking victims and the U visa for victims of certain categories of crimes. Both visas require law enforcement to contribute to the paperwork necessary to apply for these forms of relief. Thus law enforcement, civil and criminal legal assistance, and possibly even experts on the risks a victim could face if repatriated are important elements to comprehensive, multidisciplinary, victim centered service provision. Of course, law enforcement also can potentially play a role in initial victim identification.

In addition to professional categories of assistance, victims need to receive care and services that are trauma-informed and culturally appropriate from all professionals with whom victims interact.

Trauma-Informed Care

Trauma is the

> exposure to actual or threatened death, serious injury, or sexual violence in one (or more) of the following ways: directly experiencing the traumatic event(s); witnessing, in person, the traumatic event(s) as it occurred to others; learning that the traumatic event(s) occurred to a close family member or close friend (in case of actual or threatened death of a family member or friend, the event(s) must have been violent or accidental); or experiencing repeated or extreme exposure to aversive details of the traumatic event(s).
>
> (APA, 2013)

In addition, "trauma is subjective ... [A] particular event may be experienced as traumatic for one individual and not for another," and it "has lasting adverse effects on the individual's functioning and mental, physical, social, emotional, or spiritual well-being" (SAMHSA, 2016a).

Trauma-informed care takes into consideration the impacts of trauma on a person and their behavior and supports a person who has undergone trauma.

Trauma-Informed Approach

Being trauma-informed means taking the principles about being sensitive to someone's background and history and weaving those principles into everything you do organizationally. Not just as a set-aside training program, but to really see it at the culture level, that it permeates everything you do [in an organization] from the policies and procedures to the practice and training; how you recruit, how you promote. Trauma-informed care sensitizes us.

The practice of trauma informed service is less about "what" you're doing, and more about "how" you're doing it. It requires being mindful of ways in which your interactions with clients might inadvertently make them feel unsafe, either physically or emotionally. A program, organization, or system that is trauma-informed:

- Realizes the widespread impact of trauma and understands potential paths for recovery;
- Recognizes the signs and symptoms of trauma in clients, families, staff, and others involved with the system;
- Responds by fully integrating knowledge about trauma into policies, procedures, and practices; and
- Seeks to actively prevent re-traumatization.

The Substance Abuse and Mental Health Service Administration's (SAMHSA) has developed six principles that are meant to be generalized across multiple types of settings, which any organization can use to determine whether your approach is trauma-informed:

1   Safety—throughout an organization, the staff and people they serve feel physically and psychologically safe; the physical setting must be safe and interactions should promote a sense of safety.
2   Trustworthiness and Transparency—Organizational operations and decisions are conducted with transparency and the goal of building and maintaining trust among clients, families and staff.
3   Peer Support—Other individuals who have experienced trauma can serve as key partners in recovery from trauma.
4   Collaboration and Mutuality—Partnering and leveling of power differences between staff and clients and among staff.
5   Empowerment, Voice and Choice—Individual strengths are recognized, built on, and validated and new skills are developed as needed.
6   Cultural, Historical, and Gender Issues—the organization incorporates policies, protocols, and processes that are responsive to the racial, ethnic and cultural needs of individuals served; there is a responsiveness to gender and consideration for historical trauma.

From SAMHSA's perspective, it is critical to promote the linkage to recovery and resilience for those individuals and families impacted by trauma. Consistent with SAMHSA's definition of recovery, services and supports that are trauma-informed build on the best evidence available and consumer and family engagement, empowerment, and collaboration. (US Department of Health and Human Services, n.d.)

Cultural Humility

Cultural competence, more recently referred to as cultural humility, is

> the ability to interact effectively with people of different cultures,
> helps to ensure the needs of all … are addressed. In practice,
> both individuals and organizations can be culturally competent.
> Culture must be considered [in every aspect of work and service
> provision]. Culture is a term that goes beyond just race or ethni-
> city. It can [include] age, gender, sexual orientation, disability,
> religion, income level, education, geographical location, or
> profession

as well as country of origin.

> Cultural competence means to be respectful and responsive to the
> health beliefs and practices—and cultural and linguistic needs—of
> diverse population groups. Developing cultural competence is also
> an evolving, dynamic process that takes time and occurs along a
> continuum.
>
> (SAMHSA, 2016b)

This ongoing need for education and awareness is why the term has
been shifting to cultural humility, demonstrating an emphasis on con-
tinual learning for professional service providers.

Competency indicates our personal and professional approach to our
work, our clients, and our own development, and an acknowledgement
that "we are always in the process of learning and growing."

Cultural humility is a tool "for understanding and developing a pro-
cess-oriented approach to competency; it is "other-oriented (or open to
the other) in relation to aspects of cultural identity that are most important to the [person]."

Three factors can guide cultural humility:

1. A lifelong commitment to self-evaluation and self-critique. We are
never done learning; therefore, we must be humble, flexible, and able to
look at ourselves critically in order to learn more. When we do not know
something, are we able to say that we do not know? Our willingness to
identify when we can learn more, and to act on this self-awareness, is
integral to cultural humility.

2. The recognition of the value of each person. A client is the expert on
his or her own life and experiences, and has understanding outside the
scope of the practitioner. Both professional and client must collaborate
and learn from each other.

3. Develop partnerships with people and groups who advocate for others. Though individuals can create positive change, communities and groups can also have a profound impact on systems. Cultural humility, by definition, is larger than our individual selves, and so it is important to advocate for it systemically.

(Adapted from APA, 2013)

Cultural humility is a lifelong process of self-reflection and self-critique whereby the individual not only learns about another's culture, but one starts with an examination of her/his own beliefs and cultural identities. This critical consciousness is more than just self-awareness, but requires one to step back to understand one's own assumptions, biases and values. Individuals must look at one's own background and social environment and how it has shaped experience. Cultural humility cannot be collapsed into a class or education offering; rather it's viewed as an ongoing process. Tervalon and Murray-Garcia state that cultural humility is "best defined not as a discrete end point but as a commitment and active engagement in a lifelong process that individuals enter into on an ongoing basis with patients, communities, colleagues, and with themselves." This process recognizes the dynamic nature of culture since cultural influences change over time and vary depending on location.

(Yeager and Bauer-Wu, 2013)

Culturally Competent Services and Cultural Humility

Cultural competence and humility cannot be overemphasized. This includes understanding where a victim comes from, so that all professionals who interact with a victim understand the victim's cultural and other history appropriately. For example, in labor trafficking in the US, many foreign-born victims have very low educational attainment, to the extent that they may not be literate even in own language. Victims may have had very limited experience with formal systems, including attorneys, law enforcement, and anyone employed by a government agency. To give other examples, victims may not understand how to apply for job, or make police report, or even how to read a bus schedule. Victims may not have any skills for navigating even basic systems. Victims, especially once they are identified formally as a human trafficking victim, have many different services available to support them, but often the professionals working with victims do not understand each victim's ability to do basic things. Put differently, the level of support that victims may require to navigate systems and access supports that could be essential to their recovery, as well as to their participation in prosecutions and other legal proceedings for relief. This support can help victims to not fall back into the hands of traffickers.

Cultural competence and cultural humility is important, whether with rural or urban US citizen youth victims, LGBTQIA+ victims, or victims from outside the US. For example, victims from Central and South America come from very specific places, and understanding where they are coming from is crucial to providing appropriate and effective services. Professionals working with trafficking victims need to be able to understand what victims do *not* say, as well as what they say to professionals that they are working with; this includes understanding victims' expectations that professionals may already know certain things about a victim's background and country context. In cases that involve a trafficker using coercion to control a victim, the trafficker often uses a complex web of different techniques and strategies to coerce a victim to stay in a trafficking situation. Often those techniques and strategies are powerful because of the place the victim is coming from; for a victim fleeing gang violence or civil war in El Salvador, it can be tremendously powerful to threaten to not bring the person back next year or to have a person deported back to that very dangerous situation in their country of origin. Or, a victim may come from a violent and abusive home, and although a trafficker is exploiting them, a victim may feel safer and better cared for with the trafficker than in their previous situation, whether it was in the US or abroad. Therefore, if anyone working with a victim does not understand the victim's safety concerns about "home," it is then very hard to understand why "home" may be a dangerous threat. This can be compounded if the victim is present with their family, preparing to bring their family to join them, or if there is a threat to stop plans to bring the victim's family; it could also devastate a victim's extended family to stop the modest economic support a victim may have been sending home.

Cultural Competence Includes Linguistically Appropriate Services

In working with victims who speak limited English or do not speak English, it is often difficult to find therapists who provide linguistically appropriate services. While it is tremendously beneficial for victims to receive therapeutic services in the victim's own language, it can be very hard to find therapists who can provide non-English language services and work with victims in their own language. Although the next option is to work with a professional interpreter, this is both often cost prohibitive, and also less effective for the victim to have to work through an interpreter. Linguistically competent mental health services are helpful not only for the victim's own healing, but this in turn helps the victim to be more stable and therefore be better able to work with their attorney in prosecuting the victim's case and defending their legal rights, as well as working with law enforcement when that is needed.

Cultural Competence, Cultural Humility, and Human Trafficking

The dynamics of trafficking are rarely simple. Victims may be receiving pay, but not paid what was promised, or even the minimum wage. Traffickers may charge victims for clothes, medicine, housing, fines incurred in the course of doing what the trafficker demands, and other expenses so that instead of income, they have a growing debt with the trafficker. For labor trafficking victims, many foreign-born workers have an employment visa that is tied to a single employer. A worker may want to leave a job for many reasons: because the wages are not as promised, because of sexual harassment or physical violence by a supervisor or owner, because the workers are threatened with deportation for demanding their wages or basic safety provisions, or many other reasons that would create a hostile work environment. Professionals working with victims need to be able to learn the facts and circumstances of each individual victim's experience.

Complexity of Victim Experiences

Victims of trafficking, including both labor trafficking and sex trafficking, have often been subjected to physical and sexual trauma, and may have been economically exploited in different ways over time. As Wharton notes, victims subjected to "forced sex or forced labor, whether they are male or female ... often suffer sexual abuse."[2] In addition, a trafficking victim may have been "promoted" to assisting traffickers, which can create additional psychological trauma due to a victim harming their former peers, while also creating an opportunity for better conditions and treatment by traffickers and potentially exposing the victim to being charged with trafficking crimes. Some labor trafficking victims may only want back wages, while other victims may need complex care and intensive, ongoing psycho-social support over a short or extended period of time. Factors include the length of time of the trafficking experience, the safety risks based on the trafficker's connections to the victim's home community and family, physical and psychological trauma, a victim's prior trauma experiences, and the victim's resilience. Other factors, including prior abuse, gender, economic and social class, culture, and education can also impact victim resiliency and rehabilitative needs.

Addressing Complex Trauma

It is extremely important for any professional working with human trafficking victims to understand that many victims have experienced poly-victimization, meaning that they have suffered different kinds of often extensive victimization prior to their trafficking experience. In addition, many victims often will not reveal prior victimization, which can range from severe domestic violence or childhood sexual abuse to gang warfare, political instability that threatens their personal safety, or other traumatizing experiences. Trafficking victims may also have experienced trauma during their migration to the US, for example lack of access to food, water, and medical care during a prolonged smuggling experience, sexual violence to themselves or travel companions, torture, or death of travel companions during their smuggling experience. However, it is crucial to help them address these complex traumas in order to have a successful relationship in therapy and with other providers, including non-clinical professionals such as attorneys and law enforcement. Indeed, many victims are vulnerable to trafficking because of the past victimization they have suffered, especially in cases where a person survived child abuse, severe domestic violence, and trauma during their migration to the US. In addition, the trauma that a victim experienced prior to their trafficking experience is often more traumatic than the trauma they experienced in their trafficking situation. Often the trafficking trauma is not worst trauma that a person may have experienced, especially for labor trafficking victims. This can lead to confusion when professionals are focused on the trafficking trauma, but the underlying trauma is more important or was more severe to victim. The trafficking trauma definitely compounds any other traumas, though, and all professionals working with trafficking victims need to address all of the different traumas that a victim may have experienced in order for the victim to have a more complete recovery experience.

Flexibility

The more flexible that clinical professionals can be, the more successful their outcomes for trafficking victims and with non-clinical professionals. This can include flexibility on when and where to meet victims. For example, victims in rural areas who have left a trafficking situation but are in a low-wage, long-hour job do not have time to come in to offices during business hours to meet with professional service providers. Meeting with victims on Saturdays and evenings may not be ideal for the professional, but legal and law enforcement has had great success with that level of flexibility regarding when and where to meet with victims at times and places convenient to the victims, in scattered private locations such as a private room in a public library, or another service provider's space. While it means going above and beyond, this flexibility translates clearly to much better outcomes for victims. And because it is so good for victims, it means good outcomes for legal providers as well—which means improved legal outcomes for victims.

The Value of Collaborative Multidisciplinary Teams

From the perspective of non-clinical professionals, such as law enforcement and attorneys, everything that clinical professionals provide to victims of human trafficking is deeply helpful. Victims have multiple needs, but only some needs are legal and trying to address non-legal needs has a bigger impact for trafficking victims or clients than other legal aid clients who are in poverty and have legal needs. It is incredibly helpful to have social service and other professional care providers to assist trafficking victims with housing, medical care, and psycho-social services. When an attorney or investigating officer can refer a victim to a social worker and know that the victim will be in good hands, then the legal professional can focus on building the victim's case. For example, working with a very culturally competent therapist can enable legal professionals to provide their best legal services and move a case forward for resolution for the victims, whether that is an immigration law case or a case for criminal or civil remedies. When there are excellent, sensitive, competent services from clinical professionals, legal cases move more smoothly and victims are more willing to move forward with legal cases which in turn helps victims to get relief and to stop traffickers. This also reduces re-victimization in legal proceedings. Trafficking survivors have so many different needs, that their legal needs may fall lower on the hierarchy of their needs; but if they have strong support to address these more pressing needs, such as housing and food, then that frees up time and mental space for survivors to think about their legal case. When clinical professionals do their job well, then non-clinical services, including legal services work, go well for victims in terms of seeking legal justice.

Risks of Poor Collaboration and Poor Cultural Humility

In counterpoint to the good practices and success factors described above, non-clinical professionals like attorneys and law enforcement have faced problems with victims when clinical professionals do not understand the complexity of human trafficking, do not understand other factors in a victim's background, do not value the importance of linguistically appropriate services where they are indicated, and are not flexible in meeting victims where they are at to the greatest extent possible. This can be disheartening, but with increasing education, including resources such as this book, we can be hopeful that this will become the rare exception.

What Makes Excellent Clinician Work

For clinicians to do their job well in working with non-clinical professionals to assist human trafficking victims, they need to be open to collaboration and to having relationships with other providers. They need to understand that there may be confidentiality issues, such as attorney–client privilege, in addition to therapist–client privilege, but that they may have information helpful to other providers that can be shared with appropriate written consent. It is helpful, even at times necessary, to communicate and coordinate care and services.

Conclusion

While there are many elements to good victim services, and these elements can vary from victim to victim and over time, this chapter has laid out several objectives for consideration. Some include life-long learning about each victim, and about different cultures, communities, and countries. However, intentional and strategic efforts can make the difference between having a victim go back to a trafficking situation or on to another adverse situation, and helping a victim heal, move on, and live a healthy and more meaningful life.

Notes

1 Bjelland, Heidi F. (2016). *Identifying Human Trafficking in Norway: A Register-Based Study of Cases, Outcomes and Police Practices.* Sage Publications, Thousand Oaks, CA.
2 Rebecca L. Wharton (2009–2010). *A New Paradigm for Human Trafficking: Shifting the Focus from Prostitution to Exploitation in the Trafficking Victims Protection Act.* 16 WM. & MARY J. WOMEN & L. 753, 755. Marshall-Wythe School of Law; College of William and Mary. School of Law, Williamsburg, VA.

References

APA. (2013). CYF News: Reflections on cultural humility. August. American Psychological Association. Retrieved from http://www.apa.org/pi/families/resour ces/newsletter/2013/08/cultural-humility.aspx

SAMHSA. (2016a). Behind the Term: Trauma. Substance Abuse and Mental Health Services Administration. Retrieved from https://www.nrepp.samhsa.gov/Docs/ Literatures/Behind_the_Term_Trauma.pdf

SAMHSA. (2016b). Cultural Competence. Substance Abuse and Mental Health Services Administration. Retrieved from https://www.samhsa.gov/section-223/ cultural-competency

Tervalon, M., and Murray-Garcia, J. (1998). Cultural humility versus cultural competence: a critical distinction in defining physician training outcomes in multicultural education. *Journal of Health Care for the Poor and Underserved*, 9(2), 117–125.

US Department of Health and Human Services. (n.d.). Resource guide to trauma-informed human services. Administration for Children & Families. Retrieved from https://www.acf.hhs.gov/trauma-toolkit#chapter-6

Yeager, Katherine A. and Bauer-Wu, Susan (2013). Cultural humility: essential foundation for clinical researchers. *Applied Nursing Research*, 26(4), 251–256.

11 Comprehensive Coordination of Multi-Agency Coalitions

AnnJanette Alejano-Steele, Amanda Finger and Mary Landerholm

Service coordination for the trafficking survivor through a multi-agency initiative is essential. This chapter will describe survivor needs and how to build a strong community coalition for survivor support.

Thus far, this book has featured theoretical and practical approaches to provide behavioral health support to survivors of human trafficking. These key psychological resources are nested amongst an array of survivor needs, among them basic needs for safety, transportation, food, clothing, translation services, legal advocacy, education and job readiness. Survivor needs are met within a community context, and the degree of coordination within and across anti-trafficking initiatives is paramount. These multi-agency initiatives are referred to as collaboratives, coalitions and task forces; catalyzed by grant funding, government priorities, and community will. When coordination fails, survivors encounter numerous and sometimes insurmountable obstacles to accessing the care, treatment and services necessary to begin reclaiming their lives (Clawson and Dutch, 2007; Iman et al., 2009; Pierce, 2009; Raymond and Hughes, 2001; Ugarte et al., 2003). As communities gain understanding of the complexities of this crime, they do their best to cobble together available resources to support survivors and prosecute perpetrators. Scattered community efforts may result, where traffickers go unpunished, creating system-response cracks through which survivors fall.

Community partnerships bring together diverse experiences, amplifying messages and leveraging resources. Drawing from empirical evidence gathered by the Colorado Project to Comprehensively Combat Human Trafficking (End Slavery Now, n.d.), this chapter provides a range of considerations and tools for strong trauma-informed community coalitions designed to support survivors. The Colorado Project uses the Social Ecology model to illustrate the location of trauma practitioners within the larger network of Colorado service providers. This community-based research illuminates the strengths and gaps of community response.

Colorado Community Resource Scan Using the Social Ecology Model

Background

While human trafficking is a global tragedy, it is crucial to understand its local country impacts. In the United States, state, and community-level examinations help to gain perspectives on the nature of the crime and its relevance to comprehensive services. Social Ecology models (Bronfenbrenner, 1979; Centers for Disease Control and Prevention, 2014; Alpert et al., 2014) help to frame how community-level initiatives support or hinder survivor access to trauma-informed resources and support. When examining human trafficking specifically, this model constructs a deeper understanding of the interplay between complex variables at the individual, interpersonal, community, organizational, and policy/environmental levels. Drawing out the levels of analysis surrounding trafficking survivors, each is an individual with lived experiences that have shaped her/his knowledge, attitudes, beliefs. However, these experiences (both positive and negative) are often gained relationally with others such as family, friends, and work colleagues. These relationships develop in community—home neighborhoods and workplaces: this also includes community institutions (e.g., local businesses, governmental and non-governmental agencies, religious organizations, etc.). Understanding the intricate relationships between these levels and how these systems perpetuate or eradicate human trafficking is vital.

Colorado's response to human trafficking is one of 50 state initiatives benefiting from policies at the macro level of social ecology analysis. International and US (federal) policies regarding human trafficking also continue to impact and shape state-level response to the issue. At the global level, in 2000, the United Nations ratified the Protocol to Prevent, Suppress and Punish Trafficking in Persons, Especially Women and Children, referred to as the Palermo Protocol. As a signatory to the Palermo Protocol, the United States is obliged to establish legislation and policy that aligns with the Protocol's suggestions. This year also marked the passage of the Trafficking Victims Protection Act (2000) and its subsequent reauthorizations in the United States.

Effect on Community Systems

With respect to the burgeoning national anti-trafficking movement, community systems find themselves in the middle of governmental and grassroots initiatives. Whereas many social movements have historically been rooted in grassroots, community-based organizing, the national anti-trafficking movement was catalyzed by human trafficking defined as a transnational organized crime. Systems-level advocates shaped the Federal Trafficking Victims Protection Act in 2000; and the US Department of Justice (and its Office for Victims of Crime) organized systematic nationwide disbursements of task force funding for cities around the US to prioritize the development and coordination of a response to human trafficking. Like other states, Colorado's initial efforts to understand the crime began with coordination of victim services: most were initially funded by the US Department of Justice Office for Victims of Crime in the early to mid-2000s.

Further, this federal justice funding prioritized training of law enforcement agencies, funding for foreign national victims of trafficking or child victims of trafficking, or outreach to specific "at-risk" populations. Many states like Colorado were able to incorporate these priorities into a more comprehensive response. They developed protocols to serve survivors of all forms of human trafficking. The funding mandated one task force to prioritize a law enforcement response and one task force to focus upon direct victim services *with the added requirement that these efforts partner.* This partnership element thus pulled together a variety of sectors that had not necessarily collaborated on any prior issues – federal, state and local law enforcement entities sat across from community organizers, with faith-based providers (federal funding recipients) most typically facilitating the discussions.

Although any support for response is beneficial, in Colorado, funding fluctuates, creating uneven flows of federal funding to initiate and sustain human trafficking responses. Government funding to Colorado has both prioritized and professionalized responses to human trafficking, namely in the areas of law enforcement and service provider response. As a negative result, this professionalizing of response has provided few spaces to hold community voices and perspectives at the grassroots level. One key national trend has been the prioritization of domestic minor sex trafficking, which although very important, excludes other identities and experiences of violation and exploitation. Because resources have been directed to support the FBI-led Innocence Lost Task Force focus upon domestic minor sex trafficking, other forms of human trafficking have been missed.

Since these federally prioritized efforts in the mid-2000s, many non-governmental groups have been added to form service provider, law enforcement, and advocacy coalitions; and many longer-established stakeholders have taken note of new groups emerging to address human trafficking. Established agencies in the field have concerns about these coalitions surrounding trust, duplicated efforts, and inclusion. They see that these coalitions can make partnership between established and newly formed agencies challenging. For agencies joining taskforces, law enforcement-led task forces may have restricted membership; so that not all actively include service providers and community members advocating for public awareness. While ideal partnerships may be designed to promote transparency and an "all-hands-on-deck" approach, the confidential and legal nature of investigative work may prohibit that approach.

Colorado Vulnerabilities to Human Trafficking

In Colorado, adults and children, foreign-nationals and US citizens, men and women, have all been identified as victims: all share vulnerability to exploitation and violence. Community vulnerability to human trafficking in Colorado involves force, fraud, and/or coercion of individuals into illegal activities such as panhandling, drug dealing, and commercial sex work. The crime also occurs in the context of legal workplace locations, such as construction sites, restaurants, hotels, schools, or private homes. Trafficking cases have been documented in 20 distinct industries across the United States (including but not limited to agriculture, hospitality construction, domestic service) (Colorado Human Trafficking Council, 2016); and human trafficking victims/ survivors do not conform to a single demographic category (APA, 2014). Often dominant narratives of survivor experiences often end when survivors are able to leave their exploitive experiences However, community responses need to recognize that there are additional elements that create precarious conditions to push or pull survivors into different outcomes, *especially if their home community is where the trafficking occurred*. This concept is called community precarity—conditions that create (and maintain) vulnerability to violence and exploitation (Butler, 2009).

Colorado Community-Level Precarity

Precarity creates risk for human trafficking to occur. Cracks in the infrastructure of a community's economic, social, and political spheres will directly sway how basic needs are met for these populations within their communities. For example, gentrification of poor communities may lead to individual vulnerability to trafficking as individuals make forced choices to secure safe and affordable housing. Gentrification here is illustrated as a *push factor* that forces community members to seek alternative ways to supplement income, perhaps tolerating unsafe working conditions, resorting to quick cash tactics, and/or increasing their vulnerability to unregulated markets.

Given the general lack of awareness of human trafficking across the United States, this crime may not be the most pressing issue that a community faces at a given point in time. If a community denies that human trafficking occurs or is not prepared to support survivors, human trafficking will go undetected. Survivors will not feel safe or supported to come forward.

Historically, governmental and other institutions have perpetuated politically induced conditions whereby vulnerable communities suffer from failing social/economic networks for support, which in turn exposes these individuals to injury, violence, or death (Butler, 2009). Communities that work together to identify and examine the conditions that create exploitive situations (e.g., poverty, violence) have the opportunity to develop robust, comprehensive responses to human trafficking. Such communities can look beyond the myth that human trafficking is only an "end event" (e.g., a crime that occurred, or the trauma one endured). Community resources can begin to come together to understand human trafficking as a process, complex trauma, or accumulation of vulnerabilities over a survivor's lifetime (Mechanic and Tanner, 2007).

Resourcing Colorado

Across the United States, as well as in Colorado, many non-systems and systems actors (such as governmental agencies) have been grappling with ways to address human trafficking (Foot, 2016). It is simultaneously exciting and daunting to organize around a complex topic relating to violence, whether framed as a crime or human rights violation. Many stakeholders have been addressing related crimes; for example, child abuse, wage/ labor violations, homelessness; but over time have been asked to add human trafficking to their purview of services or advocacy. As a result, early efforts to organize communities around human trafficking have appeared fragmented; many agencies and issue-specific coalitions have evolved to widen their focus on vulnerability to violence and exploitation. Many communities have learned that human trafficking is a *distinct* crime requiring tailored responses that take into account survivor status, age, form, degree of complex trauma and trauma severity. Such responses demand specific protocols distinctly different from other types of crimes. In addition, community-level response to human trafficking varies widely across the country, and priorities and scope of response may narrowly frame the issue (e.g., sex trafficking as the pimping of teenage girls) (Cojocaru, 2015). As a result, many survivors (particularly men and transgender individuals) may not be served appropriately or be denied access to services.

In Colorado (as well as nationally), awareness of the crime has increased since 2005, due in part to an infusion of federal funding, improved comprehensive human trafficking legislation (i.e., House Bill 14–1273), and efforts to educate the public. In recent years, collaborative service and prosecutorial efforts have formed through the Colorado Department of Human Services, the Front Range Anti-trafficking Coalition, the FBI-led Innocence Lost Task Force, the Colorado Trafficking and Organized Crime Coalition, among others. The creation of the statewide Colorado Human Trafficking Council in 2014 is one of the few legislatively mandated coalitions endeavoring to coordinate the multiple sectors needed to address the complexities of this crime.

Statewide Coalition Development: Service Referrals

The delivery of services to trafficking victims necessitates case-by-case attention requiring coordinated efforts from several organizations. These services include a combination of needs encompassing: immigration resources; legal and criminal defense; counseling for trauma and other mental abuses; resources for health (including physical trauma and sexually transmitted diseases); and protection from violence. Indeed, attention has been placed on the immediate moments of freedom gained by survivors, much of it dependent upon the trust built with victim advocates so that they can freely share their experiences of force, fraud and coercion. There are distinct stages of action and assistance that are required, including discovery/ identification, immediate needs assessment, working with local area victim services networks, and planning for long-term resources (APA, 2014).

One example of a local area network is the Colorado Network to End Human Trafficking (CoNEHT), a statewide resource and referral network accessible by a statewide hotline. Hotline advocates often fill the role of first responders. The impact of trauma can strongly influence how survivors interact with advocates as first responders (Clawson et al., 2008), where trust and rapport must be established quickly to assess a range of immediate needs. However, collaboration between service providers requires more than the creation of a resource directory; it requires a careful assembly of a partnership with the goal of a comprehensive community response. Communities must go beyond providing basic *protection* to those who are identified, and *prosecuting* their traffickers. States must take a holistic approach to also *prevent* this crime from occurring, and *partner* effectively by leveraging resources and including key survivor and community-level voices at the table; these are the "4Ps" of comprehensive response that complement and inform one another to provide efficient responses and trauma-informed services (LCHT, 2013a). Furthermore, anti-trafficking community initiatives can (and should) vary tremendously, from one geographical area of a state to another, building upon already-existing strengths of the community. In several cases, community strengths may be catalyzed by strong leaders who can steer community will to address this crime. Anti-trafficking community leaders persevere like no other. As noted by Foot,

> whether as an assigned part of their job or via their own initiative, whether paid or as a volunteer, (community leaders) engage with the issue on multiple levels. All are touched by the cruelty of the crime and by the resilience some survivors demonstrate ... Many citizens who volunteer in anti-trafficking efforts ... bring various kinds of professional expertise to their volunteer efforts, and catalyze anti-slavery initiatives in their industry. They all wish their work was unnecessary and yet they keep going.
>
> (Foot, 2016, p. 153)

Steadfast community leaders have the power to determine where human trafficking is prioritized in the community; they do their best with the tools available and they engage others to follow their passion, which is honorable. However, in many instances, community leaders and coalition members proceeded on hunches and best guesses, and like many states, Colorado did the best it could with the fluctuating resources it possessed. It was here that researchers and practitioners alike called for data to support or refute their efforts; this was the impetus for the Colorado Project to Comprehensively Combat Human Trafficking (The Colorado Project).

Community-Based Research as Catalyst for Change

Although lagging behind services and law enforcement response, research is recognized in the quest to understand the nature of human trafficking and efforts to respond (APA, 2014). Sustainable social change to support human trafficking survivors begins with the design of community-based social justice research. Community-based research integrates research and action attentive to the values of: individual and family wellness; sense of community; respect for human diversity; social justice; citizen participation; collaboration and community strengths; and empirical grounding (Dalton et al., 2007). Further, social justice frameworks enable researchers to identify how systems of power and oppression fuel the trafficking of persons, and how intersectional identities (e.g., gender, race, class, sexual orientation, religion) create vulnerability within communities. With these questions and reflections on community in mind, LCHT began to shape the Colorado Project in 2010.

Community-Based Research Methodology: The Colorado Project

In 2010, the Colorado Project to Comprehensively Combat Human Trafficking (The Colorado Project), a three-year collaborative initiative that aimed to answer the question, *What it would take to end human trafficking in Colorado?* The project's goal was to gain a better understanding of the key strengths and gaps in response to human trafficking.

The Colorado Project was a comprehensive, interdisciplinary research project to better understand the efforts essential to combating human trafficking, and within those efforts, assessed promising practices that individuals and agencies were using to bring an end to human trafficking in the United States. Additionally, the project assessed ongoing anti-trafficking efforts in the State of Colorado under the umbrella of prevention, protection, prosecution, and partnerships (4Ps) to understand how Colorado addresses human trafficking.

Also in 2010, the national anti-trafficking field marked the 10th anniversary of the passage of the Trafficking Victims Protection Act (TVPA). Spanning the time between the Clinton and Obama administrations, there was a shift in national awareness of human trafficking as an international, organized crime to one that included domestic youth and the role of demand and economic exploitation. Marking ten years allowed for reflection of the accomplishments gained over the years and the work still needed. It also marked how quickly tools and programs could change as knowledge about human trafficking advanced. Hence, the Colorado Project captured a baseline snapshot of national and state-wide anti-trafficking efforts during 2011 and 2012. The project utilized a social ecology systems theory approach, centralizing survivor experience within a series of systems including family, community and institutions. Further, the project acknowledged the social, historical, cultural contexts that influenced Colorado anti-trafficking efforts.

More than 40 people participated in the core goals of the project, organized into three working groups—a Project Team, as well as National and State Advisory Boards. Each team operated from a survivor-centered frame of reference and shared interdisciplinary collaborative space where community stakeholders could learn from one another's disciplines equally. The core Project Team was comprised of fourteen people representing psychology, women's studies, political science, international studies, social work, criminal justice—survivors, practitioners, and researchers who carried out project work plans. The National Advisory Board held space for dialogue between leading nationally-recognized practitioners and researchers from each of the 4Ps to create the template of promising practices and the survey (see Fig. 1.1 for the template of promising practices).

During the Project's early phases, the interdisciplinary Project Team and National Advisory board developed promising practices for prevention, protection, prosecution, and partnerships, with these "acknowledgments": 1) the field's need for evidence-based practice beyond the wealth of anecdotal practitioner experience; 2) recognizing what may be "best" practice for one community may not apply to other communities; and 3) adoption of "promising practice" terminology to signify emerging and evolving community response efforts in an ever-evolving movement; in fact, practices must be tailored to community characteristics and strengths.

The Project's initial draft definitions were shaped by five global and federal protocols and legislation[1] and with these policies, the National Advisory Board refined the initial drafting of the 4P definitions. Their collective wisdom led the way toward a more comprehensive understanding of human trafficking and the ways in which the Colorado Project's research would be framed. **Prevention** plans aim to prevent human trafficking by addressing the root causes of oppression that create communities vulnerable to trafficking (e.g., poverty, racial discrimination, gender inequity). Prevention efforts address a community's systemic vulnerabilities, and include awareness campaigns, advocacy, and education. **Protection** measures ensure that victims of human trafficking are able to access mental, physical, social, educational, and legal assistance. Importantly, such services must be provided in a trauma-informed, culturally appropriate manner that promotes survivors' well-being. **Prosecution** measures ensure the development and implementation of laws that address the continuum of labor exploitation and the pursuit of criminal punishments for such cases. It is important that human trafficking is viewed as a criminal form of exploitation, rather than simply the recruitment or transportation of workers or people in prostitution. All forms of the legal and criminal system are included, from legislation through criminal prosecution. Finally, **partnership** requires that a comprehensive community response is used to combat human trafficking. By involving cooperation and collaboration among multiple sectors, the goal is to capitalize on diverse experiences and competencies, amplify messages, and leverage resources.

Most research conducted prior to 2010 focused upon efforts within each "P" (e.g., Barrett, 2010; Clawson and Dutch, 2008; Farrell et al., 2008; Foot and Vanek, 2012; Hames et al., 2010; O'Connell et al., 2009). Yet, very few anti-trafficking efforts are developed or implemented based on a *comprehensive* 4P framework (APA, 2014; LCHT, 2013a). As evidenced by the recent National Institute of Justice solicitations requiring collaboration, the field has begun to gather evidence on the effectiveness of coordination of prosecution-protection efforts. Clawson et al.'s (2009) study of US Department of Health and Human Services programs serving human trafficking victims found that collaboration—rather than providing isolated services—among agencies is critical for survivors to access care across agencies. Furthermore, the needs of survivors are complex and vary greatly from short-term emergency services to longer-term assistance requiring months or years of care.

The Colorado Project began with a comprehensive and systematic literature review on promising practices within each of the 4P framework components. Based on the literature review and an iterative development process with an 11-member National Advisory Board, the research team developed a survey to assess the degree to which communities were implementing best practices within the 4P framework. See the Appendix and Table 1.1 for the Project Team and National Advisory Board's list of protection-specific promising practices.

This comprehensive template of components was designed to establish a baseline measurement of community resources that serve survivors of human trafficking and to catalyze a deeper understanding of resource strengths and gaps. First, understanding what is present opens the door for evaluation of these efforts and the way in which they coordinate with one another to serve human trafficking survivors. Second, understanding what is absent lays groundwork to draw community partners together for dialogue and discussion of how to fill these gaps, how to proceed with respect to vulnerable populations, and how to proceed mindfully without creating unintended consequences for other movements (e.g., policy ramifications for workers' rights). With the support of this comprehensive template, communities can begin to comprehensively prioritize action steps for more efficient use of resources, coordinated and streamlined efforts, and ultimately to better assist victims and survivors of human trafficking.

National data collection followed, to test the robustness of these promising practices, as a step toward Colorado data collection. During the next Colorado phase, the project was further guided by a Statewide Advisory Board comprised of leaders from parallel movements. This board represented movements with histories focused on exploitation and violence that preceded anti-trafficking efforts—grassroots and systems leaders representing interpersonal violence, child welfare, labor rights, immigrant rights, refugee and asylee rights, and homeless advocates and coalitions. This interdisciplinary, multi-sector initiative became one of the hallmarks of how LCHT conducts its work: holding collaborative exchanges and dialogues in coordinated and comprehensive ways. For the purpose of this chapter, focus group data will be highlighted to illustrate precarious community contexts in which service provider networks may be situated.

Sample Focus Group Results: Illustrating Colorado Precarity

As noted earlier, communities across the United States have built and refined social structures (e.g., economic, political, legal, religious, cultural, etc.) to address human trafficking; efforts have ranged tremendously, many relying on funding and community will. Understanding the concept of community precarity further allows practitioners to better understand the context that surrounds individuals served as well as community factors and accompanying resources that can support or worsen progress and recovery. Precarity creates conditions with unequal access to resources, power, education, health care and legal standing (Farmer, 1999, 2004; Galtung, 1969). In more severe cases of community precarity (also termed "structural violence"), these conditions increase vulnerability to human trafficking, or curtail or deny community access to resources.

Social ecology analyses allow for focus upon individuals and the community systems and conditions that surround them. Focus group data from ten diverse Colorado communities articulated risk for individuals and precarious community response efforts that may hinder survivors. Minding community precarity helps practitioners who work with individuals to understand the challenges for access to services and the conditions that can pull people back into exploitive situations. Community precarity further poses more difficult questions of which survivors are worthy of services and whose cases are worthy of investigation. Which vulnerable groups (e.g., unhoused populations, sex workers, etc) might be framed as "problematic" or "unworthy?"

Examples of Colorado root causes that "push" community members to leave or "pull" them to the state include job scarcity, housing shortages, poor living wages, anti-immigrant sentiment, or lack of adequate education or health care/social programs. One focus group member in rural CO noted,

> Number one, is poverty. We're a poor (region). I mean that's just how it is. And if (people) see opportunity, (they) will take it whether it puts them in danger or not. Really, we're pretty isolated out here...and that makes it a lot easier (to traffic people) as well...Community members are targeted for those kinds of traps.

Focus group participants articulated identification challenges repeatedly:

Human trafficking is definitely happening all over the country, but being in a rural area, even if we haven't seen human trafficking... we know something's happening, but we don't know how to really identify it, if we don't know who to go to and what, you know, our people gonna write it off as a, an assault instead of what it truly is.

Given the small networks within the Colorado anti-trafficking movement, communities are identified as urban or rural. Colorado's 64 counties are divided into 17 urban, 24 rural and 23 frontier counties (Colorado Rural Health Center, 2018). The range of challenges begin with identification of what human trafficking entails, and include direct quotes from focus group participants.

Urban Community 1: Human trafficking cases are sometimes recognized as cases other than those involving trafficking and identified as prostitution. Generally, there is a lack of understanding in the community to recognize human trafficking. "People don't understand consequences, social services and community groups don't understand human trafficking."

Urban Community 2: Referrals are made to designated task forces, the Innocence Lost Task Force and Colorado Trafficking and Organized Crime Coalition. "It is also difficult to distinguish between individuals who are acting out of choice and those who are victims of trafficking."

Rural Community 1: Human trafficking cases are usually recognized as cases other than those involving trafficking and identified as sexual assault, domestic violence, physical violence, U-Visa, and T-Visa cases. Broadly, "it is unknown how cases are being handled."

Rural Community 2: Human trafficking cases are under-identified and tracking is difficult to achieve. "There exists poor communication between areas, a lack of protocols, and lack of understanding in the community to recognize human trafficking."

Focus group discussions revealed unique community factors, their abilities to manage cases, and what gaps remain:

Urban Community 1: has resources including the FBI, police, the Colorado hotline, organizations and non-profits, medical facilities, churches, chambers of commerce, and counselors. The community struggles with the lack of informal or formal protocols, limited awareness of the population, and failure of service providers to coordinate. **Community factors** include poverty, homelessness, discrimination against LGBT groups, as well as supply and demand for sex. There are large military and immigrant populations in the region. **These factors could be better addressed by** increasing awareness through presentations, outreach, and social media. We "need to engage non-profits and increase the ability to identify trafficked individuals," and secure funding for education, resources for runaways, mental health, and LGBT communities.

Urban Community 2: has multiple resources including organizations and non-profits, task forces, shelters. The community struggles with the fragmented state of resources, concerns of proselytizing by faith-based service agencies, and limited financial support for adult education. **Community factors** include poverty and discrimination against LGBT groups. The fact that there is a large immigration and refugee population adds to human trafficking. **These factors could be better addressed by** passing Colorado safe harbor laws, meeting the needs of victims (housing, therapy, etc.), survivor and protective services, and increasing funding to education. Barriers to these improvements include competition over resources.

Urban Community 3: has a few resources including legal, medical, DHS, and corporate service providers. The community struggles with language barriers, "the corporate sector being placed on a pedestal (not to be questioned), difficulty reaching and finding clients, as well as the guarded nature of victims" (e.g., the ability to lose their jobs if they come forward). There are no specific resources to address human trafficking and no coordinated law enforcement efforts dedicated to human trafficking. **Community factors** include supply and demand for sex "and the desire of community members to have cheap products." The fact that victims are isolated and lack familial support, possess language barriers, and have cultural difference (fear instilled by the cartels), add to human trafficking. **These factors could be better addressed by** increasing funding for services and resources, as well as outreach staff, increasing cooperation between service providers, building coalitions, unifying law enforcement responses, increasing buy-in from community leaders, as well as increasing awareness and outreach efforts. Barriers to these improvements include lack of cooperation on the part of victims, lack of resources, and limited funding.

Rural Community 1: has few resources address human trafficking given the fact that "There haven't been any cases. There are no coordinated efforts to address trafficking either, nor is the subject taken very seriously." There was mention, however, of a few small non-profits and community organizations. **Community factors** influencing human trafficking include poverty, lack of employment, and stigma of survivorship by the community itself. The fact that victims are undocumented, possess language and educational barriers, have cultural differences (patriarchal dynamics and control of the family), are isolated, and lack community support, add to human trafficking. **These factors could be better addressed by** increasing trust between asylum seekers and immigrants and service providers.

Rural Community 2: has several resources including non-profits and child protection teams and crisis response. The community struggles with lack of emergency housing, formal structures and coordination between service providers and counties, and there not being a regional advocacy center. **Community factors** include poverty and unemployment. The fact that "victims are undocumented, have access to limited resources, are isolated, possess language barriers," are untrusting of law enforcement, hired for seasonal work, young (unattended, runaways), increase risk for human trafficking. "Many victims are homeless, undocumented, ignored, minorities, possess language barriers, and are brought in for season work. Cold weather (cold), drugs, domestic violence, and gang presence contribute to the situation." Additional factors include gang activity, drugs, crime, higher cost of living, and transportation along interstate 70. **These factors could better be addressed by** identifying local contacts and service providers, increasing collaboration and partnerships, identifying leadership, increasing training for service providers and advocates, increasing the number of trained officers in law enforcements, as well as increasing public funding and awareness.

Having both focus group and survey data help to inform and guide community responses to human trafficking, by supporting data-informed discussions on strengths and gaps and how to move forward to best support survivors. The Colorado Project illustrates an approach and methodology that identifies community-level push and pull factors that make it possible to traffic people for labor and sex. Further, the Project revealed how this crime is understood/misidentified by community members, which further illustrates community or system-imposed vulnerabilities to human trafficking. The Project enables researchers to gain better understanding of the key components of a comprehensive community response to human trafficking, where services for survivors are but one component. Since 2010, this collaborative project has helped communities create comprehensive data-driven local responses.

Research into Action: The Colorado Action Plan

Embodying the principle of turning research into action. LCHT led efforts to develop the Colorado Action Plan. This plan assists in mapping the "social, cultural, economic, political, environmental, and international influences to promote positive change, health, and empowerment at individual and systemic levels" (Society for Community Research and Action, 2016). Colorado statewide data were analyzed by an interdisciplinary cross-issue State Advisory Board. The Board created a comprehensive list of statewide recommendations that evolved into the 2013 Colorado Action Plan, designed to guide and sustain community change efforts. The Action Plan is organized by the four key aspects of a comprehensive community-based response—prevention, protection, prosecution, and partnership. The Action Plan includes a total of 14 recommendations supported by 48 activities to improve community responses to human trafficking. Together, these activities operate to: 1) prioritize more efficient use of resources; and 2) coordinate and streamline efforts in order to improve survivor assistance (LCHT, 2014).

This multi-sector approach veers tremendously from other state-level plans dedicated to addressing human trafficking, typically generated by a field of experts appointed to a city- or regional-level working group. The 2013 Action Plan was the first comprehensive, statewide plan in the country driven by data and directly informed by a total of 350 project members and practitioners from a diverse array of communities around the state of Colorado.

Colorado Action Plan Recommendations

Prevention

1   Create strategic statewide human trafficking public awareness and prevention campaign(s) targeting populations that may be vulnerable to human trafficking.
2   Increase the probability of effective prevention efforts.
3   Encourage private sector participation in human trafficking prevention efforts such as through the monitoring of supply chains as well as adoption of existing private sector efforts (e.g., Luxor) (LCHT, 2013b).

Protection

1   Create a cultural shift among and between law enforcement and service providers in anti-human trafficking efforts.
2   Create a comprehensive and streamlined practice of working together across public and nonpublic agencies to address trafficking survivor service needs.
3   Increase education and networking among service providers throughout Colorado and across service areas of expertise to serve human trafficking survivors through increased membership in the CoNEHT statewide victim services network.
4   Form a statewide cohesive prosecutorial group (including law enforcement, prosecutors and judges) focusing on all forms of human trafficking (LCHT, 2013b).

Prosecution

1   Create shift in prosecutorial mindset to prioritize human trafficking with the support of public awareness initiatives and successful prosecutions throughout the state.
2   Develop system-wide protocols to increase victim-centered and evidence-based cases.
3   Consult "model" legislation and legislative efforts in other states.
4   Provide opportunities for collective learning, support, and action by encouraging leaders from community- based efforts to join existing statewide coalitions (e.g., CoNEHT) (LCHT, 2013b).

Partnership

1   Cultivate awareness and concern for the issue of human trafficking in communities across the state.
2   Encourage the development and/or growth of locally organized response groups (i.e., task forces, coalitions, alliances).

3   Encourage collaborative anti-trafficking and allied efforts at both the local and state levels to set processes for communication and conflict management that cultivate a culture of openness.

The Colorado Action Plan's strategy aligns activities as part of a larger theory of change that seeks to improve the Colorado anti-trafficking movement. The plan enables community efforts to organize cross-sector groups of partners to transform inefficient, fragmented systems, particularly in areas of service provision (protection). Since 2013, the Colorado Action Plan now includes a statewide monitoring database named the Colorado Anti-trafficking Exchange and evaluation strategy for the recommendations and activities. The exchange also includes a mechanism for public and private dissemination of Action Plan accomplishments and information exchange, including ongoing recommendations to improve on statewide policies and anti-human trafficking legislation.

2018 brings about the five-year mark to release Colorado Project 2.0, enabling Colorado to comprehensively see accomplishments and advancements in the anti-trafficking field since 2013, thus setting into motion periodic updates and measurable improvements over the course of the statewide movement. Several states have considered replication of their own state projects; replication efforts are underway in the state of Connecticut. With the help of Colorado Project methodologies, community coalitions are able to draw from project lessons learned and promising practices identified by Partnership data. The following section provides suggestions for building mindful community coalitions (LCHT, 2013b).

Lessons Learned: Building Community Coalitions

Of the various resources available on the strengths and challenges inherent in anti-human trafficking coalitions, the work of Dr. Kirsten Foot, drawing from her field of Communication, is unparalleled. Her 2016 book, *Collaborating against Human Trafficking*, is a necessary resource reviewing the dilemmas, power factors, leadership, identities, and values factored in the ways collaborations address this human rights issue. With an eye toward community-level analysis and suggestions for practitioners entering into coalitions, the following recommendations draw primarily from the Colorado Project.

1. Centralize Survivor Voices and Leadership to Inform Service Provision

Historically, survivor inclusion in the anti-trafficking movement has been in the realm of detailed storytelling with little room for elaboration on other life experiences beyond the trauma. This "victim" role marginalizes survivors into a binary representation of survivor/ non-survivor, while fostering the illusion that the experience of the crime is the only contribution a survivor has to offer (Foot, 2015). In 2016, the US Department of Justice Office for Victims of Crime (OVC) held their second annual Survivor Forum to establish the inclusion of survivor voice in policy recommendations, enabling survivors to directly guide national initiatives to combat the crime (USACHT, 2016). These groundbreaking survivor forums hold space to move beyond past assumptions that "informal" survivor input is deemed "less" legitimate due largely to lack of professional credentials (e.g., non-degree holders) (Foot, 2016). Inclusion at the national level sets precedent for survivors to take roles within community, state, and national responses to address human trafficking; the forum emphasized the point that current needs and trends in the victim service arena are tailored and inclusive of all forms of human trafficking and identities (USACHT, 2016).

Further discussion of survivor involvement in the movement is necessary, particularly non- survivor perception and the ways in which survivors are welcomed into key roles in local community response. Trauma-informed engagement of survivors is paramount, and should ideally begin with training coalition coordinators on the principles of trauma-informed system management (SAMHSA, 2014). To this end, survivor *leadership*—beyond inclusion—is critical and particularly strategic in understanding the community's unique characteristics that create vulnerability. Survivors can play a unique role in bridging invitations of community members to partnerships and coalitions, enabling them to guide effective policies. Community members bring lived experiences to bear on needs, barriers, and current relationships with other sectors. For example, responsible awareness campaigns should centralize survivor input on *community*-tailored messaging, and provide critical feedback to the use of potentially exploitive images and disrespectful language that perpetuates stereotypes. Without their valuable perspectives, siloed sectors in the movement will find it difficult to understand why their work is not fruitful.

Although stakeholders in the anti-trafficking movement value and may prioritize inclusion of survivors, the process of inclusion and how to empower survivor participation may be illusive. Coalition members need to pay attention to access to membership; coalition roles offered to survivors and community members; and support and mentorship. Coalitions should also incorporate periodic reflection points to monitor and evaluate their connection with the communities they serve. It bears repeating that without these critical contributions, coalition efforts may become segmented and disjointed.

Unfortunately, one of the realities of coalition membership is that agencies may participate without compensation of their time; the same is often true for survivors thus absorbing the financial burden for time and travel. Ideally, inclusion of individuals from a range of diverse identities (e.g., socioeconomic backgrounds) enriches the composition of a coalition and helps all members to think sensitively about survivor needs that promote economic empowerment and community inclusion; however, this is not always feasible given the volunteer nature of membership. Not every survivor has the time nor the financial status to allow for unpaid time to participate in coalitions. In order to accommodate time constraints, additional considerations for meeting accessibility should be recognized. Examples of accommodations may include language assistance (ESL), web-based platforms (e.g., Skype, Zoom), providing childcare-friendly spaces, and flexibility in times when coalitions meet. These sensitivities are ways to ensure inclusive access to meetings, while supporting survivor empowerment.

Additional supportive tools for survivor inclusion include investment in the professional development of participants, including leadership development workshops or trainings and securing funding for survivors to attend conferences throughout the community and state. From a trauma-informed approach, it is important to create and hold spaces where survivors can debrief and process their experience of holding an identity as a survivor while working within the movement.

Once survivors are welcomed as key coalition contributors, agencies and individual organizations may begin to strategize ways to incorporate survivor voice into their programmatic work. Depending on the needs of the community and the makeup of community coalitions, platforming or partnering with survivors may develop. Historically, most anti-trafficking efforts have included survivors to solely share their traumatic stories by providing details of their exploitive experiences at forums or as members of panels (Foot, 2016, p 75). An unfortunate result is the creation of two restrictive survivor categories: "victim in crisis" or "valuable coalition member;" for many, these limiting categories keep survivors from participating or entering in anti-trafficking work (Foot, 2016). Broadly, for many community members with the desire to add their perspectives to community anti-trafficking partnerships, it can be a difficult movement in which to enter. LCHT's Leadership Development Program operates to support professional development of Colorado survivors, many of whom serve on the Governor's Colorado Human Trafficking Council.

2. Attend to Coalition Focus and Roles

Understanding how a partnership was formed and honoring this history matters. For example, are there legislative mandates, formalized protocols, or Memoranda of Understanding (MOUs) to create agreements between organizations to work collaboratively to address the issue? The United Nations Office of Drugs and Crime's *Toolkit to Combat Trafficking in Persons* (UNODC, 2006) recommends that MOUs include the stated purpose, cooperation guidelines, define target population the partnership addresses and clearly define the responsibilities of each partner. The 2013 Uniform Act on Prevention of and Remedies for Human Trafficking by the National Conference of Commissioners on Uniform State Laws recommended multidisciplinary Governor-appointed councils to primarily focus on prevention and protection activities. Knowing the context in which the formal or informal partnership was established allows the mental health practitioners to know where to position her/himself, where s/he might have the most influence in advancing a particular goal or mandate. Such partnership power dynamics cannot be ignored – it is imperative for understanding what can be achieved by the partnership, what forms of human trafficking will be addressed, and whose voices are heard or ignored. Drawing from Colorado Project data, coalitions should form community-tailored responses, rather than replicating other communities.

Enter mindfully into coalitions. Serving in a multi-sector partnership requires stakeholders to be aware of their *positionality* within the coalition, or knowing where one stands with respect to power (Foot, 2016). As noted earlier in this chapter, anti-human trafficking coalitions have historically drawn a broad net of stakeholders to the table – law enforcement personnel (investigators and prosecutors), social workers, counselors, psychologists, medical personnel, community advocates, legal and social service providers, shelter operators, runaway and homeless youth outreach workers, faith-based leaders, researchers, among others. Hence, many different perspectives, disciplines, and lived experiences may be represented in such multidisciplinary groups. These partnerships also bridge stakeholders with different value sets and various approaches to their work – bureaucratic and grassroots organizers; adult-serving and juvenile-serving agencies or organizations; stakeholders who exclusively focus on immigrant communities and those who focus on domestic US citizens; researchers and practitioners; survivors and non-survivors. While these stakeholders are pulled to the table under the broad umbrella of human trafficking, it will take time to establish the common goals, mission or vision of the group (LCHT, 2013a, p. 87). Where can behavioral health practitioners engage and share perspectives at these coalitions? What cautions and considerations must be taken into account to navigate coalition membership? Below are suggested considerations as mental health providers engage in these partnerships and navigate the dynamics that accompany such endeavors.

Attend to missing roles. Behavioral health practitioners are often in the best positions to consider the communities or clients they represent and if those voices are represented in the coalition. Whose voices are missing? Does this coalition or the content that is produced represent viewpoints from your community? This exercise is not to understand who might oppose recommendations, but rather an inclusive attempt to understand who holds the power and who does not. Mental health providers will possess the sensitivities unique to the communities they represent; create spaces that are empowering for typically marginalized individuals to speak up and provide input; and often be the first to call out tokenizing behaviors from fellow partnership members (e.g., asking survivors for their input as it only pertains to the traumatic events they survived).

3. Partner with Parallel Movements

The crime of human trafficking intersects with other forms of violence and exploitation, and requires gaining a solid understanding of the history of parallel issue area initiatives and movements, including interpersonal violence, labor rights, refugee/asylee rights, immigrant rights, child welfare, and homelessness. As the Laboratory to Combat Human Trafficking engaged in the Colorado Project in 2010, it became critical that the Project partner representatives—practitioners and policy makers in each of these *parallel* fields—in order to create shared learning spaces so that each would benefit from this carefully tended set of partnerships. For example, it is important to recognize that any changes in the name of the anti-trafficking field honor and respect the history and efforts of advocates for homelessness, given the overlaps in population vulnerability. Having colleagues representing these issue areas enriched the work of the Colorado Project, for they served as members of the State Advisory Board who helped to shape the recommendations for the Colorado Action Plan. With this foundation, the Project began to pave the way for partnership and sustainability around human trafficking in other movements. Long after media spotlights and attention to this human rights abuse pass, the hope will lie with parallel movements to keep human trafficking in their sights, as it will take a comprehensive coordinated response to address this egregious crime, in Colorado and globally.

Acknowledgments

Special thanks to Carol Steele, Lindsey Breslin and David Shaw, and the Project Team for the Colorado Project to Comprehensively Combat Human Trafficking. The Colorado Project to Comprehensively Combat Human Trafficking was designed and facilitated by the Laboratory to Combat Human Trafficking, under a grant from the Embrey Family Foundation. All intellectual property associated with the data and research methodology developed for The Colorado Project belong to the Laboratory to Combat Human Trafficking and any use of this intellectual property without its prior written consent is strictly prohibited.

Appendix

GUIDING FRAMEWORKS:
THE 4Ps

LCHT conducted a substantive literature review to better understand and define the key components of promising practices within each of the 4Ps. It was via the Social Ecology Theory (see page 9) that we began to articulate that these Ps happen in specific communities with unique characteristics. We gathered diverse innovative thinkers and began to think together, learn from one another, and adapt our lenses.

What does it mean to combat human trafficking? Governments and international organizations have declared that an effective response to human trafficking must include four key elements (US State Department & UNODC):

PREVENTION	PROTECTION	PROSECUTION	PARTNERSHIPS
› Training and education programs	› Social service advocacy & case management	› Human trafficking protocols and procedures	› Private sector
› Awareness campaigns	› Housing	› Training and education	› Public sector
› Advocacy campaigns	› Medical services	› Task forces	› Third sector
› Public and private sector policies	› Mental health services	› State trafficking and trafficking-related legislation	› Protocols
› Protection services for persons who have experienced trafficking	› Outreach	› Municipal trafficking and trafficking-related legislation	› Leadership
› Programs that address root causes of trafficking aimed at universal and selected communities	› Legal services	› Attempted/ successful civil and criminal prosecutions of trafficking cases	› Group diversity
	› Training and education programs		› Resource leveraging
	› State laws on victim protection/rights		› Trust building
	› Clothing and food		› Sustainability beyond an individual
	› Interpretation/ translation		› Inclusion of vulnerable population perspectives
	› Education		› Effective communication
	› Life skills training		› Conflict management
	› Employment assistance		› Management of competing interests
	› Community re-integration		

 To understand the complexities of prevention, protection, prosecution and partnerships is to build up the strengths and address gaps in anti-human trafficking efforts.

Figure 11.1 Guiding Frameworks: The 4Ps

Table 11.1 Protection table from Table 1. 4P Components and Definitions

PROTECTION
Protection measures ensure that victims of human trafficking are provided access to, at a minimum, health care, legal aid, social services and education in ways that are not prejudicial against victims' rights, dignity, or psychological well-being. Protection also means creating an environment (social, political and legal) that fosters the protection of victims of trafficking.

Component	What Component Seeks
Social Service Advocacy and Case Management	Provision of a "person who works with other service providers and is responsible for assessing service needs, providing victims with information about their rights to services, establishing comprehensive service plans with victims, identifying and making service referrals, coordinating services, accompanying victims to appointments, advocating on behalf of victims to other providers and agencies, providing emotional and moral support, and often keeping victims informed of progress on their legal cases and T-visa and other applications."[2]
Housing	Basic needs in terms of immediate, short- and long-term housing.
Medical services	Types of medical treatment for any physical illness or injury.
Mental Health Services	Types of psychosocial services to treat various types of mental health issues.
Outreach	Informing vulnerable populations about available services and educating them about human trafficking and other potential risk and harmful behaviors.
Legal services	Legal services for persons who have been trafficked to access services, obtain immigration relief and/or asylum, obtain visas, pursue civil claims against their trafficker, and/or seek compensation. Also, criminal justice advocacy and legal defense when trafficking victim is prosecuted for criminal activity resultant from the trafficking situation.
Training and education programs	Programming that trains service providers in identifying persons who have been trafficked and/ or trafficking specific service needs.
State laws on victim protection/rights	Legislation that specifically calls for persons who have been trafficked to receive protection services.
Clothing and food	Basic needs in terms of food and clothing.
Interpretation/ Translation	Provision of language services for foreign nationals in their native language.
Education	Provision of schooling or access to schooling at primary, secondary, or tertiary.
Life Skills Training	Provision of training and education in various skills to assist a person to be able to live independently.
Employment Assistance	Provision of job training and linking individuals with internships, apprenticeships, and potential employers.
Community Reintegration	Services to assist a person in making successful transitions to their new communities or back to their home communities.

188   A. Alejano-Steele, A. Finger, M. Landerholm

Notes

1 United Nations (2000) *Protocol to Prevent, Suppress and Punish Trafficking in Persons (Palermo Protocol)*; The 2000 U.S. Trafficking Victims Protection Act (TVPA); the 2010 U.S. Trafficking in Persons Report; The July 2006 U.S. Government Accountability Office report, *Human Trafficking: Better Data, Strategy, and Reporting Needed to Enhance U.S. Anti-trafficking Efforts Abroad*; The 2008 United Nations Office on Drugs and Crime, *Toolkit to Combat Trafficking in Persons*; The 2008 Office of the High Commissioner for Human Rights report, *Recommended Principles and Guidelines on Human Rights and Human Trafficking*.
2 Clawson et al. (2009)

References

Alpert, E. J., Ahn, R., Albright, E., Purcell, G., Burke, T. F., and Macias-Konstantopoulos, W. L. (2014). *Human Trafficking: Guidebook on Identification, Assessment, and Response in the Health Care Setting.* MGH Human Trafficking Initiative, Division of Global Health and Human Rights, Department of Emergency Medicine, Massachusetts General Hospital, Boston, MA and Committee on Violence Intervention and Prevention. Waltham, MA: Massachusetts Medical Society.
APA. (2014). *Task Force Report on the Human Trafficking of Women and Girls.* APA Task Force on Human Trafficking. Division 35 Psychology of Women. Washington, DC: American Psychological Association. Retrieved from https://www.apa.org/pi/women/programs/trafficking/report.pdf
Barrett, N. A. (2010). An exploration of promising practices in response to human trafficking in Canada. Vancouver, BC:International Centre for Criminal Law Reform & Criminal Justice Policy. Retrieved from https://www.researchgate.net/publication/273134225_HUMAN_TRAFFICKING_IN_CANADA_AND_WORLDWIDE_A_CRITICAL_ASSESSMENT_OF_THE_AVAILABLE_ESTIMATES_AND_OFFICIAL_STATISTICS
Bronfenbrenner, U. (1979). *The Ecology of Human Development.* Cambridge, MA: Harvard University Press.
Butler, J. (2009). *Frames of War: When Is Life Grievable?* Brooklyn: Verso.
Centers for Disease Control and Prevention (2014). The Social Ecological Model: A Framework for Prevention. Retrieved from http://www.cdc.gov/violenceprevention/overview/social-ecologicalmodel.html (accessed April 21, 2014).
Clawson, H., and Dutch, N. (2007). *Addressing the Needs of Victims of Human Trafficking: Challenges, Barriers, and Promising Practices.* Office of the Assistant Secretary for Planning and Evaluation. Washington, DC: US Department of Health and Human Services.
Clawson, H. J., and Dutch, N. (2008). *Identifying Victims of Human Trafficking: Inherent Challenges and Promising Strategies from the Field.* Office of the Assistant Secretary for Planning and Evaluation. Washington, DC: US Department of Health and Human Services.
Clawson, H. J., Salomon, A., and Goldblatt Grace, L. (2008). *Treating the Hidden Wounds: Trauma Treatment and Mental Health Recovery for Victims of Human Trafficking.* Office of the Assistant Secretary for Planning and Evaluation. Washington, DC: US Department of Health and Human Services.

Clawson, H. J., Dutch, N. M., Solomon, A., and Grace, L. G. (2009). *Study of HHS Programs Serving Human Trafficking Victims*. Final report. Office of the Assistant Secretary for Planning and Evaluation. Washington, DC: US Department of Health and Human Services. Retrieved from http://aspc.hhs.gov/hsp/07/huma ntrafficking/final/index.pdf (accessed October 10, 2012).

Cojocaru, C. (2015). Sex trafficking, captivity, and narrative: constructing victim-hood with the goal of salvation. *Dialectical Anthropology*, 39(2), 183–194.

Colorado Human Trafficking Council (2016). *Colorado Human Trafficking Council 2016 Annual Report*. Report to the Judiciary Committees of the House of Representatives and the Senate, pursuant to C.R.S. § 18–13-505. Denver, CO: Colorado Division of Criminal Justice.

Colorado Rural Health Center (2018). *Colorado County Designations, 2017*. Colorado Rural Health Center, The State Office of Rural Health. Retrieved from http://coruralhealth.wpengine.netdna-cdn.com/wp-content/uploads/2017/07/2017-Rural-County-Designation.pdf

Dalton, J. H., Elias, M. J., and Wandersman, A. H. (2007). Citizen participation and empowerment. In Schreiber-Ganster, L. (ed.), *Community Psychology. Linking Individuals and Communities. International Student Edition*, Belmont, CA: Wadsworth, Cengage Learning, pp. 398–431.

End Slavery Now. (n.d.). Colorado project to comprehensively combat human trafficking. The Colorado Project Website. Retrieved from https://www.endsla verynow.org/colorado-project-to-comprehensively-combat-human-trafficking

Farmer, P. (1999). Pathologies of power: rethinking health and human rights. *American Journal of Public Health*, 89(10), 1486–1496.

Farmer, P. (2004). *Pathologies of Power: Health, Human Rights, and the New War on the Poor*, Vol. 4. Oakland: University of California Press.

Farrell, A., McDevitt, J., and FahyS. (2008). Understanding and Improving Law Enforcement Responses to Human Trafficking. Final Report, June. Research Gate. Retrieved from https://www.ncjrs.gov/pdffiles1/nij/grants/222752.pdf

Foot, K. (2015). *Collaborating against Human Trafficking: Cross-Sector Challenges and Practices*. Lanham, MD: Rowman & Littlefield.

Foot, K., and Vanek, J. (2012). Toward constructive engagement between local law enforcement and mobilization and advocacy nongovernmental organizations about human trafficking: Recommendations for law enforcement executives. *Law Enforcement Executive Forum*, 12(1). Retrieved from http://faculty.washington.edu/kfoot/Publications/EFJ%2012.1%20Foot-Vanek.pdf

Galtung, J. (1969). Violence, peace, and peace research. *Journal of Peace Research*, 6(3), 167–191.

Hames, C., Dewar, F., and Napier-Moore, R. (2010). Feeling good about feeling bad: a global review of evaluation in anti-trafficking initiatives. Global Alliance Against Traffic in Women. Retrieved from https://www.gaatw.org/publications/GAATW_Global_Review.FeelingGood.AboutFeelingBad.pdf

Iman, J., Fullwood, C., Paz, N., DaphneW., and Hassan, S. (2009). *Girls Do What They Have to Do to Survive: Illuminating Methods Used by Girls in the Sex Trade and Street Economy to Fight Back and Heal: A Participatory Research Study of Resilience and Resistance*. Chicago, IL: Young Women's Empowerment Project.

LCHT. (2013a). *Colorado Project National Survey Report*. Denver, CO: Laboratory to Combat Human Trafficking.

LCHT. (2013b). *Colorado Project Statewide Data Report*. Denver, CO: Laboratory to Combat Human Trafficking.

LCHT. (2014). *Colorado Action Plan*. Denver, CO: Laboratory to Combat Human Trafficking.

Mechanic, D., and Tanner, J. (2007). Vulnerable people, groups, and populations: societal view. *Health Affairs*, 26(5), 1220–1230.

O'Connell, M. E., Boat, T., and Warner, K. E. (eds.). (2009). *Preventing mental, behavioral, and emotional disorders among young people: progress and possibilities*. Washington, DC: The National Press. Retrieved from: http://www.pre vencionbasadaenlaevidencia.com/uploads/PDF/RP_Preventing_young_people_ disorders_NRCIM.pdf

Pierce, A. (2009). *Shattered Hearts: The Commercial Sexual Exploitation of American Indian Women and Girls in Minnesota*. Minneapolis: Minnesota Indian Women's Resource Center. Retrieved from http://www.miwrc.org/shattered_hearts_full_ report-web_version.pdf

Raymond, J., and Hughes, D. (2001) *Sex Trafficking of Women in the United States*. National Institute of Justice/Coalition Against Trafficking in Women.

SAMHSA. (2014). *SAMHSA's Concept of Trauma and Guidance for a Trauma-Informed Approach*. HHS Publication No. (SMA) 14–4884. Rockville, MD: Substance Abuse and Mental Health Services Administration.

Society for Community Research and Action. (2016). Who We Are. Division 27 of the American Psychological Association. Retrieved from http://www.scra27.org/ who-we-are/

Trafficking Victims Protection Act. (2000) § 7101, 22 U.S.C. (b)(2).

Ugarte, M. B., Zarate, L., and Farley, M. (2003). Prostitution and trafficking of women and children from Mexico to the United States. *Journal of Trauma Practice*, 2(3–4), 147–165. Retrieved from https://www.ncjrs.gov/App/Publications/a bstract.aspx?ID=205054

UNODC. (2006). Toolkit to Combat Trafficking in Persons. United Nations Office on Drugs and Crime. Global Programme Against Trafficking in Human Beings. Retrieved from https://www.unodc.org/pdf/Trafficking_toolkit_Oct06.pdf

USACHT. (2016). *United States Advisory Council on Human Trafficking Annual Report 2016*. Washington, DC: US Department of State.

Contributors

AnnJanette Alejano-Steele, Ph.D., is a professor of psychology and gender studies, currently serving as Associate Dean of the College of Professional Studies at Metropolitan State University of Denver. She is also the co-founder and Research and Training Director for the Denver-based Laboratory to Combat Human Trafficking. Her educational background includes a Ph.D. in psychology from Michigan State University and NIH-supported postdoctoral work in psychology and medicine from the University of California, San Francisco. Dr. Alejano-Steele has taught about human trafficking since 2000 and researched and trained on the subject since 2005. She coordinates Metro State's Human Trafficking Academic Response Team that has supported 70 survivors of human trafficking since 2007. Her expertise has focused upon multicultural psychology; health access for vulnerable populations; and comprehensive services for victims of human trafficking. She has served on five national working groups focusing on trauma and human trafficking—three for the Department of Health and Human Services Office on Women's Health on Trauma-informed care, Administration for Children and Families and Substance Abuse and Mental Health Services Administration; one for the American Psychological Association Task Force on the Trafficking of Women and Girls and the US Bureau of Justice National Institute of Justice Expert Research Working Group on Human Trafficking. In 2012, she was one of the inaugural speakers at the Denver TEDxMileHighWomen, where she spoke about human trafficking in Colorado. In 2013, she was named a CBS4 Game Changer and in 2014, she presented at the United Nation's Commission on the Status of Women on LCHT's groundbreaking Colorado Project to Comprehensively Combat Human Trafficking. Her applied work in the anti-human trafficking movement has privileged her with the knowledge of structural violence, vulnerability, community resilience, and data-informed community-led social change.

Katherine W. Bogen graduated from Clark University with a bachelor's degree in Political Science, a minor in English, and a concentration in Latin American/Latino Studies. Since then, she has worked as a research assistant in several different settings, and currently works as a Clinical Research Program Coordinator at Rhode Island Hospital within the Department of Psychiatry. Her research and scholarly interests center around supporting women who have experienced sexual abuse, having authored/co-authored several publications on this topic.

Susan Brotherton, M.S.W., is the Director of Philadelphia Social Service Ministries for The Salvation Army of Greater Philadelphia. She has been an employee of the Salvation Army for 24 years, previously serving as the director of the trauma-informed Red Shield Family Residence. Susan has represented The Salvation Army presenting promising practices in trauma-informed care, creating trauma-sensitive cultures, serving families and youth experiencing homelessness, and meeting the unique needs of survivors of commercial sexual exploitation. Susan taught for many years as an adjunct professor in Temple University's social work program. Prior to her work with the Salvation Army, she worked in the mental health field where she managed a residential program for adults whose lives were affected by mental illness, worked as a clinical case manager, and a psychotherapist serving individuals and families.

Brian D. Bruijn, Ph.D., is a Behavioral Health Consultant Fellow with Cherokee Health Systems in Memphis, Tennessee. He has a Ph.D. in Counseling Psychology from the University of Memphis and completed his internship in health service psychology at Michigan State University's Counseling and Psychiatry Services. While at Michigan State University, he earned a Certificate in Multicultural Counseling from the Multi Ethnic Counseling Center Alliance. Dr. Bruijn's research includes qualitative studies that examine the lived experiences of those involved with domestic sex trafficking aftercare (both worker and survivor). Dr. Bruijn has consulted with anti-trafficking aftercare agencies for approximately five years, and serves as a volunteer in the anti-trafficking effort in his local community. He is presently specializing in behavioral health in the primary care setting working directly with marginalized populations and those who have experienced significant health disparities.

Lucy L. Bruijn, MD, MPH, FAAFP, is a staff physician with Methodist Medical Group Primary Care in Memphis, Tennessee. She received her degrees from Emory University (BA in History, Summa Cum Laude), Ben Gurion University of the Negev in collaboration with Columbia University Health Sciences (MD), and Columbia University (MPH). Dr. Bruijn completed her residency in Family Medicine at The University of Rochester in Rochester, New York and a fellowship in Family Medicine Surgical Obstetrics at St. Elizabeth Medical Center in Edgewood, Kentucky. Prior to her current practice, she served in academic practice as a faculty attending physician teaching residents and students in several different locales. Dr. Bruijn has particular interests in global health and serving underserved populations. She is a Fellow of the American Academy of Family Physicians.

Mary C. Burke, Ph.D., is a Professor of Psychology at Carlow University in Pittsburgh, Pennsylvania where she teaches in the Doctoral Program in Counseling Psychology. Her scholarly interests include minority mental health in the context of oppressive systems, gender based violence, trauma and human trafficking. In 2004 she founded the Project to End Human Trafficking (www.endhumantrafficking.org). Dr. Burke has lectured extensively about human trafficking both in the United States and abroad. She has begun anti-trafficking coalitions (Pennsylvania and Virginia), consulted on the development of coalitions in other regions and has worked on legislation in support of strengthening trafficking laws. Current international efforts are focused in Uganda where she and her team work collaboratively with citizens to prevent trafficking through community based programming. Dr. Burke is a member of the American Psychological Association Task Force on the Trafficking of Women and Girls and is working to advance knowledge about current best practices regarding therapeutic work with survivors.

Paola M. Contreras, Psy.D., is a psychologist and an Assistant Professor at William James College where she directs the Human Trafficking Community Research Hub. She is an advanced psychoanalytic candidate at the Boston Psychoanalytic Society and Institute. She has a private practice in Cambridge, MA. Dr. Contreras provides consultation to US-based and international organizations to develop specialized services to assist individuals with histories of human trafficking. Between 2014 and 2017 she was Vice-Chair of the American Psychological Association's Committee for Women in Psychology.

Kelly O. Dillon is a student and Research Assistant in Carlow University's Counseling Psychology doctoral program. She completed her bachelor's degree in Psychology at Grand Valley State University and her master's degree in Clinical Psychology at Roosevelt University, after which, she also completed an assessment internship at The Pine Rest Psychological Consultation Center. Her scholarly and research interests center around social justice, personality, and the influence of technology on human relationships.

Amanda Finger, M.A., is the Executive Director and co-founder of the Laboratory to Combat Human Trafficking (LCHT) in Denver, which has focused on anti-trafficking efforts since 2005. Her professional background includes serving as an adjunct faculty member at Metropolitan State University of Denver teaching courses on human trafficking and women's health; health advocacy in Washington, DC; Congressional campaign organizing; serving as a Legislative Aide for the Colorado General Assembly; and field research on human trafficking and forced migration in Johannesburg, South Africa. Ms. Finger holds a Master of

Arts degree in International Human Rights from the Josef Korbel School of International Studies at the University of Denver and a Bachelor of Arts degree in Political Science and French from Kansas State University.

Leah Russell Flaherty is completing a pre-doctoral internship accredited by the American Psychological Association (APA) at the Charles George VA Medical Center in Asheville, NC. She completed her doctoral-level coursework at Carlow University in Pittsburgh, PA. Ms. Flaherty has published articles addressing issues such as reduction of medical hospitalizations using home telehealth, traumatic brain injuries among homeless Veterans, Suicide risk among LGBT Veterans, and microaggressions in therapy. She has taught graduate and undergraduate psychology courses including assessment, personality theory, and child development. As a research associate with the Department of Defense and the Veterans Health Administration she presented, analyzed, and collected data within the military healthcare system specifically aimed at PTSD, TBI, and suicide. During her doctoral training she and a group of colleagues traveled to Uganda to educate community leaders on the impact of trauma on children. She is currently collecting interview data for her dissertation research entitled "Suicidal Thoughts and Behaviors: Relation to Locus of Control"—the goal of this study is to refine the understanding of characteristics that might impact suicidal ideation, ultimately aimed at prevention.

Judy Hale Reed, Esq., MPA, has rooted her career in improving the rights of the most vulnerable and, in particular, addressing human trafficking issues, including implementation of laws, capacity building, and coordination of anti-trafficking efforts in the US and Eastern Europe. She has worked with the OSCE Mission to Moldova as the Anti-Trafficking and Gender Equality Program Manager and as a consultant to U.N. agencies on anti-trafficking programs and social service system development; she has also served as a judicial law clerk and worked as a general practice attorney. Ms. Hale Reed authored the chapter "Addressing the problem: community-based responses and coordination" in the book *Human Trafficking: Interdisciplinary Perspectives* (Routledge, 2013). Ms. Hale Reed served as a Peace Corps Volunteer in the Republic of Moldova from 1999 to 2001, and holds a Juris Doctor, a Master of Public Administration, and a Bachelor of Arts in Sociology and Women's Studies. Currently, she is the Legal Advocacy Manager for the Women's Center and Shelter of Greater Pittsburgh, is involved in the Western Pennsylvania Human Trafficking Coalition, and teaches a course on Human Trafficking as an adjunct at Chatham University.

Mary Landerholm, M.S.W., is a double degree holder from Metropolitan State University (MSU) of Denver's Department of Social Work where she began her studies on the complexities of those experiencing exploitation. Taking the knowledge of research and community organizing, Mary began her work as Interim Executive Director of Prax(us) in 2014, an agency serving street-based youth and young adults in the Denver Metro experiencing such exploitation, using an anti-oppression and public health framework. From there Mary continued her work within the anti-trafficking movement with the Laboratory to Combat Human Trafficking to support a statewide initiative to on-board a data-driven response to the crime of human trafficking using the Colorado Project to Comprehensively Combat Human Trafficking and the Colorado Action Plan. Mary currently is an Adjunct Facility at MSU Denver's Gender, Woman, and Sexuality Department teaching the human trafficking course and also the Policy course for the BSW degree out of the MSU Denver's Social Work Department. Mary was selected as a member of the Colorado Human Trafficking (Governor's) Council sub-committee to inform training recommendation for law enforcement and service providers; consultants for the Office for Victims of Crime and is currently a Fellow for the National Human Trafficking Training and Technical Assistance Center in Washington, DC.

Veronica M. Lugris, Ph.D., is a licensed psychologist and consultant. An active member of the New York State Psychological Association and the Society for Consulting Psychology, Dr. Lugris received her doctorate from the University of Illinois, Urbana–Champaign. She also holds a postdoctoral certificate in Organizational Development and Consultation from the William Alanson White Institute in New York City. Throughout her career, Dr. Lugris has specialized in issues of diversity, interpersonal relationships, organizational assessment, training and development, group and leadership dynamics, and trauma management.

Jamie Manirakiza, M.S.W., has worked in the field of anti-trafficking for over nine years. Ms. Manirakiza currently works for the Salvation Army Eastern Territorial Headquarters located in West Nyack, New York as the Anti-Human Trafficking Specialist. Prior to this role, Jamie was the Director of Anti Trafficking for | The Salvation Army of Greater Philadelphia, where she provided a wide range of comprehensive services to survivors of human trafficking. Ms. Manirakiza is an adjunct professor for the Human Trafficking Certificate program of Vanguard University of Southern California and has taught about human trafficking in the Social Work Department at Eastern University. Ms. Manirakiza has consulted for the Department of Justice on issues related to human trafficking and has been quoted extensively in the media on topics pertaining to commercial sexual exploitation in Philadelphia, PA. She has been a featured speaker at press conferences and formal trainings, sharing her insights on what makes victim services successful. Ms. Manirakiza is a founding Board of Advisor member of the Villanova University School of Law's Institute to Address Commercial Sexual Exploitation. Ms. Manirakiza earned her Bachelor's degree from Eastern University and her Master's in social work from the University of Pennsylvania.

Heather L. McCauley is a Harvard-trained social epidemiologist and Assistant Professor in the Department of Human Development & Family Studies (HDFS) at Michigan State University. Her research focuses on the health impacts of and intervention strategies to reduce gender-based violence, with emphasis on victimization among marginalized populations (e.g. sexual and gender minorities, foster youth, incarcerated women). Dr. McCauley has authored or co-authored sixty peer-reviewed journal publications and has given more than 100 regional and national addresses on her federally funded work. Dr. McCauley serves on grant review panels for the National Institute of Justice and the National Institutes of Health. She is Associate Editor of the multidisciplinary research journal *Psychology of Violence*.

Katie A. McIntyre, M.S., is a doctoral candidate in Counseling Psychology at Carlow University, currently completing her residency in pediatric behavioral health at Cleveland Clinic Children's. Her scholarly interests include medical traumatic stress and post traumatic growth among chronically ill pediatric populations as well as adjustment to chronic illness. Katie has completed clinical training at the Center for Traumatic Stress in Children & Adolescents at Allegheny General Hospital focusing on trauma-focused cognitive behavioral therapy. Additionally, in 2014, Katie spoke to a group of school administrators and community leaders in Entebbe, Uganda regarding strength-based developmental conceptualizations of children and adolescents with a history of trauma.

Elizabeth Miller, MD, PhD, is chief of Adolescent Medicine at Children's Hospital of Pittsburgh of UPMC, and professor of Pediatrics at the University of Pittsburgh School of Medicine. Trained in medical anthropology as well as internal medicine and pediatrics, Dr. Miller's research has included examination of sex trafficking among adolescents in Asia, teen dating abuse, and reproductive health, with a focus on underserved youth populations including pregnant and parenting teens; and foster, homeless, and gang-affiliated youth. Her current research focuses on the impact of gender-based violence on young women's reproductive health. She conducts research on brief clinical interventions to reduce partner violence and unintended pregnancy, funded by the National Institute of Child Health and Human Development and the National Institute of Justice. In addition, she is conducting a study of a sexual violence prevention program entitled Coaching Boys into Men, which involves training coaches to talk to their young male athletes about stopping violence against women, funded by the Centers for Disease Control and Prevention. She is also involved in projects to reduce gender-based violence and improve adolescent and young adult women's health in India and Japan.

Katherine Miller, M.A., is an award-winning activist and educator, with extensive experience in victim advocacy for survivors of interpersonal violence and human trafficking. In addition to serving as the Victim Services Coordinator for the Phoenix Center at Auraria in Denver, Katherine also teaches undergraduate students at Metropolitan State University of Denver in the Gender, Women, and Sexualities Studies department, teaches Psychology for the Community College of College online system, supervises the Colorado Network to End Human Trafficking (CoNEHT) statewide hotline, and serves as an active board member for the Laboratory to Combat Human Trafficking (LCHT). Katherine has utilized her Master's degree in International Disaster Psychology and Bachelor's degrees in Women's Studies, Psychology, and History to provide prevention education through the Blue Bench, trauma therapy at the Aurora Strong Resilience Center, psychoeducation and process groups with women in rural Southern India living with HIV, and providing direct service to students in crisis at the Institute for Women's Studies and Services. Katherine is committed to infusing intersectional feminism and praxis into advocacy work, building coalitions to support survivors of violence and exploitation, and dismantling systems and cultural norms that perpetuate violence.

Susan O'Rourke, Ed.D., is the Director of Special Education Programs and professor of education at Carlow University in Pittsburgh, Pennsylvania. She earned her doctorate in Instructional Design & Technology and a Master's degree from the University of Pittsburgh. Prior to joining the faculty at Carlow, she was a teacher of individuals with multiple disabilities at The Rehabilitation Institute of Pittsburgh. Susan is a Past President of the Division of International Special Education and Services (DISES) and founding member of the Division of Performing and Visual Arts Education (DARTS)—divisions within the Council for Exceptional Children (CEC).

Kevin Spencer, M.Ed., is an educator, artist, consultant, and social entrepreneur. After more than 25 years as an award-winning touring artist, he now devotes his time to using the power of the arts to provide access and opportunity to individuals with developmental and intellectual disabilities. He has earned a M.Ed. in Arts & Interdisciplinary Academic Education and has a Certification in Autism Studies. In addition to working with arts professionals, he is faculty in the special education program at Carlow University (PA). He is also an authorized speaker for the US State Department as a subject expert on arts integration for special populations.

Index

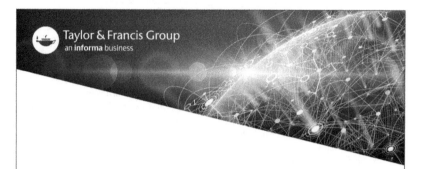

Ingram Content Group Australia Pty Ltd
Printed in Australia
AUHW011812130723
380813AU00009B/67

9 781138 924307